D1187611

THE HOLOCAUST

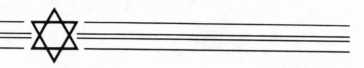

Selected Documents in Eighteen Volumes

John Mendelsohn
EDITOR

Donald S. Detwiler
ADVISORY EDITOR

A GARLAND SERIES

CONTENTS OF THE SERIES

THE HOLOCAUST

15. Relief in Hungary and the Failure of the Joel Brand Mission

Introduction by
John Mendelsohn

GARLAND PUBLISHING, INC.
NEW YORK • LONDON
1982

P.H. WELSHIMER MEMORIAL LIBRARY
MILLIGAN COLLEGE, TN 37682

REF
D
810
·J4
H655

Introduction copyright © 1982 by John Mendelsohn
All rights reserved

These documents have been reproduced from copies in
the National Archives. Dr. Mendelsohn's work was
carried out entirely on his own time and without
endorsement or official participation by the National
Archives as an agency.

Library of Congress Cataloging in Publication Data
Main entry under title:

Relief in Hungary and the failure of the Joel Brand mission.

(The Holocaust ; 15)
1. Jews—Hungary—Persecutions—Sources.
2. Holocaust, Jewish (1939–1945)—Hungary—Sources.
3. World War, 1939–1945—Jews—Rescue—Hungary—Sources.
4. Brand, Joel, 1906–   .
5. Hungary—Ethnic relations—Sources.
I. Mendelsohn, John, 1928–   . II. Series.
D810.J4H655   vol. 15   940.53'15'039240439
[DS135.H9]   81-80323
ISBN 0-8240-4889-X   AACR2

Design by Jonathan Billing

The volumes in this series have been printed on acid-free,
250-year-life paper.

Printed in the United States of America

ACKNOWLEDGMENTS

I owe a debt of gratitude to many people who aided me during various stages of preparing these eighteen volumes. Of these I would like to mention by name a few without whose generous efforts this publication would have been impossible. I would like to thank Donald B. Schewe of the Franklin D. Roosevelt Library in Hyde Park, New York, for his speedy and effective help. Sally Marcks and Richard Gould of the Diplomatic Branch of the National Archives in Washington, D.C., extended help beyond their normal archival duties, as did Timothy Mulligan and George Wagner from the Modern Military Branch. Edward J. McCarter in the Still Picture Branch helped a great deal. I would also like to thank my wife, Tish, for letting me spend my evenings during the past few years with these volumes rather than with her and our children, Michael and Lisa.

J. M.

107097

INTRODUCTION

Among the incomprehensible horrors of the Holocaust the fate of the Hungarian Jews was perhaps the most tragic of all. Although the Jews in Hungary had been persecuted at least since 1938, when major anti-Jewish legislation was first promulgated, there had been no large-scale deportations of the Jewish population until the spring of 1944. The Jews had experienced severe restrictions of their activities, they had been forced into labor battalions, and they had suffered the whim of the Arrow Cross Party and the gendarmes, but they were not in fear of being deported to the extermination camps. In fact, in March 1944, when the Russian front grew nearer to the Hungarian border, they were confident that they could outlast the Nazis, whose demise was as near as the Russians. They hoped against hope that the Nazi menace, which had destroyed the Jews in so many countries, would not be able to destroy the Jews in Hungary. They were reinforced in that hope by the fact that many Jews, particularly those from Slovakia, had fled to Hungary as a safer haven.

This feeling of relative safety changed suddenly, however, and the Jews in Hungary too were forced to confront deportation and extermination in Auschwitz when on March 19, 1944, the Germans occupied Hungary militarily. They brought with them the dreaded *Sondereinsatzkommando* Hungary or Eichmann, and in less than six months, from May 15 to the end of October, over four hundred thousand Jews had been deported. The confidence of the Hungarian Jews and the swiftness of the change that led to deportation of over one half of their number to the gates of Auschwitz impart an element of profound tragedy to their terrible fate.

The deportations of the Hungarian Jews could not and probably were not intended to be kept secret from the world. Nazi attempts to barter Jewish lives for direly needed goods, money, and industrial holdings tend to indicate that their needs to keep the deportations secret were not overwhelming. In the summer of 1944 the SS allowed members of the Weiss, Chorin, and Kornfeld families, Jewish Hungarian industrialists, to escape persecution via Vienna and Lisbon in exchange for their industrial holdings and large sums of money. While the agreements were being completed by SS *Standartenfuehrer* Kurt Becher, Himmler's representative, some members of the families were kept behind as hostages. The consummation of the agreement led to a crisis in the government of Prime Minister Sztojay, who had hoped to pocket these industrial

Jewish orphans on their way to Palestine

National Archives Still Picture Collection 306-NT-649C-27

holdings and the family wealth for Hungary rather than see them fall into the hands of the fast-moving SS. In another instance, for the sum of one and a half million dollars Rudolf Kastner, the executive vice president of the Jewish Assistance and Rescue Committee in Budapest, was able to negotiate with SS *Hauptsturmfuehrer* Dieter Wislizeny of Eichmann's staff in Hungary the transport of sixteen hundred Jews to the Bergen-Belsen concentration camp rather than to Auschwitz. In the fall of 1944 many reached safety in Switzerland.

Perhaps the largest and most complex of these "goods for blood" negotiations was the Joel Brand mission. In fact, the failure of this mission was one of the most depressing events in the tragedy of the Hungarian Jews. Although it never had any chance to succeed fully, greater sensitivity to the plight of the Hungarian Jews by the agencies involved might have spared the lives of thousands of innocent victims. Joel Brand was a member of the Assistance and Rescue Committee (Vaadat Ezra v' Hazalah) in Budapest. He left Budapest on May 15, 1944, the day the deportations to Auschwitz began, with an offer by Eichmann to release a million Jews and eventually to dismantle the killing installations at Auschwitz in exchange for ten thousand trucks and commodities such as coffee, tea, and soap. The trucks were to be used exclusively at the eastern front. Obviously, the western Allies could not agree to this deal, because it would have split their alliance with the Soviet Union wide open. Besides, the offer might have been a ruse calculated to create disunity among the Allies in the first place. Joel Brand proceeded to Istanbul with his offer and from there to Aleppo in Syria, where on June 5 he was arrested by the British, who suspected him of being a double agent. He was detained until early October, while his family was kept hostage by the SS in Budapest. With Brand incommunicado the British denounced the offer in the press as monstrous, and the deportations of the Hungarian Jews to Auschwitz continued at a rapid pace. Conceivably, the deportations could have been halted, at least temporarily, if one of the major agencies involved—perhaps the Jewish Agency through its leaders Chaim Weizman or Moshe Shertok—had at least indicated their willingness to conditionally accept the offer. Unfortunately none of them did and the slaughter continued.

A number of agencies, including the War Refugee Board, established in January 1944, helped nonetheless in several activities that saved the lives of Hungarian Jews. Foremost among these were the attempts of neutral countries, particularly Sweden through its representative Raoul Wallenberg, to extend the protection of their states to the Jews by issuing passports and letters to them. These resulted—at least temporarily—in freedom from deportation. The War Refugee Board also cooperated with the International Red Cross and the Vatican in relieving the plight of the Hungarian Jews. Thus the board was able, though often only indirectly and as a middleman, to carry out relief and rescue operations.

The records printed in this volume were selected from two sources: the records of the War Refugee Board in the Franklin D. Roosevelt Library in Hyde Park, New York, and the Pretrial Interrogation Series of the Nuernberg Trials records. The documents selected consist of reports and memoranda on Hungary by the War Refugee Board and the Vaad Hahatzala Emergency Committee. There are two transcripts of interrogations of Kurt Becher, by Rudolf Kastner among others, on the situation in Hungary in 1944 as seen through SS eyes, with emphasis on the "goods for blood" negotiations. A detailed dossier documents the tragic failure of the Joel Brand mission. Judged by the fact that almost three quarters of the Hungarian Jews lost their lives, rescue and relief operations failed; they commenced too late and accomplished too little. Nonetheless, thousands of lives were saved by these operations.

John Mendelsohn

SOURCE ABBREVIATIONS
AND DESCRIPTIONS

Nuernberg Document

Records from five of the twenty-five Nuernberg Trials prosecution document series: the NG (Nuernberg Government) series, the NI (Nuernberg Industrialist) series, the NO (Nuernberg Organizations) series, the NOKW (Nuernberg Armed Forces High Command) series, and the PS (Paris-Storey) series. Also included are such Nuernberg Trials prosecution records as interviews, interrogations, and affidavits, excerpts from the transcripts of the proceedings, briefs, judgments, and sentences. These records were used by the prosecution staff of the International Military Tribunal at Nuernberg or the twelve United States military tribunals there, and they are part of National Archives Record Group 238, National Archives Collection of World War II War Crimes Records.

OSS

Reports by the Office of Strategic Services in National Archives Record Group 226.

SEA

Staff Evidence Analysis: a description of documents used by the Nuernberg prosecution staff. Although the SEA's tended to describe only the evidentiary parts of the documents in the summaries, they describe the document title, date, and sources quite accurately.

State CDF

Central Decimal File: records of the Department of State in National Archives Record Group 59, General Records of the Department of State.

T 120

Microfilm Publication T 120: records of the German foreign office received from the Department of State in Record Group 242, National Archives Collection of Foreign Records Seized, 1941– . The following citation system is used for National Archives

Microfilm Publications: The Microfilm Publication number followed by a slash, the roll number followed by a slash, and the frame number(s). For example, Document 1 in Volume I: T 120/4638/K325518—K325538.

T 175 Microfilm Publication T 175: records of the Reich leader of the SS and of the chief of the German police in Record Group 242.

U.S. Army and U.S. Air Force Records relating to the attempts to cause the U.S. Army Air Force to bomb the extermination facilities at Auschwitz and the railroad center at Kaschau leading to Auschwitz, which are part of a variety of records groups and collections in the National Archives. Included are records of the United States Strategic Bombing Survey (Record Group 243), records of the War Refugee Board (Record Group 220), records of the Joint Chiefs of Staff, and other Army record collections.

War Refugee Board Records of the War Refugee Board, located at the Franklin D. Roosevelt Library in Hyde Park, New York. They are part of National Archives Record Group 220, Records of Temporary Committees, Commissions and Boards. Included in this category are the papers of Myron C. Taylor and Ira Hirschmann.

CONTENTS

Dossier on the Joel Brand Mission
Franklin D. Roosevelt Library,
Records of the War Refugee Board, Box 70, Folder: Joel Brand

Notes

1. *Document 1.* OWI is the abbreviation for Office of War Information. The Trianon Treaty was the peace treaty between the Allies and Hungary following World War I.

2. *Document 6.* Chaim Barlas was the representative of the Jewish Agency in Ankara; Laurence A. Steinhardt was the American ambassador there.

3. *Document 7.* Rueben B. Resnik was a representative of the American Jewish Joint Distribution Committee in Istanbul.

4. *Document 9.* Nahum Goldmann was the leading official of the World Jewish Congress and the Jewish Agency for Palestine; Edward R. Stettinius was deputy secretary of state until December 1, 1944, when he became secretary of state.

5. *Document 11.* Ira A. Hirschmann was the representative of the War Refugee Board in Ankara; Cordell Hull was secretary of state until November 30, 1944; Moshe Shertok was head of the political division of the Jewish Agency.

6. *Document 14.* Saly Mayer was the Swiss representative of the American Jewish Joint Distribution Committee; Robert Pilpel was acting European director of that committee.

7. *Document 15.* William Averell Harriman was the American ambassador in Moscow.

8. *Document 17.* Andrei I. Vyshinski was vice commissar for foreign affairs of the USSR.

9. *Document 19.* Lord Moyne was British minister resident in the Middle East; Lowell C. Pinkerton was the American consul general in Jerusalem.

10. *Document 23.* Hayden G. Raynor was special assistant to the undersecretary of state.

11. *Document 24.* Somerville P. Tuck was the American envoy extraordinary and minister plenipotentiary to Egypt.

12. *Document 26.* Joseph Schwartz was the representative of the Jewish Agency in Lisbon.

13. *Document 31.* Anthony Eden was British foreign secretary.

14. *Document 32.* SS *Obersturmbannfuehrer* (Colonel) Adolf Eichmann was chief of Amt IV B 4 in the SS Reich security main office, the office for Jewish affairs. He was tried by an Israeli court in Jerusalem and executed there in 1962. Freiherr Kurt von Schroeder was a German banker with strong SS connections. SS *Hauptsturmfuehrer* (Captain) Dieter Wislizeny was a deportation expert in Eichmann's department; he was tried as a war criminal and executed in Czechoslovakia.

15. *Document 33.* The report by Rueben B. Resnik, originally part of this document, is reproduced in Document 7 instead.

16. *Document 36.* Mnachim Bader was a representative of the Jewish Agency in Istanbul.

17. *Document 37.* Admiral William D. Leahy was formerly American ambassador to Vichy France and advisor to President Roosevelt.

18. *Document 40.* Rudolf Kastner was a leading member of the Jewish Assistance and Rescue Committee in Budapest.

19. *Document 41.* John Gilbert Winant was the American ambassador in London.

20. *Document 42.* Robert F. Kelley was chargé d'affaires of the American embassy in Ankara.

21. *Document 43.* John J. McCloy was the assistant secretary of war. The report by Ira A. Hirschmann mentioned in this document is missing.

22. *Document 52.* Roswell D. McClelland was the representative of the War Refugee Board in Switzerland.

MEMORANDUM

I

There is general agreement among those who know the
situation in Hungary that it is impossible to help out of
Hungary its 800,000 Hungarian and 100,000 foreign Jews, who,
until March 20, found tolerable and secure refuge there, or
any substantial number of them.   There will be only a few,
certainly not many thousands, who may brave the dangers and
risks of flight and reach territories under the control of
the Russians beyond the Carpathians or of Tito and Michail-
ovitch.

Therefore action for the rescue of the Hungarian Jews
must be directed to their support within Hungary and to
the improvement of their chance for survival there.

This chance for survival can be improved, among other
ways, by increasing the determination or willingness of
non-Jewish Hungarians to expose themselves to the dangers
and risks connected with the aiding of the persecuted.
In Hungary the proportion of Jews and their absolute number
are so high that the Germans will probably be unable to push
them out of economic life, to deprive them of their living
quarters and livelihood, unless they succeed in getting active support from the Hungarians, especially from the lower

and medium rank bureaucrats. The Nazis might have exchanged the ranking civil servants but the mass of the administrative personnel are holding their positions. These are the people on whom will depend ultimately the survival of the great majority of Jewry in Hungary.

It is therefore the task of propaganda to find its way to these people, to talk their language, to appeal to their sentiments. We ask ourselves, therefore, what was the American propaganda policy until March 20, 1944, and shall it be continued?

II

The OWI broadcasts (Voice of America) rebroadcast from London, the listening to which was not only free and unprohibited in Hungary, but could be technically achieved with the help of the cheapest radio set, proclaimed and preached daily that on account of her claims for the revision of the Trianon Treaty, the Hungarian Government and the Hungarian people alike were responsible for the world war because treaty revision meant attack against the world order. The same broadcasts telling the Hungarian people that they were accomplices of the German Nazis emphasized that Hungary was the only country where there was no underground resistance and sabotage, which made Hungarians more responsible for the acts of Hitler and of their own government than other peoples.

Moreover, when the lack of collaboration could not be left unmentioned, Hungarian listeners of the Voice of America were told that such attempts at resistance were not much to their credit, as they were parts of a well-schemed double game actuated by a desire to have one foot on each side of the fence.

III

This propaganda line was not very apt to strengthen, encourage and maintain Hungarian resistance. There is no Hungarian who would not take the attack on Hungarian claims for the revision of the Trianon Treaty as meant for him, since in Hungary rich and poor, landowner and peasant, employer and workman, bureaucrats, professional men, adults and children – all social classes – had one thing in common, that it would be against reason, morality and justice to acquiesce in the separation of three and a half million Hungarians from their mother country and their oppression by people of mostly inferior civilization. Every Hungarian thinks that it is his moral duty to maintain the desire for plebiscites, reparation and peaceful change.

Also, every Hungarian knew that the recrimination for lack of underground resistance and sabotage was frivolous and unjustified, since the Hungarian "overground" resistance was infinitely stronger, more efficient and more substantial than underground movements in the neighboring countries could

3

ever be.

Let us review what these underground movements have been achieving in the Central European countries:

(a) Threatening or "liquidating" the local collaborators. [In Hungary this was not necessary since the Hungarian Government put the Hungarian Nazis in jail.]

(b) Publicizing and disseminating Allied news. [This was done in Hungary not by underground leaflets but by seven Hungarian daily papers with a circulation reaching every house in the country. The two leading pro-Allied papers increased their circulation five-fold, and the Hungarian Government provided the newsprint.]

(c) Publication and dissemination of speeches of President Roosevelt, Prime Minister Churchill, Marshal Stalin, and other Allied statesmen, and the publication of American and English books dealing with war and related problems. [All this was done in Hungary publicly. Willkie's "One World" in Hungarian translation was a record-breaking best-seller in 1943, and was distributed in cheap editions.]

(d) Listening to Allied broadcasts. [This was not prohibited in Hungary and was done openly.]

(e) Supporting refugees from other countries. [In Hungary 50,000 to 70,000 Poles, many thousands of Anti-Nazi Austrians, Serbs and Italians, and 100,000 foreign Jews found safe haven in Hungary with the help of the Government. The Polish and Austrian resistance movements had important centers in Budapest.]

(f) Counteracting Nazi propaganda against democratic ideas. [In Hungary the Social Democratic Party and the Small Farmers Party held public meetings all over the country where democracy and democratic ideas were explained, preached and extolled.]

(g) Preventing or hampering deliveries of goods to Germany. [Hungary, according to The London Economist, was the only country in Europe which succeeded in restricting deliveries to Germany to the amount of return deliveries made by the Germans.]

IV

Returning to the situation of the Jews: 800,000 of them had tolerably secure life in Hungary. This was so in spite of Nazi pressure and without encouragement from American propaganda. Hungarians did not seem to need praise or promises in order to abstain from joining the Germans, Slovaks and Roumanians in the persecution of Jews. The reason for this is the nature of the Hungarian people. To quote from a book by one of the leading anti-Hungarian propagandists explaining why, in the former Austro-Hungarian Monarchy, it was in Hungary that anti-Semitism was the least prevalent:

"One reason was surely the sober and benevolent character of the Hungarian peasants, devoid of any religious or racial fanaticism, somewhat analogous to the Confucian type of philosophy which was based on agriculture, order and tradition."

Let us contrast this with a statement by the Secretary of State in the Ministry of Foreign Affairs of Czechoslovakia, according to whom, "In Slovakia anti-Semitism was native to the soil, and not entirely due to German pressure" (Gedye, "Foreign Bastions", p. 516).

V

After the occupation of Hungary by the Germans, the natural tendency of Hungarians for tolerance and humanitarian behavior will not be sufficient to afford a chance for survival to Jewry in Hungary. The destruction of the Jews need not be carried out by Hungarians. It will be planned and ordered by Veehsemayer, "the trustee of the German Reich in Hungary", by the Gestapo, by the 700,000 Hungarian Germans organized in Nazi units, and by the Hungarian Nazis who were kept under control (and some of them in jail) until March 20.

If the Hungarians remain passive and perform their duties under the law, these bandits will be able to execute their devilish schemes. The Hungarian Jews may, however, be saved with the active cooperation of Hungarian civil servants, soldiers, police staff and peasants. They must be spurred on to active cooperation with the Jews and passive resistance against the Gestapo.

VI

It cannot be hoped or supposed that Hungarians will brave
the threats and dangers of the Gestapo and the Hungarian
Quislings if the Voice of America continues the propaganda
policy outlined above.   The Hungarians are very patriotic and
are aware of the fatal situation in which they are today.
Since March 20, the Nazis have kept the country occupied; they
have taken away everything that can be moved; they have made
the country pay the "expenses" of the occupation army and feed
the Nazis.   The Hungarians know that their political leaders
are being imprisoned and murdered; that their newspapers have
been suppressed.   No great encouragement is necessary to spur
a proud nation into resistance against such brutal oppression
but some ray of hope must reach them that the merits of their
policies have been understood and if continued they can count
on justice and recognition.

We recommend that the Hungarians not only be promised
recognition if they go over now to passive resistance, underground work and sabotage, but that the American propaganda
give full credit for the achievements of their resistance
prior to March 20, 1944.

Memorandum to the Honorable John W. Pehle
Executive Director, War Refugee Board
Washington, D. C.

- -

HUNGARY:

A cold horror and fear has gripped the approximately one
million Jews of Hungary, who until the recent Nazi occupation,
lived in reasonable security and hoep that they would escape the
fate of their brethren in Poland and other lands. Now the spectre
of the horrible sadistic torture and death that met the Polish Jews,
looms before their eyes, and they live a thousand deaths in one
short hour.

From reports which seep through, among which are dispatches
from Joseph Levy, correspondent of the New York Times, our fears
are not groundless and there is every indication that the Nazis,
in desperation are working with feverish and bestial tempo to pre-
pare their infamous "gas chambers" and other inquisitional methods
to destroy the entire Jewish community of Hungary, the remnant of
an innocent people, whose only crime is their birthright as Jews.

The civilized world, cannot and dare not, consider the case
closed. It must rise in justified indignation and by the might
of justice, raise its voice and do everything possible to prevent
the impending fate. To remain quiet is to be guilty as an access-
ory and to forever bear the irremovable stain of the blood of innocent victims.

We would, in the name of Orthodox Jewry, respectfully suggest the following proposals to be carried through with the exped-
iency the emergency nature of the subject demands.

1) a- We respectfully request the Government of the United
States to give immediate and special warning to the Government of
Hungary, and to the people of Hungary, that they shall be held
responsible for the safety of the Jewish population within her
borders; that every murder and other crimes committed against these

innocent per???s shall be carefully note and full punishment exacted; that every individual, whether a leader issuing the order, or a menial carrying it through, shall be considered equally guilty before the tribunal of justice, and receive a well-merited punishment; and that obeying an order or the excuse of discipline to commit murder shall not be considered a justification or excuse to escape punishment - this warning should be administered with greatest severity and in no uncertain terms.

Furthermore, a call is to be issued to the people of Hungary, to desist from and resist any attempts made to carry out the mass murders, and any participation therein will result in economic, political and moral sanctions against Hungary, which will bear this stain on its national honor throughout the centuries.

b- It will be to their fullest advantage to counteract every outrageous act against their Jewish population and every move, step or measure taken by them to prevent the murder of Jews, and their escape from Nazi hands will be favorably considered at the peace period and react to their advantage.

c- Every possible available means are to be utilized to direct this request and warning to Hungary and her people. Fullest use of the radio, pamphlets, leaflets, newspapers and other forms of contact is to be exploited. In addition, this warning should be communicated through diplomatic channels at which time every detail could be noted and due mention made of the specific consideration Hungary can expect for a compliance with the warning.

2) We respectfully request the Government of the United States to direct a communication to the other Allied nations and to all neutrals requesting these countries to direct a strong appeal to Hungary to prevent the murder of her innocent Jewish inhabitants to warn her of the dire results she can expect from collaboration in such iniquity, and to likewise make clear to her how much can be gained from a favorable and helpful attitude.

3) The United States is requested to make a presentation to the Vatican to call upon the church dignitaries in Hungary to awaken the conscience of the pious and religious to the bloody crimes that are perpetrated within their domains, that they may give active resistance to any attempts made to carry out the diabolical plans for mass-murder, to give shelter to Jews escaping the murderers and to aid in the rescue and escape of their Jewish neighbors.

4) We would also respectfully request that measures continue for the rescue of the Hungarian Jews through the Balkan States into Turkey and through the partisan forces of Marshal Tito of Yugoslavia.

Presented by:

VAAD HAHATZALA EMERGENCY COMMITTEE

Rabbi Israel Rosenberg
Rabbi Aron Kotler
Rabbi Jacob Levinson
Rabbi L. Seltzer
Rabbi B. L. Levinthal
Rabbi Jacob Konvitz
Rabbi Ichiel M. Gordon

Presidium

Affiliated Organizations

Union Orthodox Rabbis of U.S. and
Canada
Rabbinical Council of America
Mizrachi Organization of America
Agudath Israel of America
Young Israel Council of America
Agudath Israel Young Council
Union of Orthodox Jewish Congregations

By. Baruch Korff

May 17, 1944

10

Memorandum to the Honorable Adolf A. Berle
Assistant Secretary of State
Washington, D. C.

- -

Presented by:
Vaad Hahatzala Emergency Committee
132 Nassau Street, New York City

- -

I. HUNGARY:

The Nazi occupation of Hungary, has once again clearly
and most emphatically, brought before us the tragic picture of
European Jewry. Hungary, in which close to one million Jews had
existed, has also fallen, and these Jews are in imminent danger
of the fate which had overtaken millions of their brethren in the
execution chambers of Poland and elsewhere.

We have been profoundly impressed by the earnest
desire of our government to effect measures for the rescue of the
Jewish victims of Nazi barbarity. We have seen on many occasions,
definite action resulting in actual rescue.

The problem of Hungary, however, by its very urgency
and specific nature, calls for exceptional action. The relief
necessary, cannot be accomplished through individuals, organizations or agencies. We would respectfully suggest the following,
perhaps drastic, but nevertheless, vitally and imperatively
necessary action. Our government must, if success is to be achieved and rescue effected, react to this problem, and utilize
measures, which it would use in matters pertinent to our own national interest.

A) Every effort should be made for agents well supplied
with necessary funds and preferably of Magyar and Aryan extraction
to be sent secretly into Hungary. Their entry could be made
through Yugoslavia and through the cooperation of the Allied
Military forces. These agents by taking full advantage of the

animosity of [Hun]garian populace to t[he Na]zis and their friendly
disposition to the Jews would arrange 1- forthe hiding of Jews
among the friendly populace in cities, villages and hamlets.
These agents, by a judicious use of funds, could save the lives
of thousands, as was done in Poland, where for sums of 5,000 Zlotys,
(equivalent to $55.00),a Jew would be kept in hiding; for larger
sums Jews would be rescued from concentration camps. This has
been factually reported by the Polish government. The agents
should further be instructed to utilize their funds wherever it
would help in the saving or rescue of Jews from Hungary, and,if
necessary, to bribe, that the desired result be secured. 2) The
agents should also endeavor the escape of the Hungarian Jews via
Roumania and Bulgaria into Turkey. The matter of a friendly disposition by Turkey to the entry of escaping Jews, has already been
presented by the State Department, and we were advised that
Turkey has expressed her willingness to cooperate. This problem,
however, may be of such mass proportions, that a special presentation should be made to Turkey and every assurance given that they
would be taken out immediately and brought to temporary camps.
3) That these agents be instructed to help the escape of the
Hungarian Jews towards that part of Yugoslavia which is under
Marshal Tito's control; that these agents contact and urge the
cooperation of Marshal Tito and his partisans in the rescue of
these Jews. Lest these Jews become a burden to the partisans,
they should be helped to Adriatic shores from whence they could
be brought to Allied held territory. 4) Since the wrath of the
Nazis would first be visited upon the Rabbis and religious leaders
of the Jews, the agents sent in should be instructed to give
especial concern to the rescue of these.

b) That a presentation be made to the Vatican that
instructions issue to all dignitaries calling particular attention

to the plight of the Hungarian Jews and requesting fullest cooperation in their rescue; that the population be awakened to
this rescue necessity and urge all to hide and help in the escape
of Jews. A request should be made that especial consideration
be shown the Rabbis and religious leaders, who are in greater
danger.

c) That every effort be made to enlist the good offices
and assistance of the Russian Government to do everything possible
for the rescue of the Jews from the Balkan and Baltic States.

d) We refer to a message from Isaac Sternbuch of our
Committee sent through the American Legation, Bern, in which the
following requests are made:

QUOTE: "Southern American passports for ten thousand families
would be another possibility for rescue. Through the consulates
of those countries in Switzerland, passports should be handed to
us confidentially. Since the receivers would know that these
passports are valid only during war time as a means of saving lives,
they (passports) could not be misused. Only to well known Rabbis
and other reliable persons would passports be given.

"To report on the situation a courier has been despatched by me to Hungary. It is my suggestion that the possibility
of arranging an exchange of Jews in Hungary against German civilians
from Africa or other Allied occupied territory be examined by you
with the Government of America." UNQUOTE

We would therefore, respectfully present these two
rescue measures to the State Department and urge the adoption of
these measures as positive action which would result in the rescue
of larger numbers of doomed Jews.

II. LITHUANIA:

The problem of rescue in Lithuania has been the
subject of several presentations to the State Department. We would,

however, respectfully urge that the rescue proposals for Hungary, ie: - sending agents into Hungary and requesting the intervention of the Vatican be utilized also for Lithuania.

In addition, may we suggest

a) Intervention with Sweden to grant passports or citizenships to a minimum of 200 great Rabbis and religious leaders who are in greater danger because of their status.

b) To endeavor to utilize rescue possibilities inherent in the small boats plying between Sweden and the Baltics. These boats, the smaller the better, could be used effectively in helping the escape from Lithuania. The American government would be requested to give every assurance to Sweden that those Jews escaping entering Sweden would be taken out at the first opportunity.

LL

III. VAAD HAHATZALA DELEGATION TO LISBON:

That the Vaad Hahatzala Emergency Committee be granted permission to send a delegate or a committee of two to Lisbon, Portugal which woudd 1) endeavor to investigate and make an accurate record of all Rabbis, scholars, religious leaders and communal heads presently in Europe with a view to explore the existent rescue possibilities and to extend necessary relief to them. 2} To establish contact with those in neutral countries and if possible with those in countries liberated by the armed forces of the United States and those of the Allied nations. 3) To accumulate the necessary data for the reconstruction of the Jewish communal and religious life in Europe. This work may necessitate extension of the delegates activities to include visits to Turkey, Palestine and Switzerland. We would, therefore, request the State Department to respectfully grant diplomatic status to these delegates and to facilitate the arrangements for the journey.

Presented by:

VAAD HAHATZALA EMERGENCY COMMITTEE

Rabbi Abraham Kalmanowitz

SUMMARY REPORT OF THE ACTIVITIES OF THE WAR REFUGEE BOARD
WITH RESPECT TO THE JEWS IN HUNGARY

Prior to Germany's military occupation of Hungary on March 19, 1944, and the reconstitution of the Hungarian Government as a Nazi puppet, Hungary was the only refuge for Jews in Axis Europe. Although anti-Jewish laws had been on the Hungarian statute-books since as early as 1938, their enforcement and the condition of the Jews in Hungary were such as to invite the clandestine immigration of tens of thousands of Jews from Poland, Slovakia and Rumania, and the Jewish population of Hungary was swelled to over 800,000. The refugees were cared for by the native Jewish population who tried to see to it that no large numbers of newcomers congregated in any one place. However that may be, the movement was so large that the conclusion is inescapable that it was known to and connived at by the Hungarian authorities. During the first month of the Board's existence, the clandestine movement of Jews from Poland and Slovakia into Hungary still continued and the Board facilitated the efforts of private agencies to increase the traffic. During the same period, Hungary was also envisaged as an important source of food for the International Red Cross and other relief organizations to distribute to persecuted groups in concentration camps in German-controlled areas. On the Board's recommendation, Treasury licenses were issued to permit purchases of Hungarian foodstuffs for such purpose.

There were, however, lapses in the Hungarian Government's passive attitude. Thus, it was reported that during 1941 a substantial number of Jews from Poland and Hungarian-born Jews of Polish origin but of uncertain

nationality were in part deported to Poland and in part detained in con-
centration camps. It was also reported that in December, 1943, the
Germans began to press Hungary to adopt a stricter anti-Jewish policy.
Late in February, 1944, reports reached the Board that Hungary was yield-
ing to German pressure to deport foreign Jews and to close its borders to
refugees from Poland and elsewhere. Consequently, on March 7, 1944, the
American legations at Bern and Lisbon were instructed to communicate to
Hungarian authorities, through channels known to be available, a message
expressing this Government's disapproval of such persecution and warning
them of the consequences thereof. In part, this message read:

> .....the Government of the United States is aware that
> ...../the Hungarian Government is/ pursuing programs of
> persecuting.....Jewish minorities and refugees of other
> nationalities who have escaped into...../its/ territories.
> This persecution consists among other forms in sending
> such refugees beyond the borders.....into Poland where
> they undergo various forms of cruelty and even death,
> dictated by Nazi degeneracy. Still another form of perse-
> cution consists in preventing the refugees from escaping
> to neutral countries where their lives may be saved.
>
> The Government of the United States is determined to
> do everything it can to rescue such unfortunates who are in
> danger of losing their lives and to find for them havens of
> refuge. Any continuation by...../the Hungarian Government/
> of the execution of these policies of Hitlerite persecutions
> is viewed with great seriousness by this Government and will
> be kept in mind. The President, in establishing the War
> Refugee Board, recently restated unequivocally the position
> of the United States Government in this matter.....The Govern-
> ment of the United States takes the view that...../the Hungarian
> Government/, as well as...../its/ subordinates and functionaries,
> are fully responsible for the actions of persecution committed
> on their territories and in the interests of humanity they
> should desist immediately. Moreover, they should be informed
> that in their own interest they will be well advised to take
> advantage in the future of such opportunities as may be avail-
> able to them to allow refugees to depart across their borders
> into territories of any neutral countries which may be prepared
> to receive them."

16

On March 11, we were advised by our Minister at Lisbon that this message had been delivered to appropriate Hungarian authorities. A similar response was later received from our Minister at Bern.

On March 19, however, the German military occupied Hungary and the following days witnessed the creation of a Nazi puppet government, one of whose avowed purposes was to make Hungary "Judenrein".

On March 24, the President publicly condemned the Nazi policy of exterminating Jews and other civilian populations. He made particular reference to Hungary and warned that all those who took any part in such persecutions would be punished for their crimes. He called upon the decent people in Nazi Europe to assist the victims of persecutions in their efforts to hide and escape. This statement of the President was broadcasted from United Nations and neutral radio stations in whole or in part for many weeks. It was dropped in leaflet form from the air over Hungary and other Axis controlled countries.

On the theory that the presence of foreigners in official or unofficial capacities might have a deterrent effect, the Board, under date of March 25, requested the International Red Cross to "send effective representation to Hungary in order to protect the well-being of groups facing persecution". Under date of April 13, the following reply was received through the American legation at Bern:

> In order to give it more efficacy the International Committee has as a matter of fact concerned itself for some time in enlarging its delegation at Budapest. For the time being it has not considered sending to Hungary a special delegation with instructions to assume the particular protection to which the State Department's message referred since under the present circumstances such mission might be considered as unrelated to the committee's traditional and conventional competence.

17

The International Committee shall continue to devote its entire attention to all categories of war victims as it has in the past without intruding into the domestic policy of any of those states and the War Refugee Board as well as all the humanitarian and government institutions of several belligerent states can rest assured of this. Within full scope which circumstances demand and according to means placed at its disposal it shall always attempt to broaden and increase its action along its own line of activities in favor of those victims.

The aid of the Holy See was also enlisted. Thus on March 24, the Board wrote the Apostolic Delegate in Washington:

> Recent events have brought new tragedy to millions of people in Hungary and Rumania. The occupation of these countries by German military forces will spell added persecution, if not transportation and death, to nearly two million Jews unless the people and such native regimes as may continue to exist take measures to protect them. Consequently, the War Refugee Board earnestly seeks your good offices in presenting to the Holy See the suggestion that action by the Holy See, through the Nuncios or otherwise, may be effective to foster and facilitate the adoption of such measures of protection. The War Refugee Board is cognizant of the Holy See's deep interest in the welfare of these unfortunate people and ventures to hope that the Holy See will be able to take all appropriate action.

The following day the Delegate replied:

> It is a pleasure to inform you that I have already sent a communication to His Eminence, the Cardinal Secretary of State, invoking every possible assistance by the Holy See, through its diplomatic representatives, the Bishops and clergy, that the lot of these unfortunates may be rendered less difficult.
>
> I am confident that the Holy Father personally, and the agencies of the Holy See will cooperate to the utmost in the humanitarian cause.

On April 1, the Cardinal Secretary of State informed the American representative and the British ambassador at the Vatican that instructions had already been given to the representatives of the Holy See in Hungary to do everything possible for the relief of the Jews.

18

In the meantime, reports continued to arrive that German pressure on Hungary was being intensified, and on April 12, a second informal warning was addressed to Hungarian authorities through the American Legation at Lisbon. The instruction read, in part, as follows:

> In view of the German military's reported operations in Hungary, we request that you again approach the channels to the Government of Hungary that are available to you and state again the position taken by this Government and make it clearly understood that in spite of the current pressure by the Nazis any action on the part of the Hungarian Government to inflict new and further persecutions or to continue existing persecutions designed against foreign or native Jews or the deportation to Germany itself or any territory controlled by Germany of foreign or native Jews will be considered by this Government with the greatest disfavor and will be taken into account at the end of the war.

On April 18, the Board was advised that this warning has been placed in proper channels for transmission to the government of Hungary.

In view of the rising tide of persecution, avenues for escape were explored. The most promising clandestine route at the time appeared to be through that portion of Yugoslav territory occupied by the partisan forces of Marshal Tito. Consequently, during the first week of April, 1944, one of the Board's representatives discussed at length the feasibility of such an escape route with representatives of Marshal Tito as well as American and British military authorities at Bari, Italy. On April 13, the American Minister to the Yugoslav Government-in-Exile, in Cairo, informed the Board that the British Government was also taking steps to contact Marshal Tito in this connection. On April 22, the Board informed the American Minister to Yugoslavia that it was "prepared to arrange for any assistance, including funds." On April 29, the Board was advised that

19

support in rescuing Hungarian Jews has now been promised by Tito. He will aid them to escape and join his army or be evacuated whenever possible.

The possibility of escape through emigration was also explored, and the Turkish government was urged to facilitate the departure of Jews from Hungary by issuing Turkish transit visas in considerable numbers. There was some reason to believe that the holders of Turkish transit visas and Palestine immigration certificates might obtain Rumanian and Bulgarian transit visas.

On May 2, the efforts of the Board in this connection received a severe set-back. On that day, the U. S. Embassy at Ankara reported that

> the Turkish consul at Budapest had sent word that every Jew entering the Turkish consulate in Budapest was arrested as soon as he left and transported to an unknown place.

20

While pursuing its efforts to influence the Hungarian authorities by official and unofficial pressure, and to aid in the escape of Jews from Hungary, the Board did not neglect the possibility of enlisting the self-interest of individual German and Hungarian officials in a position to alleviate the fate of Jews. Thus on April 20, in cooperation with a private agency, steps were taken to establish contact with a mysterious person known only as "Willy" who was reported to have been successful in arresting the deportation of Jews from Slovakia. An intermediary in Switzerland was asked to explore with him the

> possibility of arranging for evacuations from Hungary to neutral countries or for holding up deportations or permitting sending relief to those detained. If any such arrangements possible, please indicate amounts you consider would be involved and extent to which such amounts could remain in neutral countries.

Another effort along such lines was made three months later with
the assistance of a prominent Hungarian in this country.

On May 4, the Board was advised by the American embassy in London
that the deportation of Jews from Hungary had begun and that 24,000 Hungarians
had already been deported from Carpatho-Russia, in addition to an unknown
number of Jewish refugees from Poland.

This report was rapidly followed by reports from other sources
that the deportation of Jews from Hungary was being relentlessly pursued and
with attendant brutalities.

On May 11, the American consulate in Jerusalem was requested to
obtain from the Jewish Agency the names of Hungarian officials responsible
for the persecution of Jews.

On May 17, the American embassy at Moscow was informed of the
situation in Hungary and given the following instruction:

> Please endeavor to have Russian broadcasts in appro-
> priate languages beamed on Germany and German-satellite
> countries transmit warnings to German and German-satellite
> military and civilian personnel carrying out deportation
> proceedings that they personally will be held responsible
> by the United Nations for their actions and the deaths that
> may result from deportation. Please also approach the
> Foreign Office in an attempt to have it use its influence
> upon the satellite governments and populations by all pos-
> sible means to cause their resistance to German demands for
> the deportation and persecution of minority groups under
> their control.
>
> For your information, the OWI transmitters are carrying
> similar warnings and the American Embassy, London, is being
> requested to make similar approaches to the Ministry of In-
> formation and the Foreign Office.

A similar instruction was sent to the American embassy in London.

21

Under date of May 25, the following information and suggestions were cabled by our Minister at Bern:

According to all reliable information unmistakably steps are being taken preparatory to massive deportation and extermination of the Jewish population especially in Carpatho-Russian and Maramaros regions. The number of people immediately involved is about 200,000 and the action shows every sign of being extended to the Jewish population in Hungary proper.

This action has all the namelessly tragic and brutal earmarks of similar actions carried out in Poland by the Nazis and their henchmen. It is being most savagely taken in northeastern Hungary.....

For all reliable reports - and this is even reflected in the Hungarian press especially in the provinces - the Hungarian population have not sympathized with such brutal anti-Jewish measures. On the contrary they have openly sided with the persecuted Jews and have continually attempted to aid these wretched souls by bringing them food and clothing.

On the other hand the Hungarian authorities have taken severe measures to isolate such concentration camps and to cut off all assistance from outside.....

The lot of these Jews in such improvised "camps" is wretched. Such cattle markets, tile factories and wood yards are almost completely devoid of sanitary facilities and in many instances thousands of men women children old and sick people are forced to live in the open under conditions of frightful crowding and promiscuity. They were permitted to take nothing with them in the way of blankets or covers and it becomes tragically obvious that a great many will die of exposure disease and slow starvation even before they are jammed 80 to 100 to a wagon into cattle cars for deportation.....

It is my urgent suggestion, in close collaboration with the War Refugee Board representative here, that the Government of the USSR be prevailed upon in regard to the purpose of the occupation of Hungary by the Nazis, to associate itself with the declaration of March 24 by President Roosevelt (Eden March 31). Since the Soviet armies are standing on the frontiers of Hungary and the fear of the Russians in the hearts of a large number of "collaborators" in Hungary is mortal, a declaration by the Soviet Union would have all the more weight.

The suggestion was cabled to our ambassador in Moscow on June 10.

Among other steps taken to ensure the safety of Jews in Hungary was the extension to Hungary of this Government's emphatic demand that persons in German-controlled territory holding documents issued in the name of any American republic, or otherwise claiming the nationality of an American republic on other grounds, be accorded all rights and privileges of such nationals, unless and until the government whose nationality is claimed denies the validity of such documents or claims. In the course of a prolonged exchange of communications with other American republics, this Government succeeded, on humanitarian grounds, in securing the consent of most of them to this procedure, and they agreed to postpone examination of such documents and claims until such time as the persons in question should no longer be subject to enemy persecution. Through the protecting powers of the American republics—Spain and Switzerland—Germany and Hungary were informed of these demands. Several thousands Polish and other Jews in Axis-held territory who, in an attempt to escape death, succeeded in obtaining documents of various Latin American countries, were the beneficiaries of this program. Although many of these "Latin American nationals" were made the victims of what the German Foreign Office, in one of its notes to Switzerland, described as "the general treatment accorded to Eastern-European Jews," a considerable number of such Jews have, nevertheless been enabled to survive by reason of this measure.

Further information regarding the situation in Hungary was requested of the European neutrals between May 20 and May 23, and, on

23

May 25 and 26 American missions in Ankara, Bern, Lisbon, Madrid and

Stockholm were instructed as follows:

> Please represent to the ..... government that,
> according to persistent and seemingly authentic reports,
> systematic mass extermination of Jews in Hungary has
> begun. The lives of 800,000 human beings in Hungary
> may well depend on the restraint that may result from
> the presence in that country of the largest possible
> number of foreign observers. To this end, please urge
> appropriate authorities in the interest of most elementary
> humanity to take immediate steps to increase to the
> largest possible extent the number of .....diplomatic
> and consular personnel in Hungary and to distribute them
> as widely as possible throughout the country.

> It is hoped, of course, that all such diplomatic
> and consular representatives will use all means available
> to them to persuade individuals and officials to desist
> from further barbarisms.

Sweden agreed to comply with our request and appointed as its

special attache to its Budapest legation a Swedish businessman who had

already expressed his willingness to the Board's Stockholm representative

to undertake a similar mission in his private capacity. The Swedish Foreign

Office invited the Board's suggestions as to the new attache's activities,

and on July 7 the Board cabled its Stockholm representative:

> Since money and favorable post-war consideration may
> motivate action impeding, relaxing or slowing down tempo
> of persecution and facilitate escapes and concealments, it
> should be ascertained in what quarters such inducements may
> be effective.....If circumstances warrant funds will be made
> available at neutral bank for post-war use or in part in
> local currency now, procured against blocked counter-
> value here or in neutral bank.....Whenever a concrete
> proposal based on financial arrangements of substantial
> character or on favorable post-war consideration is broached,
> the matter should be referred to the Board for clearance,

24

which will require evidence of effectiveness and good
faith in the meantime. In order to care for less substantial transactions a fund of $50,000 will be placed
at Olsen's disposal which may be used in his discretion
in addition to the fund already available to him for
discretionary use.

The problem may be dealt with on various levels such
as high official, low official and unofficial, central and
local. In connection with unofficial channels an informed
source suggests that ships and barges going down the Danube
are generally empty and may afford a means of escape for a
limited number of refugees in the guise of seamen or otherwise. Same source suggests that skippers can be approached
on financial basis and crews through so-called communist
channels. Board is also advised that railroad line from
Budapest to Mohacs, said to be about ten miles from partisan-
controlled Yugoslav territory, might afford similar opportuni-
ties if contacts made with trainmen through what are termed
communist channels. Board further advised that Transylvania
Unitarian Church, socialist and partisan groups may be in a
position because of geographical situation and absence of
real occupation to shelter refugees if they can reach that
area. In addition, Board believes that Roman Catholic clergy
and Nuncio may be helpful both in action and with advice.

With reference to high official channels exploration
may be made of the possibility.....of evacuation of Jews
and persons similarly situated belonging to specific groups
such as (a) holders of Palestine certificates, (b) holders
of visas for entry into neutral countries, (c) persons to
whom the issuance of visas for entry into an American
republic is authorized provided they appear personally there-
for before a consular office in a neutral country, (d) persons holding passports or consular documents issued in the
names of American republics, or who are under the protection
of a neutral country.....(e) women and children, (f) aged
and infirm men, and (g) parents, husbands, wives, children,
etc., of American citizens.

You should advise.....[the new Swedish attache at
Budapest] of the foregoing to the extent that you deem
advisable and inform him that the same constitutes a
general outline of a program which the Board believes can
be pursued. While he cannot, of course, act as the Board's
representative, nor purport to act in its name, he can,
whenever advisable, indicate that as a Swede he is free to
communicate with Stockholm where a representative of the
Board is stationed. He may thus express his willingness
to lay before the Board's representative specific proposals
if in any particular case he should deem so doing to be
advisable, or if by reason of the nature of the proposal
Olsen's or the Board's approval is necessary.....

25

/He_/ should consult with the representative of the International Red Cross and impress upon him the urgent need of increasing Intercross representation in Hungary and intercession in an effort to secure permission to visit and inspect concentration camps, ghettos and other places of detention. /He_/ might undertake also to see whether such permission might be granted him and his colleagues.....

The new Swedish attache assumed his duties with vigor and in addition to his efforts generally to alleviate the condition of Jews in Hungary, soon had a substantial number of persons under effective Swedish protection.

On May 26, the following message from the Government of the United States was cabled to Rome for delivery to the Cardinal Secretary of State:

> The wave of hate which has engulfed Europe and the consequent mass persecution, enslavement, deportation and slaughter of helpless men, women and children have, we know, sorely grieved His Holiness. We know also that His Holiness, with great compassion for the sufferings of a large portion of mankind has labored unceasingly to re-inculcate a decent regard for the dignity of man. So, too, we know of His Holiness' tireless efforts to alleviate the lot of the persecuted, the hunted and the outcast. His Holiness, we are certain, is aware of the deep feeling of abhorrence which the persecutions, mass-deportations, enslavements and slaughters in France, Germany, Poland, Czechoslovakia, the Balkans, Norway and elsewhere have aroused in the American people. His Holiness, we are confident, is also aware of the deep concern of the Government of the United States with respect to these reversions to usages of ancient barbarism, and of its constant efforts to prevent their recurrence.
>
> In view of the common concern of the Holy See and the Government and people of the United States with such matters, we believe it appropriate to call to the Holy See's attention the seemingly authentic reports that the present authorities in Hungary have undertaken to persecute the 800,000 Jews in Hungary merely because they are Jews, and are planning their mass slaughter both in Hungary and after deportation to Poland. The Government of the United States has warned the authorities and people of Hungary of the material consequences that will follow the perpetration of such inhuman acts of barbarism. We believe, however, that it is both timely and fitting that

26

the Hungarian authorities and people should be reminded of
the moral values involved and of the spiritual consequences
that must flow from indulgence in the persecution and mass-
murder of helpless men, women and children. To that end we
earnestly suggest that His Holiness may find it appropriate
to express himself on this subject to the authorities and
people of Hungary, personally by radio and through the Nuncio
and clergy in Hungary as well as through a representative of
the Holy See specially despatched to Hungary for that purpose.
His Holiness, we deeply hope, may find it possible to remind
the authorities and people of Hungary, among whom great
numbers profess spiritual adherence to the Holy See, of
the spiritual consequences of such acts and of the ecclesiastic
sanctions which may be applied to the perpetrators thereof.

On June 25 the Pope addressed a personal appeal to Regent Horthy.

It was learned from the Apostolic Delegate in Washington under

date of July 24, that

> the personal appeal of the Holy Father to Regent Horthy has
> led the latter to assume a more determined attitude of oppo-
> sition to the racial laws. Likewise the members of the
> Catholic Hierarchy were encouraged to carry on a more in-
> tense activity in favor of victims of racial laws.

27

> It seems that the Government of Hungary has now given
> assurance to His Eminence, Cardinal Seredi, Primate of Hungary,
> that deportations of Jewish people will cease. The Apostolic
> Nunciature adds that in fact the whole racial situation is
> somewhat improved.

In a direct effort to confront the Hungarian authorities with
their responsibility for the treatment of Jews, the following instruction
was sent on June 6 at the urgent request of the Board, to our legation at
Bern:

> In view of consistent neutral press reports carrying
> Berlin and Budapest date lines and other information to the
> effect that the eight hundred thousand Jews in Hungary are
> being segregated in ghettos and concentrated in camps, there
> seems little doubt that the pattern heretofore set in Poland
> and repeated elsewhere is again being followed. In an effort
> to develop means to forestall the effectuation of the ultimate
> ends of such program, that is mass-executions either before or
> after deportation, consideration has been given to the advis-
> ability of requesting the Swiss Government to address an
> inquiry on behalf of this Government to appropriate authorities

in Hungary asking them to state their intentions with respect
to the future treatment to be accorded to Jews in ghettos and
concentration camps and specifically whether they contemplate
forced deportations to Poland or elsewhere or the imposition
of discriminatory reductions in food rations, or the adoption of
other measures which like those mentioned will be tantamount
to mass-execution. At the same time, the Swiss government
would be requested to remind the same authorities of the grave
view that this Government takes with respect to the persecution
of Jews and other minorities and of the determination of this
Government to see to it that all those who share the responsibility for such acts are dealt with in accordance with the
President's statement of March 24, 1944.

Please give the foregoing your most careful consideration
and unless you are of the opinion that to do so would involve
positive disadvantages you should proceed promptly to make the
requests outlined above.

A note in the tenor indicated was transmitted to the Swiss Foreign

Office on June 13, and was communicated to Hungarian officials two weeks

later.

28

From the very outset of the German military occupation of Hungary,

the Board cooperated closely with private agencies in organizing clandestine

escapes. Thus, the Board made available to representatives of private

rescue agencies in neutral countries the names and addresses of persons in

Hungary who were believed, on the basis of available information in the

United States, to be inclined and in a position to be of assistance. Every

facility was extended for the transmission of private funds to finance such

operations and the Board communicated to private agencies information con-

cerning acceptable sources of pengo currency. The Board's representatives

abroad were on the constant lookout for underground groups that might be

of assistance and through their efforts arrangements were concluded between such groups and private rescue agencies.

The Board also extended its facilities fully for the transmission of applications for the issuance of Palestine immigration certificates to people in Hungary and, after Rumania was induced to abandon the persecution of Jews as a national policy, the Board exerted pressure upon the Rumanian Government to permit the entry of Hungarian refugees. On June 2, the Prime Minister of Rumania advised the Rumanian Delegate to the International Red Cross that he might give formal assurances that Jewish refugees from Hungary would be allowed to enter Rumania notwithstanding formal declarations to the contrary, and that "their safety would be looked out for by the Rumanians".

In addition to the above steps, wide publicity over a period of many months was secured in Hungary, by radio and otherwise, for a series of warnings and appeals to the people of Hungary. These included the President's statement of March 24, statements by the members of the Senate Foreign Relations Committee, by the House Foreign Affairs Committee, by Archbishop Spellman of New York, by a group of representative leaders of American opinion headed by Governor Alfred E. Smith, and by Hungarian leaders in this country.

On July 6, our Minister to Stockholm advised us that the King of Sweden addressed a strong personal appeal to Admiral Horthy. Finally, on July 13 the Board was advised that as the result of persistent suggestions by the Board's representative and private organizations that the International Red Cross intervene in the Hungarian situation, Professor Huber, President of the International Red Cross, addressed a personal letter of protest to Admiral Horthy on July 6.

29

Meanwhile, the reports regarding the situation in Hungary became more alarming. On June 24, the American legation in Bern cabled the following information:

Now there is no doubt that the majority of the Jewish population east of the Danube especially in eastern, northern, and north eastern Hungary has been deported to Poland. Further reliable information confirming this fact has come in in the course of the past two weeks from the following independent sources: (a) Swiss official employee just returned from Budapest, (b) Railway workers in Czech resistance movement, (c) other reliable secret source. Regard information as to sources as absolutely confidential since any publicity regarding them would endanger lives.

Prior to the deportations, there were two weeks to a month of brutal concentration during which thousands of Jews were crowded together in primitive quarters with insufficient food, clothing and water, regardless of state of health, sex or age. The Hungarian gendarmerie on Laszlo Endre's orders largely carried out this action.....

Some 350,000 Jews have already been concentrated in Budapest and environs. This began around June 16 and on the 21st it was to be finished. In the city proper they have been settled in requisitioned blocks of houses in a chess board pattern so that they will not escape bombardment.

In an effort to check such continued deportations..... we recommend British and Soviet broadcasts and especially leaflets. If it is possible, the Vatican should be prevailed upon to associate itself with such protest.

There is little doubt that many of these Hungarian Jews are being sent to the extermination camps of Auschwitz (Oswiecim) and Birkenau (Rajaka) in western upper Silesia where according to recent reports, since early summer 1942 at least 1,500,000 Jews have been killed. There is evidence that already in January 1944 preparations were being made to receive and exterminate Hungarian Jews in these camps. Soon a detailed report on these camps will be cabled.

On July 14, our Minister in Bern reported that, according to information received by him from the Swiss Foreign Office on July 6, some

250,000 Jews had been deported from Hungary.

Although it was at first reported that the deportations were being conducted by German authorities, on August 18, our legation in Stockholm informed us of reports from several sources that

> in the main the Hungarian police have themselves been the instrument for arresting and deporting Jews from Hungary under conditions which are tragically cruel.

In the same message, the legation related the following incident witnessed by a member of the Swedish legation in Budapest and related by him to a friend in Stockholm, one of the most prominent personalities in Sweden:

> Approximately 20,000 Hungarian Jews, children, men and women, had been concentrated in the open air for 4 or 5 days with nothing even to sit on except the ground. Then they had been herded into boxcars 80 persons per car, the car then nailed up and sent off to foreign destinations. The people are packed in the cars like sardines with no possibility of sitting or even moving. Many must have been dead on arrival. The friend was specifically asked by this source if the Germans were instrumental in this operation and he was assured by his friend that the people handling this affair were not Germans but Hungarian Gerdarmes.

31

In a message of August 22 concerning that incident the American legation at Stockholm identified the place as Budakalasz. The message added that

> the informant was particularly impressed by the ruthless demeanor of Hungarian gendarmes. They were described by him as bloodthirsty as the Gestapo of Germany. Jews old, young and children, male and female were herded into boxcars by gendarmes who drove them on with rifle butts and a whip was even used by one gendarme.
>
> From Jewish girls of Hungary now in Hamburg and other places soldiers of Germany have brought back messages to Budapest to their friends. After having been deported from Hungary these girls have been turned over to German armed forces and wear armbands inscribed war harlot (kriegshure).
>
> In provincial Hungary, camps of Jews were emptied before a halt was made to deportations by officials of Hungary. As a rule while the camps were still operating

they were managed by Hungarian personnel aided by an SS adviser thought competent in giving instructions in competent managing of Jews to the Hungarians.

In view of persistent Hungarian denials of the complicity of Hungarian officials in the commission of atrocities (see Hungarian note transmitted by American legation in Bern under date of August 5, below), our legation in Bern was instructed on August 25 to request the Swiss Government to bring this incident and other reports of Hungarian participation in atrocities to the attention of appropriate Hungarian authorities.

On July 19, the American legation *at Bern* cabled as follows:

A note from the Foreign Office, dated yesterday, states that according to a telegram from the Swiss Legation at Budapest, authorization has been given by the Government of Hungary for the departure of all Jews from Hungary who hold entry permits for another country, including Palestine.

This same message states that transit through occupied territories will be permitted by the German Government. As soon as possible the Swiss Legation, in collaboration with the Palestinian Bureau, Budapest, will take necessary measures for evacuation. It is probable that Hungarian police passports will constitute travel documents.

In order to take the fullest possible advantage of this development, the European neutrals were requested on July 28 to advise Germany and Hungary that they were prepared to receive all Jews permitted to emigrate. This request was accompanied by assurances that this Government would undertake to make arrangements for the support and early evacuation of such refugees. The British government was urged to join us in the request and commitment. Thus, the American legation at Bern was instructed as follows:

You are requested to consult with your British colleague and either in collaboration with him or alone, as the circumstances may develop, approach appropriate officials of the Swiss Government with the request that Switzerland advise the Hungarian Government that it is prepared to receive Jews released by Hungary and permitted to go to Switzerland. You may assure appropriate Swiss officials that if Switzerland so advises the Hungarian Government, Jews arriving in Switzerland from Hungary will be evacuated to United Nations territory as promptly as possible and that in the meantime the United States will undertake to make arrangements for their maintenance and support in Switzerland. You should inform the Department and the Board promptly of the results of your consultation with your British colleague and your approach to the Swiss Government."

On the same day, our embassy in London was instructed as follows:

This Government is prepared to advise the Hungarian and neutral governments that all Jews arriving in neutral countries from Hungary will be afforded havens in United Nations territory just as promptly as military considerations permit, neutral governments to be given adequate assurances as to the maintenance of such persons in the meantime and to be requested to advise the Hungarian Government of their willingness to receive such persons. Please endeavor to ascertain from the Foreign Office whether the Government of the United Kingdom will join this Government in this attempt to save lives. American missions in neutral countries are being instructed to take appropriate action along these lines in collaboration with their British colleagues if possible, alone if necessary. Since time is of the essence, British missions should be advised of Foreign Office views promptly.

Please keep Department and Board advised.

Please advise Sir Herbert Emerson of the Intergovernmental Committee of the foregoing and endeavor to ascertain from him some indication as to the extent to which IGC funds may be available for the maintenance of such refugees from Hungary as may arrive in neutral countries following such approaches. The War Refugee Board would appreciate as early a response to this inquiry as possible.

Under all of the circumstances it might prove tragic if the fullest advantage of the present opportunity were not (repeat not) taken. Consequently, you are requested urgently to propose to the Foreign Office the necessity of

33

P.H. WELSHIMER MEMORIAL LIBRARY
MILLIGAN COLLEGE, TN 37682

immediately making available to Jews in Hungary Palestine certificates in substantial additional numbers. In this connection, the possibility should not be overlooked that once the holders of such additional certificates arrive in Turkey or Spain, they may be routed to havens other than Palestine if circumstances should be deemed to preclude their entry into Palestine. Please advise the Department and Board of such views as the Foreign Office might express.

Realizing that such a broad program might meet with difficulties, European neutral countries were requested, at the same time, on the basis of a commitment similar to that mentioned above, to express to enemy countries their willingness to receive persons for whom American immigration visas had been authorized after July 1, 1941. American consular officers in such countries were simultaneously authorized by the Department of State to

34

issue new American immigration visas to any such person to whom an American visa was issued or for whom such visa was authorized after July 1, 1941, provided that (a) such person other than a child under 16 years of age is found upon telegraphic reference to the Department for security check not to be the subject of an adverse report dated subsequent to the previous approval, (b) such person is not affirmatively found by the consul to be inadmissible into the United States under the law, or (c) the consul does not consider that the case is one which should be recommended for consideration under the committee procedure.

The Swiss government was asked to advise Germany and Hungary that

American consular officers in neutral countries have been authorized to issue an immigration visa to any person to whom an American immigration visa was issued or for whom a visa was authorized on or after July 1, 1941 and who has been in areas controlled by Germany or any of Germany's allies since December 8, 1941, provided that such person presents himself to an American consular officer in a neutral country and is found not to have become disqualified for the issuance of a visa.

This authorization was in accordance with a program proposed by the Board as early as March 16 pursuant to which American immigration visas authorized after the present security checks had been put into effect, but which had become invalid by lapse of time, would be replaced in the case of persons in enemy controlled territory and subject to enemy persecution. The Department of State agreed to this program on July 20.

Turkey was also requested to admit all persons in enemy territory holding Palestine certificates and to advise enemy governments of its willingness to do so. The assurances given by this Government regarding maintenance and evacuation of refugees were extended to cover such refugees as well.

In pursuance of our request, Sweden and Turkey advised the Hungarian Government of their willingness to receive holders of American immigration visas, and Turkey also agreed to receive holders of Palestine certificates.

In the meantime, the following letter, dated July 25, was received from the Washington delegate of the International Committee of the Red Cross:

We have received today the following communication from the I.C.R.C. in Geneva:

The Hungarian Government is willing to make possible the emigration of certain categories of Jews and has advised the I.C.R.C. of its readiness in this respect.

Very obviously from the viewpoint of maintaining the principle of neutrality, which in effect is based on reciprocity, the I.C.R.C. feels that the number of emigrant Jews to be admitted to the United States should be substantially increased, and that a corresponding number of Entry permits should be accorded.

35

It would, furthermore, be desirable if the United States Government would make a public statement on this subject, indicating the number of Entry permits accorded. The I.C.R.C. is of the opinion that such a statement would impress the Hungarian Government as the visible sign of a favourable reaction to their decision to cease the persecution of the Jews also on this side. Moreover, the possibility of an eventual withdrawal of the concession granted would be made difficult by a public declaration, as suggested above, which would at the same time also forestall an attempt on the part of the countries of emigration to throw the blame for an eventual failure on the countries of immigration.

The I.C.R.C. would like to be informed whether the United States Government would be willing to transmit and support this proposal to the Governments of the South American Republics or whether the I.C.R.C. should do so directly.

The I.C.R.C. reserves the right to issue a communique concerning this proposal, which has simultaneously been submitted to the Government of Great Britain.

The letter did not elaborate on what categories of Jews would be

36

permitted to emigrate.

Despite the vague nature of the Hungarian "offer," it seemed

imperative to reply to it as soon as possible and to stress that this

Government's acceptance thereof was not limited to any special category

of Jews, but embraced all who should be permitted to leave Hungary. In

the opinion of the Board, engaging in protracted negotiations with Latin

American governments as to the number of entry permits they would be

willing to grant would have further endangered the lives of Jews in

Hungary. As, however, the Red Cross inquiry was addressed to the United

Kingdom as well as to the United States, an exchange of views with

Great Britain ensued.

On August 11 the following reply was handed by the American

Minister at Bern to the Red Cross:

The United States Government has learned through the
ICRC of the Hungarian Government's willingness to permit the
emigration from Hungary of certain categories of Jews.
This Government, despite the substantial difficulties
and responsibilities involved, has consistently made clear
its determination to take all practicable steps to rescue
victims of religious or political oppression. In view of
the overwhelming humanitarian considerations involved concerning the Jews in Hungary, this Government now repeats
specifically its assurance that it will arrange for the
care of all Jews permitted to leave Hungary in the present
circumstances who reach neutral or United Nations territory,
and will find for such people temporary havens of refuge
where they may live in safety. These assurances have been
communicated to the governments of neutral countries who
have been requested to permit the entry of Jews who reach
their borders from Hungary. This Government now awaits information concerning the concrete steps to be taken by the
Hungarian Government to carry out its proposal.

On August 16 we were advised that the British had agreed to

join the United States in this response. On August 17 the following

joint statement was issued by the two governments:

37

The International Committee of the Red Cross has communicated to the Governments of the United Kingdom and
the United States an offer of the Hungarian Government
regarding the emigration and treatment of Jews. Because
of the desperate plight of the Jews in Hungary and the
overwhelmingly humanitarian considerations involved the
two governments are informing the Government of Hungary
through Intercross that, despite the heavy difficulties
and responsibilities involved, they have accepted the
offer of the Hungarian Government for the release of Jews
and will make arrangements for the care of such Jews
leaving Hungary who reach neutral or United Nations territory, and also that they will find temporary havens of
refuge where such people may live in safety. Notification
of these assurances is being given to the governments of
neutral countries who are being requested to permit the
entry of Jews who reach their frontiers from Hungary. The
Governments of the United Kingdom and the United States
emphasize that, in accepting the offer which has been made,
they do not in any way condone the action of the Hungarian
Government in forcing the emigration of Jews as an alternative to persecution and death.

Following this reply to the Red Cross, further steps were taken

to increase the number of Jews in Hungary who would be likely to obtain Hungarian and German permission to leave the country and the consent of neutral countries to receive them.

Thus, earlier arrangements made by the Board for havens in Latin-American countries and Ireland for refugee children from France, were, with the approval of such countries, extended to cover Jewish children from Hungary. On August 21, American consuls in Switzerland, Spain and Portugal were authorized to issue up to five thousand immigration visas within the limits of existing quotas, to refugee children from Hungary who succeeded in reaching these neutral countries.

On May 24, the Board had proposed to the Department of State that the issuance of visas be authorized for victims of enemy persecution so related to American citizens and alien residents of the United States as to be entitled to non-quota or preference visas. The Board's purpose in this, as in its proposals that lapsed visas be renewed and that visas be authorized for refugee children, was to facilitate the escape of persecuted persons into neutral territory, and not to foster immigration into the United States.

On August 5, the Department of State gave its approval to this. Several weeks passed in clearing various technical details with the Department of Justice. By then, information from abroad made it very doubtful whether German authorities would permit the exit of any Jews from Hungary or other German-controlled areas, whatever permits or visas they might have. Nevertheless, the Board decided to continue its efforts to rescue Axis victims by all possible means. Accordingly, the following instruction was cabled

38

on August 24 to the American legation at Bern:

Notwithstanding recent developments.....this Government
intends to pursue further the reported offers of Hungarian
authorities.....

Accordingly, please request appropriate officials of the
Swiss Government to advise enemy governments, particularly
neutral countries have been authorized to issue an immigration
visa to the alien husband, wife, parent, and unmarried minor
child of an American citizen, and the wife and unmarried
minor child of an alien resident of the United States who has
been in an area controlled by Germany or any of Germany's
allies, provided that such person presents himself to an
American consular officer and is found not to be disqualified for a visa. At the same time, please attempt to secure
the prompt agreement of the Swiss Government to advise enemy
governments of Switzerland's willingness to permit the entry
into Switzerland of persons falling within the categories
described above. You may assure Swiss officials that any
such persons so admitted will be adequately maintained and
that any who may be found not to be qualified for the issuance
of a visa will be evacuated as promptly as possible.....

Consular officers in Switzerland are hereby authorized
to issue immigration visas to any alien who is the husband,
wife, parent, or unmarried minor child of an American citizen
and on whose behalf nonquota or first preference status has
been established by the approval of the Department of Justice
of a petition filed by such citizen relative, or who is the
wife or unmarried minor child of an alien lawfully admitted
into the United States for permanent residence and as such
is entitled to second preference immigration status. The
issuance of visas is subject to the proviso, however, that (a)
such person other than a child under 16 years of age is found
upon telegraphic reference to the Department for security
check not to be the subject of an adverse report or to be
open to reasonable suspicion because of the circumstances of
the case such as those attending the release of a male applicant
of military age, (b) such person is not affirmatively found by
the consul to be inadmissible into the United States under the
law, or (c) the consul does not consider that the case is one
which should be recommended for consideration under the committee procedure.

Similar instructions were cabled to our missions at Ankara,
Lisbon, Madrid and Stockholm.

39

Private agencies in this country were advised by us of the visa procedures above described, and with their help lists of persons who could benefit thereby were compiled. Upon certification by the Department of State (in the case of holders of lapsed visas) and by the Department of Justice (in the case of relatives) of the eligibility of the persons listed, their names were transmitted to our missions abroad for action in accordance with our instructions of July 28 and August 24.

Practically no Jews, however, were evacuated from Hungary as the result of the foregoing. Under various pretexts, the German authorities refused to grant the Jews in Hungary permission to leave the country or to travel through German territory to adjoining neutral countries. Thus, under date of September 12, the International Red Cross reported:

40

> .....at the present time emigration from Hungary towards Rumania and Bulgaria is absolutely impossible. On the other hand emigration towards the other neutral countries which are accessible, namely, Sweden and Switzerland, meets with very serious obstacles.
>
> The Governments of those two countries are undoubtedly quite ready to receive a large number of Hungarian Jews but the difficulty for those emigrants is to reach those countries.
>
> While the Hungarian Government declared that it was disposed to let the Jews emigrate to countries which are willing to receive them particularly Palestine on the other hand the German Government is little inclined to deal with requests for permission to leave Hungary or to cross Germany in transit.

The Germans similarly denied exit permits and transit visas to substantial groups of Hungarian Jews who had been granted Swedish and Spanish entry visas.

At first, the Germans explained that their friendship for the Arabs made it impossible to permit Jews to emigrate unless it was assured that they would not go to Palestine. Then they demanded assurances that

all Jews permitted to emigrate would go to Britain or America. Finally,
however, it became clear that the Germans were willing to let the Jews
go only in exchange for such articles as trucks, tractors, machine tools,
and similar material to support the German war effort. Gestapo agents
were reported by our Minister at Bern on September 16 to have demanded
$25,000,000 in neutral countries for the purchase of war materials, as
well as Allied permission for the export to Germany of the commodities
which they might buy.

The attitude of the Hungarian authorities during the period
after their July offer is not too clear. There were several reports from
neutral, Vatican and Red Cross sources that deportations had stopped and
that the International Red Cross was being afforded an opportunity to
supervise the treatment being accorded to the remaining Jews. On the
other hand, the Hungarian government attempted to gloss over and, indeed,
to justify its persecution of the Jews. An illustration of this attitude
is provided by the Hungarian reply to our inquiry transmitted by Switzerland
to Hungary on June 26. The reply, cabled to us by the American minister
at Bern under date of August 5, is in part as follows:

41

> Military events on eastern front and approach of
> Soviet Army to Hungarian frontier made it necessary
> fully to mobilize all military material and moral forces
> of country for defense of nation's existence. This also
> meant elimination of everything that would undermine or
> diminish the country's resisting power. As defeatist
> propaganda and agitation of Jews—as in 1918—became
> more and more perceptible in this decisive phase of the
> war and in order to prevent repetition of tragic events
> of 1918-1919 government was obliged to eliminate on in-
> creased scale influence of Jews. They were consequently
> separated from rest of population and put to more useful
> work—either in country itself or abroad. In so doing
> Government and its functionaries did not fail to consider
> laws of humanity and justice. If individual cases of in-
> justice occurred they were always due to sporadic [apparent
> omission in the cable] of some subordinate organs which in
> each case responsible.

22

Numerous Jews were placed at the disposal of German Government as workers as was case for years for tens of thousands of workers of Hungarian nationality and Christian faith.

Our minister at Bern was instructed on August 19 to request the Swiss Foreign Office to convey the following reply:

With.....reference to Hungarian communication.....the Government of the United States notes the explanation contained in said communication regarding Jews deported from Hungary to the effect that they have been "placed at disposal of German Government as workers as was case for years for tens of thousands of workers of Hungarian nationality and Christian faith."

In view of the policy of the German Government with regard to Jews, which, the U. S. Government assumes is well-known to Hungarian Government, the Government of the United States would appreciate a statement of such measures which have been taken and are being taken by Hungarian authorities to insure humane treatment of Jews placed at Germany's disposal and to safeguard them against starvation and other forms of persecution.

The Hungarian authorities will readily perceive that unless such measures are taken with respect to all Jews "placed at disposal of German Government" the explanation offered would appear to be at utter variance with the facts and any cases of abuse will be imputed to those Hungarian authorities responsible for placing such Jews at Germany's disposal.

Prompt response to the inquiry herein made is being awaited by the Government of the United States with extraordinary interest.

On August 23 the following additional instruction was cabled to Bern:

Please request the Swiss Foreign Office to inform Hungarian authorities that although this Government has taken note of the communication.....it does not accept the reasoning therein contained and reserves the right to return at a later date to the purported facts therein related. Hungarian authorities should further be informed that the limited assurances contained in such communication serve only to prompt a reiteration of this Government's warning that all those who share in the responsibility for the persecution of Jews and other minorities will be brought to justice. Hungarian authorities should also be informed

42

that it is the Government's strong view that the deportation
of any category of Jews comes within the foregoing and that
permission freely to emigrate and Red Cross supervision of
treatment and living conditions must as a minimum be extended
to all categories of Jews.

On September 6, both messages were conveyed to the Hungarian
Government by the Swiss Minister at Budapest.

At the same time, it came to the knowledge of the Board that in
a note to the Swedish Foreign Office, the Hungarian legation in Stockholm
stated that

It was further ordered that future deportees for labor
service will have right of supervision by Hungarian Red
Cross representatives in order to avoid further charges
of brutality.

Taking advantage of this opening, the following instruction was
cabled on August 19 to the American minister at Bern:

In view of issue involved, i.e. possible extermination of
400,000 Jews already said to have been deported, please suggest to Intercross the urgency of contacting Hungarian authorities and Hungarian Red Cross with a view to establishing immediate supervision of Red Cross over all camps to which Jews
from Hungary have been deported in the past as well.

According to a report from the American legation at Bern dated
September 15, as many as 360,000 Jews had been deported from Hungary.
These were admitted by the Gestapo to have been exterminated. 160,000
Hungarian Jews had been put at forced labor in German-controlled territory
outside Hungary. These are presumably alive. 200,000 Jews remained in
Hungary, principally in the new Budapest ghettos.

There are indications that the Jews who have not yet been
deported from Hungary have of late found themselves in a somewhat better

43

position, due, perhaps, to the combined pressure of this Government

and its Allies, of neutral governments, of the Vatican, and of the

necessity of utilizing all available manpower for the defense of Hungary

against the United Nations' advance. On September 25, the Apostolic

Delegate in Washington wrote to the Board:

> I have been just informed by the Holy See that
> according to a report of the Apostolic Nuncio in
> Budapest the situation among the Jewish people of
> Hungary is now much less acute. This is attributed
> to the fact that the officials responsible for the
> atrocities previously committed have now been
> eliminated from power.

However, beginning in the middle of September renewed reports

of a disquieting nature began to arrive regarding the situation in Hungary.

44 Cables from the legation at Bern, dated September 15 and September 28, advised

us that Hungarian authorities were preparing to remove the bulk of the Jews

from Budapest to camps in rural areas. It was hinted from Hungarian

sources that in such camps the Jews would be more immune to sudden

German mass-extermination moves than if they stayed in the capital.

Thus on September 15, the legation at Bern reported:

> There follows a summary of the material portion of
> the Swiss note of September 13 which states that report
> from the Swiss Legation in Budapest indicates that it has
> followed the development of the situation of Budapest Jews.

> It is currently established that the Hungarian Govern-
> ment, under German pressure, has decided on transfer of
> Jewish residents of Budapest to Hungarian provinces and
> that this is to occur in the immediate future.

> After assembly Jews of both sexes from 14 to 70 years
> of age must be incorporated in the Hungarian labor service
> while persons above and below these age limits must be con-
> centrated in provincial camps.

It seems that the Hungarian Government is to O.K.
these measures to protect Jews against whom the German
Government for its part, without consulting Hungarian authorities, would otherwise have taken measures.

Later the same day, the legation reported:

.....during the past fornight we have received reports.....
that the Government of Hungary is planning to take the dis-
positions given below with respect to about 200,000 Jewish
individuals remaining in Hungary, in Budapest mainly.

Every physically able bodied man and woman will be
placed in compulsory work in agriculture and industry in
various parts of the nation in the interests of national
defense.

As early as August 24, preparations were being made to
establish two large camps having a combined capacity of
120,000 individuals for all Jews from Budapest who were
not suited for work from a physical standpoint.

On the other hand, there was suspicion that there was no manpower or

material to build and equip such camps, and that the move was merely

intended to get the Jews away from the eyes of neutral observers in

the capital and to isolate them in rural camps where they could easily

be killed or left to die. Consequently, under date of October 6

our Minister at Bern was instructed to request the Swiss to deliver

the following message to appropriate Hungarian authorities:

The Government of the United States has learned
of the plan of Hungarian authorities to remove the
Jews still remaining in Budapest to putative work camps
in the provinces. In view of the fate of Jews who were
removed in previous months from other cities to similar
camps, and in view of the approach of winter, the
Government of the United States has good reason to
regard the present plan as a further measure of mass
extermination, for mass extermination may be accomplished
either by the methods employed at camps of final destination in Poland, or by subjecting large numbers of people to
under-nourishment, hard physical labor and unhygienic

45

living conditions in improvised camps. Consequently, the
United States Government considers it appropriate to remind
Hungarian authorities of its determination, as expressed
by the President of the United States on March 24, that
"none who participate in these acts of savagery shall go
unpunished..... All who share the guilt shall share the
punishment." This determination was publicly reaffirmed on
May 31 and June 28 by members of the Senate Foreign Relations Committee and the House of Representatives Foreign
Affairs Committee, respectively.

The Government of the United States, however, recognizes the possibility that the present plan may in
fact have been evolved to achieve genuine humanitarian
ends as has been claimed by various Hungarian authorities.
To the extent that the plan, if put in operation, may
achieve such ends, the Government of the United States
will, of course, recognize the validity of such claims.
On the other hand, should the removal of the Jews from
Budapest to provincial camps be but a prelude to their
further removal to extermination centers or otherwise
result in their deaths, Hungarian authorities are fully
apprised of the attitude of the people and Government of
the United States.

Despite the unwillingness of the German authorities to permit

emigration from Hungary, the Board continued to the last its efforts in

this direction. Thus, upon learning that the Germans had given some

vague indication that they might permit the emigration of about 2000

Jews from Hungary, the Board, on September 30, sent a cable to our legation

in Bern, stating:

> With regard to your suggestion that perhaps efforts
> could be made to facilitate the emigration of children
> and others who do not have Palestine certificates, your
> attention is called to the fact that the Legation in Bern
> already has broad authority to grant visas for entry into
> the United States.

> Particular reference is made to.....[previous communi-
> cations] which made available approximately 4,000 American
> visas for children in Hungary;.....which made special provi-
> sions in favor of persons to whom American immigration visas

were issued or authorized after July 1, 1941; and.....
making special provisions in favor of close relatives
of American citizens and alien residents in the United
States.....

        You were requested to bring the foregoing arrange-
ments to the attention of the Swiss Government and the International Red Cross, and through them, to the attention
of the German and Hungarian authorities in an effort to
effect the evacuation from Hungary of as many as possible
of the refugees for whom arrangements have thus been made.
We assume that you have done everything possible to execute
these instructions, and if anything further can be done
in this regard, we are sure that you will proceed to do
so under the already existing authorizations. You will
note that the authorizations above referred to are applicable
to substantially more than the 2,000 refugees referred to in
...../previous communication/.

Other, less conventional methods of rescue were also followed

up to the last. Thus, upon learning the names of some persons in Hungary

who might be able to assist in the temporary hiding of Jews in that country,

these names were cabled on October 2 to our minister in a neutral capital,

who had contacts with a member of a neutral legation in Budapest, with the

following instruction:

        Please request.....if feasible, to ascertain
whether they have any programs which he can facilitate.
If they need any funds for any projects which give any
reasonable promise of success, you may, in your discretion,
make funds available to them. If their requirements for
any such projects exceed the amount you have available for
such purposes, please advise the Board.

47

~~RESTRICTED~~

Restricted Classification
Removed Per
Executive Order 10501

OFFICE OF U.S.CHIEF OF COUNSEL FOR WAR CRIMES
APO 696-A
EVIDENCE DIVISION
INTERROGATION BRANCH

- - - - - - - - -

INTERROGATION SUMMARY NO.4772 √

Interrogation of : Kurt BECHER, SS Standartenfuehrer, Chief of
SS Operational Command Economic Staff in
Hungary, - Index No. 2710 a

Interrogated by : Mr. Norbert G. Barr, 2 March 1948, Nuremberg

Division & Att'y : Ministries Division - Mr. Hardy

Compiled by : H.T.E.Schwarz

- .

Doc. 4

48

PERSONS MENTIONED:

- - - - - - -

EICHMANN	–	SS Obersturmfuehrer, Chief of IV A 4 b (Solution of Jewish Questions), RSHA (pp.1,2)
KASZTNER,Dr.Reszo	–	Head of Jewish Rescue Committee in Hungary (pp.1-3)
BRAND ,Joel	–	Assistant of KASZTNER in JRC (pp.1,2)
WINKELMANN	–	Higher SS and Police Fuehrer in Hungary (pp.1,2)
WEISS, Manfred	–	Hungarian Industrialist (p.1)
BIELITZ	–	Director of Manfred WEISS Concern (p.1)
KURRIN	–	Hungarian Manufacturer, Concentration Camp Inmate (pp.1,2)
KORNFELD	–	" " " " (p.1)
SCHELLENBERG	–	Brigadefuehrer, Chief of Security, Occupied Territories (pp.3-5)
MEYER, Sally	–	Financier (p.3)
MUESY	–	Former Swiss Bundesrat (pp.3,5)
GROTHMANN	–	Adjutant of HIMMLER (p.3)

SUMMARY

- - - - -

BECHER asserts that it was EICHMANN who, in connection with
the Jewish rescue action, established contact for him with KASZTNER
and Joel BRAND, probably in cooperation with WINKELMANN, who was

~tor Classification
Removed Per
~utive Order 10501

aware of informant's negotiations with HIMMLER in regard to taking
over the Manfred Weiss works.

During one of his economic missions in Hungary, Dr. BIELITZ,
a full-blooded Jew and the manager of the Manfred Weiss concern,
approached informant and suggested that he employ the help of the
leading Hungarian industrialists in carrying out his mission. He
particularly referred him to KURRIN who, however, proved to be un-
available as a buying agent due to his internment in a concentration
camp. BECHER informed HIMMLER that he required the assistance of
a Hungarian company for a successful completion of his mission and,
upon request, obtained the release of KURRIN and KORNFELD from the
concentration camp in order to use them as sales agents in his deals.
KURRIN offered to sign over to informant the entire Manfred WEISS
property in exchange for getting the WEISS family out of the country.
Some members of the family were in hiding, while others were in
concentration camps. Although through arrangement between the two
governments a commissioner had already been appointed for the Weiss
concern, it was practically without central management. Informant
attracted HIMMLER's attention to the deal by telling him that the
foremost industrial family in Hungary, Manfred WEISS, was willing
to give him a controlling influence in the concern. HIMMLER obtained
HITLER's approval for the deal and the stage was set for the transaction. Informant took the people from Stuttgart to Lisbon and
Zurich. The whole affair caused great excitement in Budapest and
WINKELMANN and EICHMANN were annoyed by informant's success in obtaining through HIMMLER the release of Jews whom they had arrested
at his orders. EICHMANN told BECHER that he was holding some Jews
who wanted to do business with him. Thus he got in touch with
Joel BRAND, who claimed to be able to obtain through channels any
and all commodities the SS desired, offering among other items the
delivery of 10,000 trucks, provided that informant would use his
influence with HIMMLER in obtaining farreaching concessions in the
Jewish question. HIMMLER instructed informant to take everything
the Jews could obtain for him and to promise them anything they
asked for in return, without worrying about keeping his promise.

BRAND flew to Ankara to arrange for the delivery of the trucks
but never returned, because he found out that it was impossible
to obtain them. ROOSEVELT and the American War Department had put
an embargo on them. Shortly after BRAND's departure, KASZTNER
and informant managed through skillful manipulations to obtain,
in addition to the release of the WEISS family, that of one transport of 300 Jews, another of 1400, a shipment of 75 to 80 persons,
and finally, in February 1945, a transport of 1100 persons for which
SCHELLENBERG claims credit, although BECHER insists that he

Restricted ... ...
Reproduced for ...
Executive Order 10501

negotiated with KASZTNER about this transport as early as November 1944, after having previously conferred with Sally MEYER concerning customs and border questions.

An attempt was made by Altbundesrat MUESY, an old acquaintance of HIMMLER's, to get in on **this** transaction, but MEYER advised against his participation and informant succeeded in having him withdrawn by HIMMLER. He doubts that SCHELLENBERG had anything to do with this attempt.

At the end of January informant received permission by HIMMLER to get in touch again with MEYER, HIMMLER putting 1000 more Jews at his disposal for trading purposes. When he was about to leave, GROTHMANN informed him that he had to report to SCHELLENBERG before going on his mission to Switzerland. The latter told him of MUESY's visit to HIMMLER which, he said, had opened new aspects of the case which required BECHER's withdrawal from it. He declared that the truck deal was a failure and that he, SCHELLENBERG, intended to use the Jews for a political deal, as a result of which HIMMLER, through a publicity campaign in the eight largest newpapers of the United States, would become within   two weeks an internationally recognized personality. BECHER protested to HIMMLER about SCHELLENBERG's interference and was told to resume his negotiations in Switzerland. With the exception of that shipment, no further shipments of Jews to Switzerland were carried out, however, as the Swiss refused to accept any more Jewish refugees. Nevertheless, the main purpose of the negotiations, to induce HIMMLER to rescind the order of complete extermination, was accomplished.

50

REGULAR DISTRIBUTION.
- - - - - - - - - - - -

RESTRICTED

Restricted Classification
Removed Per
Executive Order 10501

Interrogation # 2710-a

Mr. Hardy - Ministries

Vernehmung des Kurt BECHER
vom 2. 3. 1948 1400 - 1500
durch Mr. Barr
Stenografin Frl. Helma Schmidt

1. F. Wie kommt es, dass Schellenberg die sogenannte Rettung der ungarischen Juden fuer

sich in Anspruch nimmt? Wie hat sich die Sache in der Tat abgespielt? Durch wen

haben sie zum ersten Mal von dem Wunsch einer solchen Moeglichkeit gehoert?

A. Von SCHELLENBERG ueberhaupt nicht. - Ich bin durch AICHMANN zusammen gekommen

mit KASZTNER und Joel BRAND. Ob diese Vermittlung EICHMANN ueber den Hoeheren-

SS- und Polizeifuehrer WINKELMANN gegangen ist, weiss ich nicht, moechte ich aber

sogar annehmen. WINKELMANN wusste, dass ich die Sache Manfred WEISS mit HIMMLER

gemacht hatte.

2. F. Wie haben Sie das bekommen?

A. Ich habe durch Zufall einen Direktor der Firma kennengelernt. Ich bekam eine Ein-

weisung in das Haus der Familie WEISS. Ich habe dann die Familie in die Schweiz

gebracht.

3. F. Was hat sie dazu bewogen?

A. Das war der sehr starke Einfluss des Herrn Dr. BIELITZ, der Volljude und Direktor

von Manfred WEISS war, und in sehr guter Weise das eine mit dem anderen verband.

Er sagte zu mir: "Herr Becher Sie sollen hier Pferde kaufen, Sie brauchen dazu

einen Apparat, Sie brauchen dazu die Hilfe der fuehrenden Industriellen." Er

schlug mir dafuer Herrn KURRIN vor. Das liess sich aber nicht durchfuehren, weil

er schon in einem Konzentrationslager sass. Herr KURRIN machte mir den Vorschlag,

die Familie Weiss herauszubringen, die zum Teil im KZ und zum Teil in Verstecken

sass. Er wollte mir dafuer den ganzen Manfred-Weiss-Konzern uebereignen.

4. F. Wie haben Sie das Himmler schmackhaft gemacht?

A. Ich habe ihm gesagt, dass ich mit meinem Auftrag nicht weiter komme, ich brauche

dazu die Hilfe einer ungarischen Gesellschaft die fuer mich kauft. Er solle mir

erlauben Herrn KURRIN aus dem KZ zu holen. Ich erreichte Ehrenhaft fuer KURRIN und

KORNFELD. Herr KURRIN konnte mir aber nicht mehr behilflich sein, weil sich in-

zwischen die Moeglichkeiten verschoben, sodass auch KURRIN kein Leder mehr sink

51

fen konnte. KURRIN hat mir die Uebereignung des Konzerns angeboten. Es war fuer
den Konzern schon in Uebereinstimmung zwischen den beiden Regierungen ein Kom-
missar eingesetzt. Aber der Konzern war praktisch ohne Kopf. Ich bin zu HIMMLER
gegangen und habe gesagt: "Ich habe eine grosse Sache. Der wesentlichste Konzern
in Ungarn gehoert einer Fmilie Manfred Weiss. Die Familie ist bereit Ihnen den
gesamten Einfluss ueber den Konzern zu geben." Es handelte sich um die arischen
Teile. Das war der ungarischen Regierung gegenueber wichtig. Ich habe das alles
HIMMLER sehr schmackhaft gemacht. HIMMLER hat sich das von HITLER genehmigen lasse
Die Sache ist ueber die Buehne gegangen. Ich habe die Leute von Stuttgart nach
Lissabon und Zuerich gebracht. Es war eine Sache die in Budapest grosses Aufse-
hen erregte. Es war bei HIMMLER nur moeglich, weil ich ihm nur ein nach seinen
Begriffen verlockendes Angebot machte. Dadurch bin ich bei WINKELMANN und EICH-
MANN in einen schlechten Ruf gekommen. Sie sagten sich: "Wir bringen die Leute
ins Gefaengnis und er hat bei HIMMLER das und das erreicht." Daraufhin hat mir
EICHMANN in irgend einer Form gesagt: "Hier sind Juden, die wollen Geschaefte ma-
chen. Sie haben was abzuliefern, kommen Sie doch mal und sprechen Sie mit ihnen."
So kam ich mit Herrn Joel BRAND zusammen. Der sagte mir: "Ich kann Ihnen alles
liefern, wenn Sie irgend welche Konzessionen in der Judenfrage erreichen koennen.
Ich kann Ihnen alles liefern aus der ganzen Welt, ich kann Ihnen Last-wagen liefern." Lastwagen war ein grosses Problem. Es wurde also von Lastwagen gesprochen,
und zwar von 10 000 Lastwagen. Es gab viele Verhandlungen. HIMMLER sagte zu mir:
"Nehmen Sie von den Juden was Sie kriegen koennen. Versprechen Sie ihnen was Sie
wollen. Was wir halten ist eine andere Sache."

5. F. Was war BRANDS Stellung?

A. Er war wahrscheinlich unter Dr. KASZTNER im juedischen Hilfskommitee. Er war
ungarischer oder rumaenischer Staatsangehoerigkeit. Er flog also in unserm
Auftrag nach Ankara und kam nicht zurueck, weil er dort einsah, dass die Sache
unmoeglich ist. Ich habe gehoert, dass ROOSEVELT und das Wardepartment gesagt
haben, das ginge nicht. Kurz nachdem BRAND weg war kam Herr KASZTNER zu mir.
Mit dem habe ich nun Schritt fuer Schritt - ohne damals zu glauben was wir erreichen wuerden - eine Sache aufgebaut, aus der entscheidende Konzessionen entstanden sind. Durch meine ausschliesslichen Verhandlungen sind - ausser der Familie
Manfred Weiss - herausgegangen: ein Transport von etwa ueber 300 Leuten, ein

Transport von 1400 Leuten, dann 75 - 80 Personen und dann noch ein Transport von rund 1100 Leuten, den Herr SCHELLENBERG auf sein Konto schreiben will. Es ist zumindest nicht ganz klar wie die Sache gelaufen ist. Ich kann es nur von meiner Seite aus erzaehlen.

6. F. Wie ist SCHELLENBERG da hineingekommen?

A. SCHELLENBERG ist in meine Sache ueberhaupt nicht hineingekommen. Er hat seine eigene Geschichte.

7. F. Wann war SCHELLENBERGS Transport?

A. Im Februar 1945. Aber das war mein Transport. Wenn er ihn auf sein Konto bucht, dann hat er ihn mir weg genommen. Herr SCHELLENBERG weiss auch, dass ich anderer Meinung bin. Im November hatte ich mit Herrn KASZTNER Besprechungen in der Schweiz. Vorher hatte ich eine Grenzbesprechung mit Sally MEYER. (Financial Key Position, Joint). Als ich anfangs November in die Schweiz ging merkte ich zum ersten Mal, dass ich von SD-Leuten ueberwacht und ueberhoert wurde. Kaum war ich in Bregenz angekommen, da sagte mir mein Herr KETTLITZ: "Ein Hauptsturmfuehrer will Sie gerne sprechen." Er hatte SS-Uniform an. Ich kannte mich nicht aus, ich war viel zu naiv um hinter die Dinge zu gucken. Die boten an: "Hoeren Sie, wenn Sie Briefe in die Schweiz zu vermitteln haben, wir koennen Ihnen da gerne helfen." Mein ganzes Gefuehl war, ohne dass ich konkrete Unterlagen dafuer hatte, dass hier andere Leute im Spiel sind und versuchen mich abzuhoeren. Ich hatte ja meine eigene Linie. Die Sache ging vorueber und ich ging wieder nach Budapest. Es hatte sich der Altbundesrat MUESY an HIMMLER gewandt. Der kannte HIMMLER irgend wie aus frueherer Zeit. HIMMLER sagte mir eines Tages: "Es hat mir da der Altbundesrat MUESY geschrieben, der moechte mich sprechen und moechte sich einschalten in Ihre Verhandlungen." MUESY war dann da. MEYER sagte, er halte die Einschaltung von MUESY fuer verfehlt, denn a) hatte er gesagt, das waeren Hirngespinster und b) sagte MEYER, wolle MUESY nur verdienen. Ich habe HIMMLER von Herrn MUESY abgebracht. MUESY war bei HIMMLER. Meiner Meinung geschah das ohne Einschaltung von SCHELLENBERG. Ende Januar, glaube ich, war ich wieder bei HIMMLER. Er hat mir genehmigt mich wieder mit Sally MEYER zu treffen. Er hatte mir gesagt: "Rund 1000 Juden koennen Sie wieder rausgeben." Ich war kaum weg, da kriegte ich einen Anruf: Bevor ich in die Schweiz fahre, wuensche mich der Reichsfuehrer dringend zu sprechen. Ich muss mir ueberlegen, ob ich vorher schon wuesste, dass MUESY wiederkomme. Ich komme also zu GROTHMANN und der sagt mir, ich solle mich vorher noch bei Brigadefuehrer SCHELLENBERG melden. Der sagt mir ungefaehr folgendes: "Der Altbundesrat MUESY war beim Reichsfuehrer." SCHELLENBERG war fuer mich ein grosser Mann, er trat auch entsprechend auf. Er sagte mir also: "MUESY war da. Ich war sein Betreuer. Daraus haben sich Konsequenzen oder Moeglichkeiten oder Initiativen ergeben, die Ihre bisherige Taetigkeit ausschalten. Das mit Ihren Lastwagen ist ja alles Unsinn. Ich mache ein politisches Geschaeft." Das war Ende Januar, Anfang Februar 1945. Daraufhin sagte ich: "Brigadefuehrer, das verstehe ich nicht." Ich war auf das tiefste erschrocken, denn das bedeutete eine Torpedierung der ganzen Angelegenheit. Ich hatte mit groesster Sorge bis dahin alles geheim gehalten. Ich hatte bei HITLER keinen Mann dazwischen. Ich hatte ihm das so souffliert, dass er mit keinem darueber sprechen koenne. Es war fuer mich bei Schellenberg eine sehr schwierige Situation. Ich habe ihn gefragt: "Was fuer ein politisches Geschaeft, Brigadefuehrer?" Seine Antwort: "Ich will den Boden fuer den Reichsfuehrer im Ausland aufbessern oder gutmachen." Innerhalb von 14 Tagen werden in den 8 groessten amerikanischen Zeitungen Berichte und Leitartikel ueber den Reichsfuehrer erscheinen, die ihn mit einem Schlage faehig machen international aufzutreten." Ich habe ihm gesagt: "Brigadefuehrer, das glaube ich nicht."

54

8. F. Hat er das tatsaechlich geglaubt, oder hat er auch Sie angelogen? Haben Sie mit anderen Leuten ueber die Anklage SCHELLENBERG gesprochen? Ist dabei mein Name gefallen?

A. Nein. Ihr Name ist mir im Zusammenhang mit SCHELLENBERG kein Begriff.

9. F. Sie sind also nicht ins Vertrauen gezogen?

A. Ich sage also zu Schellenberg etwa: "Das ist unmoeglich." Er sagt: "Das koennen Sie nicht beurteilen." Nun war die Sache so, dass ich doch unbedingt dranbleiben wollte. Ich sagte Schellenberg: "Dann muessen wir zusammenarbeiten." Er sagte: "Das wird nicht gehen." Ich sagte: "Dann muss einer Ausscheiden." Darauf er: "Das sind Sie." Ich habe ihm gesagt: "Das hat der Reichsfuehrer befohlen. Der Reichsfuehrer hat mich zu Ihnen geschickt, damit ich mich mit Ihnen auseinandersetze." Darauf sagte er: "Es gibt nichts anderes, als dass Sie aufhoeren." Ich sagte ihm, dass ich am anderen Morgen zum Reichsfuehrer fahren wolle. Als ich zu Himmler kam, war auch Herr Schellenberg da. Ich hatte General WINKELMANN gebeten mit mir zu HIMMLER zu gehen und mich zu unterstuetzen. Als ich aus der Tuer ging, war es klar, dass ich wiederum in die Schweiz gehe auf Grund meiner bisherigen Verhandlungen. Ich sagte das dem Adjutanten im Vorzimmer. Der sagt:

"dann muessen wir ja umbestellen, das ist schon auf einem anderen Kanal gelaufen."
Himmler hatte mir gesagt: "Sie sind selbstverstaendlich nicht ausgeschaltet."
Denn ich hatte ihm gesagt, dass jetzt gerade mein Stab in der Schweiz daran ist,
die Sachen zu uebernehmen. Fuenf Minuten spaeter kam Schellenberg herein. Vielleicht hat er ihm das Gegenteil gesagt. Ich war jedenfalls froh, dass ich erreicht hatte, dass meine Sache weiterlaufen koenne.

10. F. Haben Sie danach noch einen Transport durchgefuehrt?

A. Das war dieser Transport, der ist aber pressemaessig ausgewertet worden fuer
RUESY-SCHELLENBERG.

11. F. Warum haben Sie keine weiteren Transporte ausgefuehrt?

A. Da muss ich Ihnen ganz offen sagen die Schweiz wollte keine. Das wichtigste war
ja, dass wir durch die Verhandlungen die Zurueckziehung des Vernichtungsbefehls
erreicht hatten, denn ich habe bei HIMMLER einen Befehl zur Aufhebung der Vernichtung insgesamt erwirkt.

55

RESTRICTED

RESTRICTED

Restricted Classification
Removed Per
Executive Order 10501

OFFICE OF U.S. CHIEF OF COUNSEL FOR WAR CRIMES
APO 696 A
EVIDENCE DIVISION
INTERROGATION BRANCH

INTERROGATION SUMMARY NO. 2675

Interrogation of : Kurt BECHER, Standartenfuehrer

Interrogated by : Mr. Ponger, 7 July 1947, Nuremberg

Division & Att'y : SS - Mr. McHaney

Compiled by : H.C. Schwarz

- -

PERSONS MENTIONED

Doc. 5

56

EICHMANN	- Standartenfuehrer, expert on Jewish affairs (pp.4,7,11,17)
WINKELMANN	- Higher SS and Police Leader in Hungary (pp.46,11,21)
WEISS, Manfred	- (pp.4,10,5)
BRANDT	- (pp.7,8,11)
SCHELLENBERG	- Head of Amt VI RSHA (p.10)
PISTER	- Camp Commander of Buchenwald and later inspector for KL in Southern area (p.13)
BARNEWALD	- Hauptsturmfuehrer, administrative officer of Buchenwald (p.13)
GROTHMAN	- Adjutant of HIMMLER (p.14)
VEESENMEYER	- Envoy to Hungary (p.16)
BISS	- (p.20)
PFEFFER-WILLENBRUCH	- (p.21)
POHL	- Head of WVHA (p.12)
JUETTNER	- Obergruppenfuehrer, chief of SS Main Operations Office (p.12)

SUMMARY

Kurt BECHER states that after he had succeeded in getting the Manfred WEISS family out of Hungary he was approached by either EICHMANN or WINKELMANN who told him that the Jews were

RESTRICTED

-1-

able to make large shipments of material and that informant
should concern himself with this. Informant states that 8
days after he learned that the Jews had requested aid in return for equivalent compensattion, he went to HIMMLER to discuss this affair. At this time HIMMLER was in Salzburg with
his staff. Informant was alone with HIMMLER during 99% of
his talks. Prior to his visit with HIMMLER, informant discussed the matter with WINKELMANN, who told him that he did
not want to be involved and that subject should go to HIMM-
LER himself. Informant told HIMMLER that a Jewish Council
in Hungary wanted promises for the Jews in return for materials (trucks, etc.). For this purpose one of their leaders would have to be allowed to go to a foreign country.
HIMMLER asked what they could give and informant replied
10,000 trucks if he wanted them. EICHMANN had mentioned
this amount to informant. HIMMLER told him to check on
this and report again. Subject cannot remember whether it
was during this visit or another that HIMMLER told him to
take what he could get and that HIMMLER would do nothing
in exchange. EICHMANN and BRANDT had a conference in Schwabenberg, where BRANDT stated that 10,000 trucks could be delivered. EICHMANN threatened that if BRANDT did not carry
this out he would have all Jews deported or killed, especially the BRANDT family. EICHMANN said that he would let
"the mill in Auschwitz work".

57

Informant claims that HIMMLER had only material interest
in him. During the trip to Bergen-Belsen when informant asked HIMMLER whether he was to have police duties, HIMMLER ans-
wered no. Subject also visited KALTENBRUNNER, who stated
that no one in a foreign country would carry on negotiations
with a concentration camp commandant. Subject did not know
what KALTENBRUNNER meant until he saw Bergen-Belsen and realized what its aims were. This also cleared up for subject
the BERNADOTTE affair.

HIMMLER gave complete authority to informant. HIMMLER
told BECHER to send Dr. KASTNER to Theresienstadt and to
visit the other camps himself. A few days later HIMMLER
said that he could not live up to his promise but that informant was to go and make suggestions. Subject states that
he knows today that HIMMLER did not intend it, and that there
was clear order from HITLER that no inmate was to fall alive
into the enemy's hands.

Subject is of the opinion that HIMMLER carried out the
Manfred WEISS affair under the protection of HITLER but that
he carried out the whole transaction involving the transpor-
ting of the 1100 Jews into Switzerland without HITLER's know-

ledge until the moment that SCHELLENBERG found out about it,
and HITLER was informed through the Swiss papers. There was
a sharp difference of opinion and HITLER stated that no Jews
were to be allowed to go to foreign countries. Subject does
not know whether HIMMLER did this in order to get the trucks
or to gain a political victory over GOERING, SPEER, etc.

Subject states that, at the time of the transaction,
there was a shortage of trucks. It is possible that informant mentioned to EICHMANN that HIMMLER was interested in
trucks or that WINKELMANN told him this. It is possible
that EICHMANN or some other person besides BRANDT suggested the use of trucks as compensation.

Informant states that HIMMLER, in revoking his authority, said, "I must remain true to HITLER". HITLER had issued
new orders and therefore HIMMLER said that he could not
keep his promises. PISTER, appointed concentration camp inspector for Southern Germany, received entirely different
orders. These orders were that no inmate was to fall alive into
the hands of the enemy.

Subject believes that HIMMLER was true to HITLER until
the last few months when he started to make his own policy.
This, however, was after the time of the deportations, kill-
ings and the march from Budapest.

Informant was told by BARNEWALD, an administration officer of Buchenwald, that PISTER had been appointed concentration camp inspector for the southern area. Subject saw HIMM-
LER for the last time on 15 April 1945. HIMMLER's adjutant
told him that HIMMLER would stay in Berlin. Informant states
that if no indiscretions were committed VEESENMEYER knew
little or nothing about the operation. Informant's relations
with VEESENMEYER were already strained before the "Action
KASTNER" or the Manfred WEISS affair. Subject went to Hungary solely as a member of the SS Main Operations Office and,
among other things, he was to buy horses. Upon his arrival
he went immediately to VEESENMEYER, who did not even receive
him for two or three days.

Hauptsturmfuehrer GRILL was with VEESENMEYER as a spe-
cialist on Jewish problems. VEESENMEYER considered GRILL
very "dirty" but got along very well with EICHMANN. Subject last saw EICHMANN on the 15th of April.

Subject states that his relations with EICHMANN were very
difficult, that he had never met a man that could lie so much.

BISS and a member of the Swiss Legation intervened
with subject in the middle of December concerning a transport of Jews.

~~RESTRICTED~~

-4-

~~RESTRICTED~~

Interrogation-Nr.929

V E R N E H M U N G

von Kurt B E C H E R ,
am 7.Juli 1947, von 14 Uhr 30 - 17 Uhr,
durch Mr.Curt PONGER,
in Anwesenheit von Dr.Rudolf KASTNER,
auf Veranlassung von Mr.HART, SS-Sektion.
Stenographin: M.Fritsche.

1.Fr. Sie haben vor einiger Zeit einen Brief geschrieben, der den Inhalt gehabt

hat, was mit Dr.KASTNER los sei?

A. Ja, nachdem Sie mir damals seinen Besuch avisiert haben.

2.Fr. Was versprechen Sie sich von dem Besuch Dr.KASTNER'S?

A. Ich verspreche mir das, dass er als der Mann, der damals meine Arbeit ge-

60   sehen hat bezw. er derjenige ist, mit dem ich am engsten zusammengearbeitet

habe, die Dinge hier zum Ausdruck bringt und dass dadurch sich in meiner La-

ge endlich mal eine weitere Entwicklung zeigt. Ich bin jetzt 10 Monate hier

in Nuernberg und bin praktisch kaum vernommen worden und wissen Sie, ein

Mann, der immerhin meines Erachtens gemacht hat, was kaum ein Deutscher auf-

zuweisen hat, - ich habe bisher in den Vernehmungen und Protokollen nie ge-

sehen, dass ein Mann etwas derartiges geschafft hat wie ich - , dem muss

doch mal geholfen werden. Dass Dr.KASTNER in dieser Sache eine ganz entschei-

dende Rolle gespielt hat, er war sozusagen mein Partner, trotzdem ich SS-

Fuehrer war, ist klar und ich moechte annehmen, dass Dr.KASTNER der Wahrheit

die Ehre gibt und auch das aussagt, was wahr ist.

3.Fr. Ich kenne die Geschichte von Ihnen und Dr.KASTNER. Sie sind hier nicht ange-

klagt. Was koennte Dr.KASTNER fuer Sie machen?

A. Sehen Sie, ich bin hier nicht angeklagt und man hat mir auch angezeigt, dass ich als Zeuge in Kuerze nicht mehr benoetigt werde. Die Frage ist die, ich hatte urspruenglich gedacht, dass man einem Mann, der das gemacht hat, was ich gemacht habe, auch von amerikanischer Seite Gehoer schenkt und dass man einen solchen Fall auf einem Sonderweg pruefen und regeln wuerde. Diesen Glauben habe ich jetzt nicht mehr, nachdem ich 26 Monate im Gefaengnis sitze und habe mich deswegen auf das eingestellt, auf Grund dessen wie die Dinge nun in Deutschland laufen. Ich sehe die Dinge so, dass wenn Dr.KASTNER trotzdem was erwirken koennte, dass dann ich den Weg gehen muss wie jeder andere von hier aus fertig in ein deutsches Lager gehen und von dort aus meine Entnazifizierung betreiben muss. Ich bin in der Reiter-SS gewesen, ich bin dadurch aus der verbrecherischen Organisation heraus. Ich bin ausserdem eingezogen in die Waffen-SS. Ich gehoere also nach dem Urteil nicht zu der verbrecherischen Organisation. Das schliesst aber nicht aus, dass die deutschen Lager mich nicht freigeben und sagen, wir halten dich hier, bis du entnazifiziert bist.

4.Fr. Was koennte faktisch durch ein Gespraech mit Dr.KASTNER gemacht werden?

A. Ich denke es mir so, er koennte hier an den massgebenden Herren sagen, wer ich bin, er koennte dem Operation Officier sagen, Herr BECHER ist der und der Mann. Ich habe ein Interesse daran, nachdem er alle Aussagen gemacht hat und nachdem er 26 Monate im Gefaengnis gesessen hat, dass diesem Mann jetzt geholfen wird, dass er jetzt auf direktem Weg der Spruchkammer zugefuehrt wird. Hier ist ein Fall und die amerikanische Behoerde wuenscht, dass dieses Verfahren endlich durchgefuehrt wird. Das wuerde zur schnellsten und klarsten Loesung ~~finden~~ fuehren. Wenn der Operation Officier den Weg zur Spruchkammer ebnet, dass ich dort vorgefuehrt werde, das hoffe ich.

61

5.Fr. Ich kenne den Betrieb nicht und weiss daher nicht, welche Machtmittel wir in
Bezug auf eine Entnazifizierung haben.

A. Ich habe hier im Arbeitsdienst mitgearbeitet. Ich habe Uebersetzungen gemacht
und auch Bodendienste. Ich habe kuerzlich Captain BINDER gesprochen und er
sagte zu mir, sammeln sie ihre Urkunden zusammen, die Sie zu ihrer Entnazifizierung brauchen. Sie sind kein Automatiker. Ich habe damals Ihren Stand-
punkt genau verstanden, dass Sie nicht glauben konnten, wer ich bin.

6.Fr. Wie rasch moechten Sie Dr.KASTNER sprechen? Er ist hier im Hause, also ungefaehr in 5 Minuten?

A. Das ist allerdings toll. Wenn ich nochtmals kurz auf die Sache in Oberursel
kommen darf. Ich war mir immer klar, dass diese Aussage allein entscheidend
war in Bezug auf Dr.KALTENBRUNNER.

7.Fr. BEGRUESSUNG ZWISCHEN Dr.KASTER und Kurt BECHER.

Sie sehen gut aus?

A. Ich habe mich sehr zusammengenommen und habe versucht alles an mir ablaufen
zu lassen.

8.Fr. Ich glaube, es ist die Sache zu schaffen.

A. Wie geht es Dr.SCHWAIGER?

9.Fr. Er ist schon weg nach Palaestina.

A. Sie werden ihm bald folgen?

10.Fr. Wahrscheinlich in einigen Monaten. Er hat mir ganz ausfuehrlich erzaehlt
ueber seinen Auszug aus Mauthausen und wie man sich um ihn gesorgt hat. Er
hat auch mit mir zusammen eine Erklaerung unterschrieben. Was aus dieser
Erklaerung geworden ist, muss abgewartet werden. Ich moechte mit Ihnen jetzt
Einiges von der Vergangenheit durchsprechen. Ich moechte sagen Dinge bespre-

10.Fr. chen, die Sie damals nicht in der Lage waren, zu besprechen. Ich moechte

Sie bitten sich zusammenzunehmen und Ihr Gedaechtnis laufen zu lassen.

A. Ich denke, dass ich die Materie noch einigermassen beherrsche.

11.Fr. Zunaechst vielleicht moechte ich von Ihnen hoeren, wie die Sache in Budapest begonnen wurde. Vielleicht werden Sie sich erinnern, die Initiative
ist von uns aus gegangen. Einmal WISLICENY, dann EICHMANN und was ist dann
spaeter geschehen?

A. Herr Dr.KASTNER, Herr WISLICENY ist mir ueberhaupt kein Begriff geworden.
Ich habe ihn hier in Nuernberg gesehen und dann ist er mir 1 mal im Vorzimmer von EICHMANN begegnet. Sie erinnern sich an die Sache Manfred WEISS?

12.Fr. Ja.

A. Meines Erachtens hervorgerufen durch meine Verhandlung in der Sache Manfred
WEISS und dem Erfolg, dass ich bei Nacht und Nebel die Familie WEISS aus
Ungarn herausgefahren habe ist entweder der EICHMANN selbst oder ueber
WINKELMANN zu mir gekommen; denn ich glaube nicht, dass Sie zuerst zu mir
gekommen sind. Entweder ist der EICHMANN bei mir gewesen oder WINKELMANN
hat mich mit EICHMANN bei sich in ein Gespraech zusammengebracht; jedenfalls wurde mir gesagt, dass die Juden grosse Leistungen bezw. grosse Lie-
ferungen liefern und ich sollte mich doch mal um die Sache kuemmern. Ich
weiss nicht, ob der EICHMANN zu mir gekommen ist oder ich zu WINKELMANN,
das ist die dunkle Entwicklung.

13.Fr. Ich habe WISLICENY nur erwaehnt, weil unser Vorschlag durch ihn an eine
hoehere Instanz weitergeleitet wurde. Seine hoehere Instanz war EICHMANN.
Es ist ein Punkt, der mich besonders interessiert. Vielleicht koennen Sie
sich doch erinnern, wann und auf welche Art und Weise Sie von dieser Sache
erfahren haben?

63

A. In der Nacht vom 17. auf den 18.Mai brachte ich die Familie WEISS heraus. Ich glaube ganz bestimmt, dass ich in diese Unterhaltung erst kurz nachher gekommen bin. Wenn Sie mir sagen koennen, wann BRANDT nach Ankara geflogen ist, dann - -

14.Fr. Darf ich Sie unterbrechen. Hier stimmt etwas nicht. BRANDT hat ebenfalls am 17. oder 18.Mai Budapest verlassen. Bevor er abgefahren ist, war er mit EICHMANN und Ihnen am Schwabenberg zusammen?

A. Jawohl.

15.Fr. Haben Sie damals zum 1.x von dieser Angelegenheit erfahren?

A. Einige Tage vorher ist darueber gesprochen worden, - es muss immerhin eine Zeit von 14 Tagen gewesen sein - .

16.Fr. Wer hatte den Flug arrangiert?

A. Technisch von mir arrangiert, denn ich habe die Plattform geschaffen, denn ich bin vorher zu HIMLER gefahren.

17.Fr. Das ist das, was mich interessiert.

A. Herr Dr.KASTNER, da ich mit diesem Vorschlag, vielleicht nach 3 Tagen, nach
dem ich ihn erfahren habe, dass die juedische Seite an uns herantritt zu helfen gegen entsprechende Equivalente, wozu ich von vornherein eingestellt war, zu HIMLER gefahren oder geflogen. Ich hatte ja viel zu besprechen in Bezug auf Manfred WEISS. Ich habe eingehend mit HIMLER ueber die Sache ge-sprochen.

18.Fr. Sie sagten, Sie haben manches damals vorzutragen gehabt. Wollen Sie sich mal ein bisschen konzentrieren und sich an dieses Gespraech mit HIMLER erinner Das wuerde mich naemlich in allen seinen Einzelheiten interessieren.

A. Sie haben mich wahrscheinlich etwas falsch verstanden.

19.Fr. Ueber den Komplex Manfred WEISS werden wir ein anderes Mal darueber sprechen.
Jetzt moechte ich Sie bitten auf diesen Sektor des Gespraeches zurueckzu-
kommen. Das dueffte wie Sie sagen, ungefaehr 14 Tage vor dem Abflug von
BRANDT gewesen sein.

A. 8 - 14 Tage.

20.Fr. Wo war HIMMLER?

A. Meines Erachtens in Salzburg.

21.Fr. Wo?

A. Er hatte ein Quartier in Salzburg, in Eigen. Wenn HITLER z.B. auf dem Berg
war.

22.Fr. Was war das fuer ein Quartier?

A. Das war eine Villa, da sass HIMMLER mit seinem engeren Stab. Er nannte es
Feldquartier. Eines war in Salzburg und eines in Ostpreussen.

23.Fr. Fand Ihre Audienz bei HIMMLER unter 4 Augen statt oder war sein Adjutant anwesend?

A. Zu 99 % immer unter 4 Augen. Es war ueblich bei HIMMLER unter 4 Augen empfan-
gen zu werden.

24.Fr. Hatten Sie ueber diese Angelegenheit ausser WINKELMANN noch jemand anderen
zu konsultieren, bevor Sie zu HIMMLER gefahren sind?

A. WINKELMANN hat zu mir gesagt, er will sich in diese Dinge nicht einschalten,
ich soll zu HIMMLER gehen. Da FEGELEIN frueher mein Kommandeur war und zu-
gleich Verbindungsmann zwischen HIMMLER und HITLER, ist es mir ueberhaupt nur
gelungen zu HIMMLER zu kommen. Sie sagen, ich soll mich konzentrieren auf die
Unterhaltung bei HIMMLER. Der Sinn war der, - -

25.Fr. Wollen Sie womoeglich wortwoertlich zitieren?

A. Das kann ich nicht.

65

26.Fr. Womoeglich?

A. Der Sinn war der, ich habe HIMMLER gesagt, es ist ein juedischer Rat in
Ungarn, der fuer die Juden Zugestaendnisse wuenscht und der dafuer Mate-
rialien, Lastwagen usw. im grossen Rahmen anbietet. Dazu muss aber einer
der fuehrenden Maenner ins Ausland fliegen oder fahren koennen, um darueber Verhandlungen zu fuehren. Herr HIMMLER hat mich damals gefragt, was
koennen Sie von den Leuten kriegen? Ich habe ihm gesagt, nach meiner Auf-
fassung sehr erhebliche Leistungen; Sie koennen, wenn Sie wollen 10 Tausend Lastwagen haben. Das war auch das, was Herr EICHMANN mir gesagt hat.
Die Reaktion von Herrn HIMMLER war, dass er sagte, pruefen Sie, was an
dieser Sache dran ist und tragen Sie mir sie wieder vor. Das glaube ich
war der 1.Extrakt fuer die 1.Unterredung mit der Genehmigung, dass ich
die Reise von BRANDT erwirkte. Ich weiss nicht Herr Dr.KASTNER, in wel-
cher folgenden oder ob in dieser Unterredung, das glaube ich aber nicht,
sagte mir HIMMLER, nehmen Sie, was Sie kriegen koennen; ich denke gar
nicht daran was dagegen zu tun und dann verschwinden Sie. Worauf ich gesagt habe, nein, das geht nicht. Wenn diese Sache gemacht wird oder gemacht werden soll, dann muss sie serioes auf beiden Seiten sein. Das ist
ueberhaupt der Punkt, dass ich bei kritischen Dingen bei HIMMLER fuer
mich Boden gewann. Aber ich weiss nicht, ob es das ist, was Sie wissen
wollen. Ich wuesste nicht, was sonst ueber die Sache gesprochen wurde.
Ich bin dann zurueckgekommen und habe EICHMANN gesagt, dass BRANDT nach
Ankara fliegen kann und gebeten, dass ich mit BRANDT, bevor er abfliegt,
noch sprechen kann. An einem Nachmittag war die Besprechung auf dem Schwabenberg, wo zwischen EICHMANN und BRANDT sehr klare Worte gesprochen wurden; wo EICHMANN fragte, koennen 10 Tausend Lastwagen zur Verfuegung ge-

66

A. stellt werden. Antwort: Jawohl. Ich weiss, dass Herr EICHMANN Herrn BRANDT dann sehr mahnende und sehr klare Worte gesagt hat und damit war die Unterredung erledigt.

27.Fr. Koennen Sie vielleicht diese Worte auch zitieren?

A. Ich habe so vielseitige Aussprueche von diesem Mann gehoert.

28.Fr. Er hat ihm gedroht, wenn die Sache nicht erledigt wird, wird er alle Juden deportieren oder ausrotten, vor allem die Familie BRANDT.

A. Das Wort ausrotten hat er nie gebraucht, hoechstens gesagt, die gehen nach Auschwitz zum Arbeiten.

29.Fr. Er war sehr waehlerisch in seinen Worten und sagte nur transportieren. Er hat wohl gesagt, ich lasse die Muehle in Auschwitz arbeiten.

A. Aber nicht in meinem Beisein.

30.Fr. Nein. zu mir. - Nun, was Sie gesagt haben, deutet eher an einen fast ausschliesslichen geschaeftlichen Charakter dieser Abmachungen

A. Von Seiten HIMMLER'S.

31.Fr. Keine spaeteren Eindruecke haben diese Annahme nicht bestaetigt, im Gegenteil, ich habe immer mehr den Eindruck gewonnen, wenn auch nicht ausgesprochen, dass aber bestimmt in ihren Anfaengen existierende politische Hintergedanken auch dabei waren. Politisch, das kann man vielfach auslegen. Es kann kriegspolitisch, ja sogar innenpolitisch sein und kann sogar eine Form von einem Versuch sein, den Kurs zu aendern. Das ist aber nicht ganz plastisch geworden.

A. Ich habe bei HIMMLER im Anfang und auch in der Folgezeit immer nur sein materielles Interesse mir gegenueber gekannt. Erinnern Sie sich Herr Dr. KASTNER, dass ich Ihnen sagte, als wir nach Bergen-Belsen fuhren, dass ich HIMMLER gefragt habe, ob ich polizeiliche Auftraege haette. Er sagte nein.

67

A. Und ich bin dann noch zu KALTENBRUNNER gefahren und er sagte, was denken

Sie denn, mit einem K.L.-Kommandanten fuehrt das Ausland keine Gespraeche.

Es war mir nicht klar, was er meinte, allerdings auf Bergen-Belsen sah ich,

was er fuer ein Ziel verfolgte. Die Sache BERNADOTHe ist mir heute klar, dass

er deswegen die Sache Bergen-Belsen gemacht hat. Dass ich aus der Sache Ber-

gen-Belsen die Konzession Theresienstadt erwirkte gegen den Befehl, das ist

ja nun wirklich nur noch 100 %ig auf meinem Ruecken gle gelaufen. Darueber

muessen wir uns noch eingehend unterhalten. Ich habe damals noch geglaubt,

Herr Dr.KASTNER, - wissen Sie noch, dass mir HIMMLER die Vollmacht gegeben

hat und sagte, also Herr Dr.KASTNER fahren Sie nach Theresienstadt und ich

in die anderen Lager. HIMMLER sagte am naechsten Tag, ich kann den Befehl

nicht halten, aber fahren Sie hin und machen Sie mir Vorschlaege. Heute

weiss ich, dass Herr HIMMLER 1.gar nicht daran gedacht hat und 2., dass ein

ganz klarer Befehl von HITLER da war, dass kein Haeftling lebend in die Hand

der Gegener fallen darf und dass ich die Sache Mauthausen geschafft habe,

da hat das Schicksal mitgespielt. Dass ich es geschafft habe, dass Herr

ZIERREIS, das war ein BLUFF von mir, HIMMLER haette mit mir gar nichts zu tur

Dann habe ich mich hingesetzt und habe KALTENBRUNNER angerufen und dieser

sagte zu mir, melden Sie meinetwegen Herrn HIMMLER ueber Ihre Juden, aber

kuemmern Sie sich nicht um Mauthausen. In der Nacht vom 25. auf den 26.April

habe ich ihn in Salzburg endlich erwischt und habe dann am naechsten Morgen

Herrn Zierreis neue Vorschlaege unterbreitet, dass er am 1.Mai endlich den

Befehl gab, die Lager sind zu uebergeben. Ich glaube Herr Dr.KASTNER, Sie

koennen stolz sein darauf, denn Ihre Arbeit war entscheidend.

32.Fr. Ich bin auch stolz darauf.

A. Das kann kein Mensch nachweisen, was Sie im Jahre 1944 gemacht haben. Ich

A.   kenne ja Ihren Brief an Ihren Freund SCHWALBE. Ich kenne all Ihre Schwierig-

keiten. Ich glaube, Sie kennen auch meine Schwierigkeiten. Auf Grund meiner

schoenen blauen Augen hat mir HIMMLER keine Konzession gemacht.

33.Fr. Eigentlich haben Sie sehr wenig ueber die Bestimmung HITLER'S zu dieser

Frage gesprochen. 1 mal haben Sie angedeutet, dass es zu einem Krach zwi-

schen HIMMLER und HITLER gekommen ist?

A.   Ich bin der Meinung, dass HIMMLER fuer die Sache von Manfred WEISS unter

Deckung von HITLER gemacht hat, dass er aber dann ohne Deckung HITLER'S

die ganzen Transaktionen gemacht hat bis zu dem Moment, wo naemlich der

Herr SCHELLENBERG dazwischenkam, bei dem Transport der 11 Hundert Juden in

die Schweiz, wo HITLER durch die schweizerischen Zeitungen informiert wur-

de und HITLER nach einer scharfen Auseinandersetzung gesagt hat, ein deut-

scher Jude kommt nicht mehr ins Ausland. Hat HIMMLER es nur getan wegen

der Lastwagen, um seine Position gegenueber GOERING, Speer usw. zu heben,

"Heinrich HIMMLER bringt 10 Tausend Lastwagen aus dem Ausland." Waren es

die Lastwagen oder der Triumpf den anderen gegenueber, dass er die Sachen

machte. Wissen Sie noch wie Sally MAYER sagte, es ist ja unmoeglich Ihnen

Lastwagen in diesen Mengen zu geben? Wissen Sie noch, wie wir gegruebelt

haben, was zu tun sei? Wissen Sie noch, wie ich 3 Wochen spaeter nicht zur

Besprechung gegangen bin, damit ich nicht zu HIMMLER kam? Erinnern Sie sich

an die Rote-Kreuz-Pakete? Und der"BECHER" hat das von Mitte August auf sich

genommen und gesagt,"jawohl, Sie kriegen Ihre Lastwagen!"

34.Fr. Darf ich zurueckkommen auf die Lastwagen-Angelegenheit. Ich weiss nicht,

wer der Schwiegervater dieses Gedankens gewesen ist? Der Gedanke ist nicht

von uns gekommen, unser urspruengliches Angebot lautete auf Geld. Das Ge-

genangebot d.h. die Forderung wurde von EICHMANN an BRANDT gestellt. Im

69

34.Fr.   Gegenteil ich wurde ausgeschaltet; wissen Sie warum?

A.   Nein. Sie erschienen kurz vor der Abreise von BRANDT in meinem Gesichts-
kreis.

35.Fr.   EICHMANN hat mich bei Ihnen eingefuehrt. Sie erinnern sich nicht mehr?

A.   Nein.

36.Fr.   Ich erinnere mich genau. Er brachte mich hinunter vom Schwabenberg und
wir warteten dort auf Sie und Sie traten ein und er sagte, das ist Dr.
BECHER und Sie reichten mir die Hand.

A.   Ich erinnere mich jetzt wieder an die Begegnung.

37.Fr.   Sie erinnern sich nicht, wie das mit den Lastwagen kam?

A.   Ich weiss nicht, wie das entstanden ist. Dass damals in Deutschland Lastwagen ein besonderer Engpass war, das duerfte auch Herrn EICHMANN klar gewesen sein. Was ich Ihnen sage, moechte ich moeglichst wissen, dass es
so war. Es kann vielleicht auch so gewesen sein, dass ich mit EICHMANN
gesprochen habe und sagte, dass HILLER ein besonderes Interesse an Lastwagen hat oder dass ihm das WINKELMANN gesagt hat, es kann sein, dass das
Stichwort "Lastwagen" nicht von BRANDT sondern von EICHMANN gekommen ist
oder von anderen Leuten.

38.Fr.   Wenn ich von KLAGES oder von dieser dunklen Figur LAUFER absehe - -

A.   Herr Dr.KASTNER, darf ich ohne Protokoll einige Fragen an Sie stellen?

39.Fr.   Bitte.

Besprechung ohne Protokoll:

40.Fr.   Dann ist dieses Gespraech damals, bevor Sie sich persoenlich eingeschalte
haben, voraussichtlich mit EICHMANN gefuehrt worden? Die Frage der Lastwagen ist interessant aus einem anderen Gesichtspunkt, naemlich der Gedanke an und fuer sich war ja, milde gesagt, ein gefaehrlicher und dieses

RESTRICTED

40.Fr. Quantum von 10 Tausend schaute von vornherein so aus, dass man es formu-
liert, aber nicht durchfuehren kann.

A. Herr Dr.KASTNER, ich habe darueber nachgedacht, aber da ist mir eine sehr
wesentliche Sache zu Hilfe gekommen, die Oberflaechlichkeit von HIMMLER.
Mein bester Helfer auf der Seite war, 1., dass ich HIMMLER immer wieder
klar gemacht habe, das muss ganz diskret gemacht werden, Sie werden da
nicht POHL oder JUETTNER einschalten und 2., dass HIMMLER absolut ober-
flaechlich und unsachlich war, dass er diesen Faden nicht zu Ende dachte,
sonst haette er mir sagen muessen, "wie wollen Sie die Sache allein technisch machen." Einen Monat spaeter war schon die Invasion, da gab es als
neutrale Grenze nur die Schweiz. Also seine Oberflaechlichkeit und dann
habe ich HIMMLER in den Gedanken verliebt gemacht; das haengt mit seiner
Eitelkeit und dem Machtgedanken den anderen gegenueber zusammen.

71

41.Fr. Am 28.April machte HITLER ein Friedensangebot an die Alliierten. Es ist
ausserdem ohne Zweifel, dass Ihre Mission Bergen-Belsen mit der Sache
Bernadote zusammenhaengt. Wenn Sie den Faden weiterfuehren, so ist Ihre
Erklaerung bezueglich der Oberflaechlichkeit und Eitelkeit allein kaum
genuegend; verstehen Sie, was ich damit meine? - Ist dieses Sonderangebot
im Einvernehmen mit HITLER gemacht worden?

A. Mit Ihnen zusammen war ich in Berlin am 16.April. Ich habe HIMMLER auch
nicht mehr gesprochen. Nach meinen Eindruecken, war es nicht in Uebereinstimmung mit HITLER.

42.Fr. Sie sagten, dass die Aktion "KASTNER" ohne vorherige Deckung HITLER gefuehrt worden ist?

A. Das ist meine felsenfeste Ueberzeugung.

43.Fr. Glauben Sie, dass die Weiterfuehrung der Sache ohne vorherige Deckung bei

HITLER und dem Willen HITLER'S ein und denselben Gedanken oder Tendenz

bilden?

A. Der Gedanke liegt absolut nahe, aber ich suche in mir nach Anahaltspunk-

ten. Mir hat HIMMLER an dem bewussten Sonntag, als er mir die mir am Abend

vorher gegebene Vollmacht zurueckzog, gesagt, ich muss dem Fuehrer treu

bleiben. Der Fuehrer hat heute Nacht befohlen und deshalb kann ich das

Ihnen gegebene Zugestaendnis nicht einhalten. Man hat jetzt im Laufe der

letzten Jahre soviel gehoert ueber die Wankelmuetigkeit HIMMLER'S in den

letzten Wochen, auf der anderen Seite hatte er mehr als 2 Sinne, sodass

alles nicht wahr sein braucht, was er zu mir sagte. Als er mir die Voll-

macht zurueckzog, soll er in demselben Moment den Kommandanten von Buchen-

wald PISTER als den K.L.-Inspekteur fuer den Sueden ernannt haben und dem

ganz andere, naemlich die Befehle, die er von HITLER bekommen hat, gegeben

haben.

44.Fr. Das heisst?

A. Dass kein Haeftling lebend in die Haende des Gegners fallen darf. Es ist

sehr schwer diese beiden Pole zu verbinden ohne dabei die Fanthasie spielen

zu lassen. Ich glaube, dass HIMMLER bis in die letzten Monate an sich HIT-

LER treu war, dass er aber dann geschwankt hat. Das liegt aber nach der

Zeit der Deportation, nach der Vernichtung und nach dem Fussmarsch von Bu-

dapest.

45.Fr. Wer hat Ihnen das ueber PISTER gesagt?

A. Das hat erzaehlt ein Verwaltungsfuehrer, der hier mal im Zeugenbau war, ich

glaube BARNEWALD hiess er.

46.Fr. Er sagte?

A. Dass PISTER von HIMMLER zum Inspekteur fuer die K.L. fuer Sueddeutschland

A. ernannt worden ist.

47.Fr. Wann haben Sie HIMMLER das letzte Mal gesprochen?

A. Am 15.April 1945.

48.Fr. Koennen Sie daraus schliessen, was er fuer Plaene fuer sich und die SS

gehabt hat?

A. Er hat mir nur in der Begruendung, dass er mir meine Vollmacht zurueck-

zog erklaert, "ich hatte heute Nacht eine scharfe Auseinandersetzung mit

dem Fuehrer und die Ursache ist das, was in Buchenwald passiert ist, -

Schweinereien in der Presse - -. Da hat er mich entlassen und zwar habe

ich nur die Vollmacht fuer Theresienstadt. Dann ging er im Wald mit Ober-

gruppenfuehrer HEISSMEIER spazieren und entgegen jeder Ordnung bin ich

ihm dann nachgegangen, habe ihn nochmals angesprochen, "Reichsfuehrer, ich

kann mich nicht mit Ihrer neuen Weisung zufriedengeben; aus rein techni-

schen Dingen ist es mir nicht moeglich Ihnen einen Vorschlag zu machen.

Er hat mir gesagt, ich kann trotzdem nichts an der Sache aendern, ich muss

dem Fuehrer treu bleiben."

49.Fr. Ich moechte auf diesen Punkt "Schweinereien in Buchenwald" zurueckkommen.

Schliesslich entsprechen die Schweinereien, die die auslaendische Presse

aufgegriffen hat, den Befehlen HITLER'S.

A. Zweifelsohne. Ich weiss nicht, was damals die Auslandspresse gebracht hat

50.Fr. Ich glaube, dass HITLER sich ueber Einiges aufgeregt hat. Die Tatsache,

dass bei dem beruehmten Zug von Buchenwald nach Dachau 12 Hundert ver-

hungert sind, unter Fuehrung von MEHRBACH. - Meine Frage war, wurden Zu-

kunftsplaene von HIMMLER gemacht, was mit der SS und ihm geschehen soll?

A. Ich habe mit seinem Adjutanten GROTHMANN gesprochen, der sagte, der Reich

fuehrer bleibt dort oben.

73

51.Fr. Hat er was gesagt, dass er sich stellen will?

A. Sie muessen sich denken, dass man mit HIMMLER nicht ueber diese Dinge
sprechen kann. Selbst nicht am 15.April.

52.Fr. Wie waren Ihre Beziehungen zu VEESEMAYER? Ich habe ihn 1 mal bei Ihnen
gesprochen.

A. Bei mir, wann?

53.Fr. Kurz nach der Flucht FREUDIGER'S, wo mich EICHMANN so angeschnauzt hat.

A. Ich kenne mein Verhaeltnis zu VEESEMAYER. Wenn ich jetzt schwoeren sollte,
dass VEESEMAYER in meinem Buero gewesen ist, dann muesste ich luegen.

54.Fr. Ich werde Sie erinnern; KRUMM haette den Auftrag bekommen sollen, nach
Bergen-Belsen zu fahren; es waren 300 Leute fuer die Schweizer Grenze vor-
zubereiten. Ich habe in Ihrem Zimmer VEESEMAYER, EICHMANN und KRUMM
gesehen.

74

A. Er Dr.KASTNER, VEESEMAYER war nie bei mir. Ich glaube, Sie irren sich,
VEESEMAYER ist nie zu mir gekommen, unser Verhaeltnis war so, dass er nie
zu mir kommen konnte. Ueberlegen Sie mal, der grosse Herr VEESEMAYER kommt
zu mir! - Ich habe ihn sicher bei WINKELMANN getroffen.

55.Fr. Ist VEESEMAYER hier?

A. Ja.

56.Fr. Ist WINKELMANN auch hier?

A. Ich nehme an, dass er in Budapest ist. - Ich weiss auch, dass ich mit VEES
MAYER nie ueber diese Dinge diskutiert habe. Wenn Sie meinen, dass er bei
einer Besprechung dabei war bezuegl. des Transportes in die Schweiz, das
glaube ich nicht.

57.Fr. Ob er in diesem Zusammenhang dabei war, darueber kann ich keine Auskunft
geben. Vielleicht hat er seinen Freund begleitet. Wie war die Einstellung

57.Fr. VEESEMAYER'S in dieser Aktion?

A. Wenn VEESEMAYER nicht durch Indiskretion darueber etwas erfahren hat,
von mir hat er nichts oder nur ganz am Rand erfahren. Mein Verhaeltnis
zu VEESEMAYER war so, dass ich schon vor Manfred WEISS und der Transak-
tion "KASTNER" mit VEESEMAYER Krach bekam. Das war so: Ich bin ja urspruenglich als reiner Mann des SS-Fuehrungshauptamtes nach Ungarn gekommen und
sollte unter anderem Pferde beschaffen. Ich ging gleich in den ersten Tagen meiner Ankunft zu VEESEMAYER und VEESEMAYER empfing mich nicht, auch
am 2.u.3.Tag nicht.

58.Fr. Wann sind Sie nach Budapest gekommen, am 1.Tag der Besetzung?

A. Einige Tage spaeter. PETTKO-LANDSER brachte mich zusammen mit dem Acker-
bau-Ministerium und mit dem Minister JODULECK und ich traf eine Verein-
barung ohne VEESEMAYER, die nachher abgeschlossen wurde zwischen dem O.K.H.
und dem ungarischen Ministerium ueber die gemeinsame Aushebung der Pferde.
Daraufhin liess mich VEESEMAYER das 1.mal kommen und machte mir eine grosse
Szene, wie ich dazu kaeme mit dem ungarischen Ministerium Verhandlungen
zu fuehren. Ich weiss auch nicht, was fuer einen Eindruck Sie hatten, wie
ich mit VEESEMAYER stehe? Ich bin im November das 1.Mal zu VEESEMAYER ein-
geladen worden. Mein Verhaeltnis zu VEESEMAYER war von vorneherein ein
sehr kuehles und skeptisches und wenn ich bei VEESEMAYER eine Sache erreichen wollte, habe ich mich hinter KONTINKOSKY gesteckt.

59.Fr. Wie hiess der Hauptsturmfuehrer bei VEESEMAYER?

A. GRELL. Das war der Sachbearbeiter fuer die Judenfragen.

60.Fr. Hat sich der sehr bereichert?

A. Ich habe nichts mit ihm zu tun gehabt. Ich glaube VEESEMAYER ist der Meinung, dass dieser ein sehr schmutziger Mann ist.

75

61.Fr. Stand nach meinem Einblick gut mit EICHMANN?

A. Sehr gut. Sie waren jedenfalls auch privat zusammen.

62.Fr. Wann haben Sie EICHMANN das letzte Mal gesehen?

A. Am 15.April.

63.Fr. Haben Sie mal gehoert von ihm?

A. Nein.

64.Fr. Nie Geruechte gehoert, wo er sein kann?

A. Nein.

65.Fr. Dass er in die Tschechoslowakei wollte?

A. Nein. Das Verhaeltnis zu EICHMANN war immer ein sehr schwieriges. Ich glaube, ich habe nie in meinem Leben einen Menschen getroffen, der so ueberzeugend luegen konnte wie der EICHMANN. Er erzaehlte Ihnen eine story, die war so wahrheitsgetreu, dass Sie nicht glauben konnten, dass sie nicht stimmt. Er hat auch sehr gern getrunken. Wenn er zu mir kam, habe ich ihm immer zuerst eine Flasche Kognak hingestellt.

66.Fr. Ob dann VEESENMAYER mit dem Auswaertigen Amt ueber diese Angelegenheit irgendwelche Beziehungen unterhalten hat, das wissen Sie nicht?

A. Ich will darueber nachdenken. Ich habe, trotzdem VEESENMAYER mich nur 1 oder 2 mal zu sich bestellt hat und gefragt hat, "was wollen Sie in der Judensache machen", erklaert, er habe eine Fuehrerweisung.

67.Fr. Fuehrerweisung sagte VEESENMAYER? Wissen Sie da etwas Naeheres darueber?

A. Er hat sie mir nicht gezeigt, mir aber in jeder Unterhaltung damit gedroht. Die musste aber im Auswaertigen Amt bekannt sein.

68.Fr. Dasselbe galt fuer EICHMANN, diese Fuehrerweisung?

A. Sie meinen, dass er sich auch bei Herrn EICHMANN auf die Fuehrerweisung bezog? Ich weiss, dass EICHMANN mit VEESENMAYER verhandelt hat.

69.Fr. Stichwort ist Budapest: Die Frage des Budapester Ghetto's wurde verschie-
dentlich ausgelegt. Ich moechte mal ganz ohne aeusseren Einfluss Ihre story
darueber hoeren; dann werde ich einige Fragen an Sie stellen.

A. Herr Dr.KASTNER, der Begriff Budapester Ghetto - , da muessen Sie mich kurz
auf den Weg bringen. Meinen Sie damit die Columbus-Strasse?

70.Fr. Nein, ich meine diejenigen, die nach dem Fussmarsch, die von EICHMANN als
nichtmarschfaehig in Budapest geblieben sind und in einem bestimmten Stadtteil untergebracht wurden.

A. Die Juden, die in Budapest blieben, nachdem wir den Fussmarsch abgestoppt
haben?

71.Fr. Nach der Abstoppung des Fussmarsches.

A. Ich weiss leider nicht sehr viel darueber. Ich wusste bis zu diesem Moment
nicht genau, waren diese Menschen ghettorisiert.

72.Fr. Wollen Sie sich bitte zuerst sammeln, denn es ist ein sehr wichtiges Kapi-
tel. Sie werden sich erinnern, Ende November bin ich nach einem 2.Telegramm
zur Schweizer Grenze gefahren, um SALLY MAIER wieder einmal zu sprechen.
Erstmals hat KETTLITZ an Sie telegrafiert, dass die Sache mit SALLY MAIER
nicht laeuft. Daraufhin haben Sie mich erstmals aufgefordert die Fragen zu
nennen. Sie fuhren in der Zwischenzeit ab zu HIMMLER und ich habe eine Bot-
schaft telegrafisch weiterleiten lassen durch den Adjutanten LUEBEN. Dann
kam das 2.Telegramm von KETTLITZ und daraufhin war eine letzte Besprechung
in Budapest in Ihrem Zimmer und auch EICHMANN war anwesend. Am darauffol-
genden Tag bin ich an die Schweizer Grenze gefahren. Damals wurden bestimmte Telegramme zwischen uns gewechselt.

A. Nachdem Sie an die Grenze gefahren waren?

73.Fr. Ja. Erinnern Sie sich noch an den Inhalt dieser Telegramme?

77

A. Ich erinnere mich eben im Moment nicht.

74.Fr. Sagen Sie ganz offen, ob Sie sich erinnern oder nicht?

A. Nein. Das muss gewesen sein, - Budapest ist am 24.Dezember eingeschlossen
worden, wir sind Anfang November aus der Schweiz gekommen und ich bin einige Tage spaeter wegen der Abstoppung des Fussmarsches zu HIMMLER gefahren.

75.Fr. In der Zwischenzeit kam das e 2.Telegramm von KETTLITZ. Die Telegramme, die
Sie von der Grenze erhielten, waren von KRELL-KETTLITZ unterschrieben.

A. Das war also wie Sie schon an der Grenze waren? Ich glaube, da kann ich mich
erinnern. KETTLITZ schimpfte laut und deutlich ueber -.

76.Fr. Augenblick, Sie verwechseln 2 Sachen. 1. sind die Telegramme von KETTLITZ
gekommen und 2. gingen sie von Bregenz nach Budapest und zurueck. Erinnern
Sie sich an diesen Telegrammwechsel?

78

A. Daran erinnere ich mich, aber ich muss schaerfer nachdenken.

77.Fr. Also eine 2.Frage, ich werde ueberspringen. Wir sind in der Hohenstaufengasse
in Wien.

A. Sehen Sie diese Strasse habe ich auch nicht mehr gewusst.

78.Fr. Sie kamen unlaengst von HIMMLER zurueck und Sie erzaehlten mir von einem Be-
richt des Kommandeurs von Budapest an HIMMLER und zwar ueber die Rolle, die
die Juden in dem eingeschlossenen Stadtteil spielten.

A. Ja.

79.Fr. Erinnern Sie sich noch an den Inhalt der Unterhaltung?

A. Als ich bei HIMMLER war - -

80.Fr. Das ist Anfang Januar 1945.

A. Ich war damals 2 mal bei HIMMLER, 1 mal Ende Dezember und 1 mal am 9.Januar,
das weiss ich genau, denn da hat mich HIMMLER zum Standartenfuehrer befoerde
Da war ein Funkspruch aus Budapest von dem General PFEFFER-WILDENBRUCH

A. bei HIMMLER, wo er anfragt, wie er sich den Juden in Budapest gegenueber
zu verhalten habe.

81.F. Das ist aber zu allgemein.

A. Ich glaube, da ist von dem juedischen Ghetto oder Raum , - ich muss vorweg
etwas einflechten.

82.F. Das sind zwei Pole. Dieses Gespraech bezueglich des Berichtes des Kommandeurs und auf der anderen Seite der Telegrammwechsel Budapest-Bregenz.

A. Ich kann den Zusammenhang nicht verstehen.

83.F. Erinnern Sie sich daran, dass Sie bereits in meiner Abwesenheit gegen
Mitte Dezember/BIS besucht worden sind, und Sie um eine bestimmte Intervention gebeten hat?

A. War das ein aelterer Befehl. Die Herren haben sich bei mir wegen eines Zuges
Judentransportes in Budapest interveniert, zusammen mit einem Herren
der schweizerischen Gesandtschaft.

84.F. Das stimmt, das war eine Intervention, wobei BIS bestimmte Garantien zu
uebernehmen hatte. Der Herr war nicht von der schweizerischen, sondern von
der schwedischen Gesandtschaft.

A. Das ist ganz etwas anderes. Das war Herr BIS oder GOMOLI. Da stand irgendein
Transport von Zuegen auf dem Bahnhof; der Zug war abgeschlossen. Ich habe
den GESCHKE angerufen und da ist das zunaechst das von GESCHKE abgelehnt
worden und dann habe ich mir irgendeinen von den Herren bei EICHMANN kommen
lassen und es ist mir gesagt worden, der Zug wuerde ausgeladen, weil keine
Maschine oder Geleise da waeren.

85.F. Augenblick mal.

A. Das meinen Sie auch nicht? Sagen Sie mir doch bitte was Sie meinen.

86.F. Was ich meine, das sind die Juden, die in Budapest geblieben sind, nachdem

79

86.F.   der Fussmarsch abgestoppt war.

A.   Herr Dr. KASTNER, ich weiss, dass gelegentlich meiner Anwesenheit bei
HIMMLER ein Funkspruch von PFEFFER-WILLENBRUCH gekommen ist; ich weiss nicht,
welche Weisung gegeben worden ist; ich weiss nur eines, dass ich sofort nach
meiner Rueckkehr mit WINKELMANN gesprochen habe, nachdem mir HIMMLER gesagt
hatte, WINKELMANN koennte sich mit PFEFFER-WILLENBRUCH zusammen- . Stimmt
das?

87.F.   Nein.

A.   Dann bringen Sie mich bitte auf den Weg.

88.F.   Der Fussmarsch war abgeschlossen; es war eine bestimmte Zahl von Juden in
Budapest. Ich nehme an, dass es kein Zufall war, dass diese am Leben geblieben sind. - Nun die Frage ist, diese Menschen haben ihr Leben den Pfeil-
kreuzlern zu verdanken.

A.   Bestimmt nicht.

89.F.   Erinnern Sie sich nicht, dass gegen Mitte Dezember die pfeilkreuzlerische Regierung den Beschluss gefasst hat, die in Budapest gebliebenen und im Ghetto
lebenden Juden auszuschalten. Ist diese Frage nicht zu Ihnen gekommen?

A.   Mir schwant etwas, aber ich kann heute darueber noch keine praezise Antwort
geben.

90.F.   Sie muessen sich das notieren und wir werden darauf zurueckkommen.

A.   Da ist irgendetwas gewesen.

91.F.   Im Allgemeinen lag es nicht in der Praxis der deutschen Behoerden, vor allen
Dingen des EICHMANN-Stabes, Eine solche Anzahl von Juden zu hinterlassen.

A.   Ja.

92.F.   Es ist anzunehmen, dass da irgendeine deutsche Intervention folgen sollte.

A.   Ja. Herr Dr. KASTNER, ich habe damals, als HIMMLER diesen Funkspruch von

~~RESTRICTED~~

A. General PFEFFER-WILLENBRUCH erhielt, - die Anfrage von PFEFFER-WILLENBRUCH war, was soll mit diesen Juden geschehen, - da habe ich HIMLER sofort gesagt, selbstverstaendlich darf den Juden nichts geschehen.

93.F. Das sagten Sie mir seinerzeit.

A. Und ich weiss, dass HIMLER mir dann gesagt hat, ich solle mit WINKELMANN darueber sprechen. Ob HIMLER an PFEFFER-WILLENBRUCH irgendeinen Befehl herausgegeben hat, habe ich Ihnen das gesagt?

94.F. Ja.

A. Und welche Weisung?

95.F. Positiv. Es musste ja daran etwas stimmen.

A. Ich versuche mir zu vergegenwaertigen, wie ich im Sonderzug in TRIBERG (Schwarzwald) mit ihm gesprochen habe.

96.F. Wo liegt das ungefaehr?

81

A. Etwa 100 Kilometer von Baden-Baden entfernt. Kann es sein, dass ich Ihnen gesagt habe, HIMLER hat einen Befehl gegeben, dass die Juden geschont werden sollen und dass WINKELMANN sich mit ihm in Verbindung setzt. Ich habe WINKEL-MANN ganz kurz darauf gesprochen. Da sass er auf einem Donauschiff zwischen Budapest und Wien. - Der Funkspruch wurde von einem Adjutanten, waehrend ich bei HIMLER im Zimmer war, gebracht und von HIMLER vorgelesen. Meines Erachtens war der ganze Funkspruch -

7.F. Nach Ihrer Ansicht handelte es sich darum, dass die Juden auf deutsche Soldaten in der belagerten Stadt schiessen sollten und dass sie an den Widerstandskaempfen teilnehmen sollten und demgemaess fragt er an, was soll mit den Juden geschehen?

A. Und Antwort?

8.F. Sie haben mich damals beruhigt, dass ihnen nichts passieren wird. - Wir

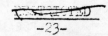

98.F. muessen jetzt abschliessen. Noch eine Frage, war Herr STEGER damals mit
Herrn BIS zusammen ("itte Dezember). Erinnern Sie sich an eine Auto-Ange-
legenheit?

A. Drei oder fuenf Lastautos aus Pressburg.

82

War Ref Bd
(Mr. Ol...

1 copy only

FROM: American Embassy, Ankara

TO: Secretary of State, Washington

DATED: May 25, 1944

NUMBER: 950
        x

CONTROL COPY

Following is Ankara No. 63 from the Ambassador for the War Refugee Board.

Reference is made herewith to Department's cable dated May 23, No. 458.

I am informed by the Turk authorities that their information regarding treatment of Jews in Hungary is limited because of the fact that since former Minister Kallay took refuge in the Turk Legation in Budapest, the German Gestapo has guarded the building and contacts and/movements of the Turk Minister and his staff have been severely restricted.

It is indicated from such information as the Turk authorities have been able to furnish me, supplemented by information from other authoritative sources, that at the time of the German occupation there were about 750,000 Jews in Hungary including about 25,000 Jewish refugees mostly from Slovakia and some from Poland. Approximately 200,000 of this total are to be in various concentration camps in Hungary. It is said that large deportations to Poland have begun from these concentration camps. Up to May 15 it is believed that no Jews have been removed from Budapest or its environs. However, a report has been received since that date to the effect that the transfer of Jews from Budapest to concentration camps in Hungary is imminent.

Two days ago an individual by the name of Joel Brand, documented as the representative of the Jewish Community of Budapest, arrived in

Istanbul

Doc. 6

83

DECLASSIFIED
State Dept. Letter, 1-11-72
By R. H. Parks Date SEP 27 1972

Istanbul and submitted to Barlas of the Jewish Agency a proposal which it is said originated with the Commissioner for Jewish Affairs, Eichman, to the effect that the exchange for two million cakes of soap, two hundred tons of cocoa, eight hundred tons of coffee, two hundred tons of tea, and ten thousand trucks Eichman would agree to stop the deportation and extermination of Jews in all areas which the Germans occupied including Rumania, and he would further agree to permit the exit of Jewish limited numbers to Palestine and in unlimited numbers to Spain.

STEINHARDT

DCR:VAG:HL   5/29/44

84

CONTROL COPY

No. 676.   Ankara, June 5, 1944.

Subject: Transmitting Memorandum on the Arrival
          in Istanbul of Representatives of the
          Jewish Community of Budapest.

The Honorable
    The Secretary of State,
        Washington.

Sir:

    I have the honor to enclose as of interest
to the Department and the War Refugee Board a copy
of a memorandum prepared for me by Mr. Rueben B.
Resnik, the able representative in Istanbul of the
American Joint Distribution Committee, dealing with
the recent arrival in Istanbul of Joel Brand and
Andre Gyorgy (alias Gross), bearing the proposal
referred to in my telegram No. 950 of May 25th.

                            Respectfully yours,

                            Laurence A. Steinhardt.
                             Laurence A. Steinhardt.

Enclosure:

    1. Copy of Memorandum.

File No. 840.1

LAS/pe

Original only (for Ozalid machine)

Doc. 7

85

DECLASSIFIED
State Dept. Letter, 1-11-72
By R. H. Parks Date SEP 27 1972

C O P Y

MEMORANDUM

I. INTRODUCTION

This report is being prepared at the request of His
Excellency, Laurence A. Steinhardt, Ambassador of the
United States to Turkey. It is based on personal interviews with Mr. Brand and interviews and conferences with
persons who have had close contact with Mr. Brand during
his visit in Istanbul and while he was a resident of
Budapest. The report is incomplete in some details,
especially with respect to the activities of one André
Gyorgy, alias André Gross, but the United States Military
Intelligence, the American Consulate General of Istanbul
and other allied services have fuller details on the
nature and scope of his varied operations and his possible relationship to the subject matter of this report.

II. This report will contain the following:

    A. Statement of Facts.
    B. Description of the Principals.
    C. Possible Interpretations.
    D. Developments and Likely Developments.

III. STATEMENT OF FACTS

On Friday, May 19, 1944, one Joel Brand and André
Gyorgy, alias Gross, arrived on a German courier plane
in Istanbul, Turkey. These men, it is reported, were
placed on this plane at Vienna, Austria, after having
been taken to the airport in a Gestapo car from Budapest
to Vienna. Their names were not added to the official
passenger list and it is reported that Mr. Brand had a
letter of instructions from the Gestapo or their representatives to German Government and Military representatives in Sofia to facilitate his movement to Turkey. I
do not know whether Mr. Gyorgy had similar credentials.
In addition, Mr. Brand had letters of introduction from
the Central Rat der Juden, Budapest, signed by Samuel
Stern and Baron Freudinger. These letters were in the
nature of "To whom it may concern" and were designed to
place a badge of authenticity on Joel Brand, at least
from the standpoint of that Jewish organization. In
connection with this and other letters in Brand's possession, it is important to make the following observations. It is quite possible that this letter was given
under duress. It conceivably could have been prepared
by the Gestapo or it might have been given freely and
voluntarily. In any event, the important fact is that
the Gestapo and/ or other German government or military
organizations were fully aware of the contents of this
letter. In addition, Brand had two other letters, one
from a relief committee with whom certain persons in
Istanbul had established a contact beginning in March,
1943 for purposes of extending relief and assistance to
needy persons in Hungary and also for the transmission

of relief

86

DECLASSIFIED
State Dept. Letter, 1-11-72
By R. H. Parks Date SEP 27 1972

of relief to other occupied areas. This letter said in
effect that everything possible be done to carry out the
major proposal which Brand was bringing because according
to the committee it was serious and it represented the
only means of rescuing a large number of people who might
otherwise be doomed. The third letter was from a United
Youth Movement urging favorable consideration of the
major plan and urging that specific plans for youth be
carried out, among which was the transfer of substantial
numbers from Hungary to Roumania through underground
methods. Brand was permitted to take all of these letters
and was not searched; as a matter of fact, he was instructed
to say that if he were asked if he had anything on his
person to say that he had nothing. He was also permitted
to carry twenty-five hundred American dollars.

Brand travelled on a German passport issued in Vienna
in the name of Engineer Eugene Band. He did not have a
Turkish visa although efforts were made here by people
whom he was to see to secure such a visa for him
immediately upon his arrival. Brand had previously cabled
to one of the persons in Istanbul with whom he had
previously established contact when he was a member of
a relief committee in Hungary. For several days after
Brand arrived, he was free to make contact with persons
with whom he had previously established relationships
but on May 25 he was taken into custody by the Turkish
police because he did not have a Turkish visa. A series
of negotiations followed which ultimately released him
from custody on Wednesday, May 31, 1944, although during
the time he was under protective custody, he was permitted
to sleep at the Pera Palas Hotel in Istanbul.

Shortly after Brand arrived a cable was received from
Bratislava sent by a person regarded as trustworthy and
with whom contact had been previously established by
local persons. This cable requested large scale assistance
for Hungarian Jews, reported that 10,000 Jews (Brand said
12,000) were being deported daily to concentration
centers in Poland and that the railroads carrying these
persons between Budapest and the Polish frontier be
bombed by the Allies in order to decelerate, if not stop,
the deportation.

On June 1, 1944 another cable was received from
Bratislava urging that the suggestions in the first cable
be implemented simultaneously, that is to say, that relief
be sent and that the railroads be bombed and further that
the proposals that Brand brings be given serious consideration.

The proposal, which is known to you and which was
made by the German Bureau for Jewish Affairs in Hungary
and had the consent and approval of one Eichmann (a
leading figure in carrying out Nazi policy with respect
to Jewish matters) is as follows: for goods, including
10,000 trucks, 2,000,000 bars of soap, 800 tons of

87

coffee

coffee, 200 tons of cocoa, and 800 tons of tea, etc., the Germans would liberate all of the Jews in Nazi-occupied countries and permit them to travel to neutral areas, mainly in the west; for example, Spain and Portugal and a limited number to Turkey. They are willing to permit the first transport of Jews to leave immediately after negotiations are completed between a responsible person representing the German bureau and a representative of responsible Jewish organization and/ or the Allied governments. (There seems to be a difference of opinion with respect to the latter matter. Brand claims that his instructions were to have a representative of a so-called responsible Jewish organization negotiate with the representative of the German bureau. Gyorgy claims that the German bureau insisted that a representative of the Allied governments be designated as the person to negotiate). It is understood that the first shipment of goods would follow immediately after the first transport of Jewish persons left the border of German-occupied territory.

The Germans also added that they would agree not to use the trucks on the western front.

IV. DESCRIPTION OF PRINCIPALS

I did not meet Gyorgy. He left Turkey for some point in the Middle East on June 1, 1944. André Antol Gyorgy, also known as André Gross, is said to be in his early forties. He is known to the British and American Intelligence and it is also reported that he has worked for the German Intelligence. Because Gyorgy acted as a courier for persons in Istanbul who were responsible for extending relief to occupied areas, he had established contact with a relief committee in Hungary of which Brand was one of the leading members. The reports are that Gyorgy performed his duties without difficulty and carried them through in a satisfactory and helpful manner. It is reported that he assisted Jewish persons to perform underground activities in occupied areas on numerous occasions. It is significant, however, that on his recent visit persons with whom he has had previous contact did not see him. It is said that American and British Intelligence regard him as a Gestapo agent and as completely unreliable.

Joel Brand appears to be in his late thirties, is a well-dressed, neat appearing, articulate person who speaks English fairly fluently. He was born in Budapest, but lived during the greater part of his life in Germany and returned to Budapest about nine years ago. In recent years he operated a small knit-wear factory which employs about forty persons. He is married, has two children, and the other members of his family who reside in Hungary include a mother and three sisters. He has been associated with a relief committee in Budapest for about two years, and during the past year and a half has taken a leading part in its activities. He has had contact with people in Turkey and in Switzerland and has received relief funds for use in occupied areas. He impressed most observers here as straight-forward, sincere and direct. I had several interviews with Brand and saw him shortly after

he was

he was released from custody and after he had been under
considerable pressure, both by the authorities and by the
people with whom he conferred.   I had the impression that
he was not as sincere and straight-forward as other observers throught him to be.   He had ready and direct answers
for all questions and was apparently very cooperative and
reiterated on several occasions the seriousness with which
he was carrying out this mission.   It is important, of
course, to observe that Brand is not completely without
anxiety and fear about his assignment and its possible consequences and any subjective judgments about him should be
evaluated in terms of this man's present uneasiness.

The question naturally arises as to why Brand and
Gyorgy were chosen for the present assignment.   The Gestapo had known that Brand had received funds from sources
in neutral countries for relief purposes in Hungary and
other occupied territory and was regarded by persons in
neutral areas as a responsible person.   Therefore, any
proposal addressed to the Jewish interests would have to
be made to a person known to these interests, and regarded as responsible by them.

The German authorities knew that André Gyorgy had acted as a courier for persons in Turkey calling Brand and
others in Hungary and it was known that these persons regarded Gyorgy as having performed his functions satisfactorily.   It appears also that the German authorities regarded Gyorgy as a trustworthy person from their standpoint
and finally it appears Gyorgy had other functions to perform on this trip of which Brand claims he did not know the
details.

V. Possible Interpretations

A. These proposals, if carried out in their entirety
or partially, would inure to the benefit of a small group
of Germans in control of Hungarian matters.

B. The proposals brought by Brand and Gyorgy are a
cover for the beginning of peace proposals and they are designed to enlist the interest of persons who might ultimately
be used for these purposes.

C. These proposals may be designed to enlist so-called
Jewish influence to disrupt the present efforts on the part
of the Allies to have neutrals break commercial relationships
with the Axis.

D. These proporals may be designed to:

    1. Place the Allied Governments in a position
       of being unable to comply with the demands
       and therefore the Germans would be in a
       position to say that the Allies too are
       refusing to assist the Jewish people and
       therefore the anti-Jewish policy of the

89

Germans . . .

Germans has validity in that the Jewish people
of Europe are in effect being ignored by the
Allies.

2. Underground propaganda in Germany and other
    occupied areas says that Germany is losing
    the war, among other reasons, because of
    its strong anti-Jewish policy.   By these
    proposals it can be said that Germany is
    adopting a new policy favoring the Jews and
    it would follow then that those who were
    responsible for carrying out the strong anti-
    Jewish policy could have it said later in
    mitigation of their acts that they ultimately
    established a program favoring the Jewish
    people.

3. Used as a means of effecting a split between
    the Allies — that is — United States and
    Great Britain from Russia.

E. It is conceivable that if the Germans are more or
less serious about these proposals, they desire the large-
scale transfer of Jews from occupied territory because they
want to be relieved of the responsibility of providing even
a minimum subsistence for these persons while they may be
in concentration centers or even awaiting death.   Moreover,
if the present proposals are not carried out, it is thought
that these might lead to other offers of assistance to the
Jewish persons who may remain in occupied areas, and in this
way the Germans will be relieved of the responsibility of
whatever care they might be compelled to give.

F. It is also conceivable that a sharper conflict has
developed between the various German groups and that one
group is prepared to effect some type of "Putsch" and in
order to swing Allied sympathy to their contemplated plans,
have made this offer.   In this connection, it is thought
that possibly Gyorgy may have carried word about the plans
for this "Putsch."

VI. Developments and Likely Developments

A. Gyorgy left for some point in the Middle East with
the full knowledge of American and British Intelligence.
Brand expects to leave for Palestine on June 5, 1944, to confer with leaders of the Jewish Agency.

B. The American and British Embassies in Turkey and
the Palestine Government have more or less full knowledge
of these proposals.

C. These proposals are known to American and Palestinian philanthropic agencies in Turkey and also in Switzerland.

D. Brand . . .

D. Brand states that he must not return to Hungary without Gyorgy.

E. Brand claims that he has the approval of the German authorities and of his own group in Budapest to travel further to carry on these negotiations and while time is of the essence no definite deadline has been set. Brand or persons acting for Brand at his request, or with his consent and approval, have communicated with persons in Budapest indicating that Brand has been received and that his proposals are being examined and that one of the first conditions toward further exploration is that there be immediate cessation of deportation of Jews from Hungary. Brand, or others for him, also intends to inform Budapest that he will leave for Palestine and perhaps other centers where he believes his proposal can receive more authoritative consideration. It is clear that the United States Government and His Majesty's Government will have to be kept fully informed of all developments as they occur and that any proposals should first be discussed with representatives of these governments.

F. It has been suggested that the German Gerschaefsdienst for southeastern Europe is probably completely informed of these proposals and possibly some representative of that group should be authorized to come to a neutral country for further discussion with persons designated by the governments interested.

G. It is clear that it appears advisable to keep all avenues for negotiation open, first because of major military and political implications involved and also because of the possibility of effecting the rescue of a substantial number of Jews.

H. Everyone with whom I have talked recognizes the impossibility of carrying out the proposals as they have been stated, but everyone believes that all should be done to continue exploration until it is definitely determined that no further good can be served by its continuance.

Finally, I wish to state that this report represents an analysis of the views of persons with whom I have talked and my own views. I cannot vouch for all of the facts but I am reporting them as I learned them.

May I also say that the report has been prepared in great haste and under considerable pressure and I should ask your indulgence on that score.

Respectfully submitted,

(Signed)

RUEBEN B. RESNIK

June 4, 1944.

In care of the American Consulate General,
Istanbul, Turkey.

RBR/MCS

Copied: HAS-AFH

91

AIDE MEMOIRE

Attached to this Aide Memoire is the text
of a telegram received by the Foreign Office from the
High Commissioner, Jerusalem. His Majesty's Ambassador
is instructed to inform the United States Government of
the proposal set out in that telegram and to put before
them the reactions of His Majesty's Government which
are as follows:

(a) Assuming suggestion was put forward by
Gestapo in form conveyed to us, then it seems
to be sheer case of blackmail or political
warfare. Implied suggestion that we should
accept responsibility for maintenance of additional million persons is equivalent to asking the
Allies to suspend essential military operations.

(b) We could not bargain over any scheme
with Gestapo and agree to trade lives against
military and economic concessions calculated to
stave off Germany's defeat. Demand that we should
in effect raise blockade is totally inadvisable;
to give Germany 10,000 lorries would bring important
access of military strength to the enemy, and German
stipulation of Spain and Portugal as sole exodus
seems clearly designed to embarrass Allied military
operations.

(c) Once committed to this kind of blackmail coupled
with raising of blockade, which seems inseparably
connected with it, the Allies would be driven to
even further lengths.

/(d) It would appear

(d)   It would appear that selection of persons, if exchange were agreed, is to be in Hitler's hands. On this we think should be borne in mind that immense numbers of Allies are held by the Germans under terrible conditions and that to arrange any exchange on a basis to be determined by Hitler, leaving Allied internees and prisoners in German hands, would lay Governments open to extremely serious protest.

(e)   While however refusing to deal with this scheme and channels through which it has come, we realize importance of not opposing a mere negation to any genuine proposals involving rescue of any Jews and other victims which merit serious consideration by Allied Governments. Whole record of United States Government and His Majesty's Government over refugees is a proof of their active sympathy with victims of Nazi terror. Accordingly if the German Government were willing to release Jews in position of extreme distress or danger, His Majesty's Government and United States Government would be willing to examine the possibilities of moving to and accommodating in Spain and Portugal such persons as could be handled without prejudice to vital military operations.

2.   His Majesty's Government are informing Dr. Weizmann in strictest confidence of this proposal, but are making no comment beyond saying that they are in touch with the

/United States Government.

United States Government. It is presumed that the latter
will similarly inform Dr. Goldman. His Majesty's Government
are anxious to learn at the earliest opportunity the views
of the United States Government on what action, if any,
should be taken. In particular they would be glad to know
whether the United States Government would agree to instruct
their Ambassador at Ankara, if he is approached by the Jewish
Agency, to associate himself in a reply on the lines set
forth above. His Majesty's Government would suggest that
Dr. Shertok should be told that we cannot sanction him or
any other Allied citizen having any dealings with the Gestapo,
but that we would agree to his conveying the substance of our
observations to his Zionist friend from Hungary. This would
show that, although we cannot enter into the monstrous
bargain now proposed by the Gestapo, we are yet far from
indifferent to the sufferings of the Jews and have not shut
the door to any serious suggestions which may be made and
which are compatible with the successful prosecution of the
war.

3.   His Majesty's Ambassador at Ankara has been
instructed to communicate the foregoing information in strictest confidence to his United States colleague, informing him
that it has been transmitted to Washington in order that
the reaction of His Majesty's Government may be coordinated
with that of the United States Government. His Majesty's
Ambassador has been instructed to return no definite reply
to Dr. Shertok until the essential common line of action
has been established between the two Governments.

                              /4. The Department

4.   The Department of State may be interested
to know that, on being informed of the Gestapo's proposal,
Dr. Waizmann merely observed that it looked like one
more German attempt to embarrass the United States
and United Kingdom Governments. He said, however,
that he would like to reflect on the affair and receive
news of any developments.

                              BRITISH EMBASSY,

                                 WASHINGTON, D.C.

                                    5th June, 1944

To:Foreign Office

From:High Commissioner, Jerusalem.

Ben Gurion and Shertok came to see me this morning and stated as follows:

Special messenger started from Turkey on May 22nd and reached Jerusalem May 24th bringing them statement from their representatives in Istanbul (Barlas etc.) to following effect.

On May 19th well known and trusted Zionist representative in Hungary Joel Brandt arrived in German aircraft in Istanbul from Vienna accompanied by a Hungarian Gestapo agent who has several aliases (e.g. Andrew George, Andrew Gross) and who so far as is known is still in Turkey. Brandt has been sent to Turkey with this man as watchdog by high German Gestapo chiefs in Budapest to place the following order before Jewish leaders in Palestine, England and America, and before the high Allied authorities.

As an alternative to complete annihilation of all Jews remaining in Hungary, Rumania, Czechoslovakia and Poland, the Nazis are ready to evacuate one million Jews from these countries to Spain and Portugal (though not, as they specifically stated, to Palestine). In return they require delivery of 10,000 motor lorries and certain quantities of coffee, tea, cocoa and soap. As an act of good faith they are prepared, once the offer has been accepted in principle to release first batch of five to ten thousand Jews before receipt of corresponding consideration. They are also prepared to exchange Jews against German prisoners of war. If the offer is rejected they will proceed with their programme of wholesale liquidation. The emissary must return to Budapest with a reply within a fortnight from May 19th.

2. Brandt has the impression that these negotiations can be prolonged if evidence is forthcoming that scheme is being earnestly considered in high Allied quarters. It is also believed that substitution of cash payments in Switzerland for deliveries in kind wholly or in part is not to be excluded and both sides barter transaction, namely evacuation and compensation can be realised by successive stages.

3. Brandt reports that 300,000 Hungarian Jews are already herded in concentration camps as a preliminary to deportation. The rounding up of other Jews is in progress. Plans have been made for daily deportation to Polish slaughter houses of 12,000 Jews of means but this is presumed to have been deferred pending negotiations. This report of the position in Hungary is said to be fully corroborated by various Hungarian Jewish eye witnesses who reached Palestine on May 24th.

4. In the light of the above and past experience agency fears that the fate of Hungarian, Czechoslovak and Roumanian Jews is sealed unless they can be saved in time and "they firmly hope that the magnitude and seemingly fantastic character of the proposition will not deter the high Allied authorities from undertaking a concerted and determined effort to save the greatest

/possible

possible number.   They fully realise the overwhelming difficulties but believe they might not prove insurmountable if
the task is faced with boldness demanded by unprecedented
catastrophe".

5.   Shertok is proceeding to Istanbul as soon as he can
(i.e. probably within a few days) for a more complete elucidation of the facts and will report to His Majesty's Ambassador Ankara.

6.   Agency is keeping all the above information strictly
secret and wishes us to do likewise but they ask that His
Majesty's Government should at once communicate it on the same
terms to Washington and that the sole exceptions to the official
secret should be

    (A) Dr. Weizman personally to be informed by His Majesty's
Government.

    (B) Dr. Goldman personally to be informed by the United
States authorities.

    I enquired whether the agency desired any other specific
action than communications referred to in preceding paragraph
pending Shertok's enquiries and report to His Majesty's Ambassador Ankara, and they replied in the negative.

97

THE JEWISH AGENCY FOR PALESTINE

7/19/44
Rec'd from
Dir. Warren

June 7, 1944

Mr. Edward R. Stettinius, Jr.
Under-Secretary of State
State Department
Washington, D. C.

Dear Mr. Secretary:

After I left you this morning I gave some further thought to the information you were kind enough to give me, and I would like to make one or two suggestions which I did not think of while we were discussing the matter.

1. I think it would be advisable to inform the Soviet Government about it. It is quite likely they will learn about it through their contacts in Istanbul, and you know how touchy they are, they may be inclined to be suspicious. I do not believe they will have the slightest objection to the policy you intend to pursue, and it would be much better for them to learn about it through you than through their own channels.

2. I am glad you do not take the line that the offer should be flatly refused, but that the impression should be given that it is being considered. I have been told by Mr. Russell of the British Embassy that the Foreign Office is inclined to take the same line.

It may be necessary to make some counter offers, so as to give the impression of serious consideration. Would it not be possible to offer some financial compensation through funds deposited in Switzerland, if they are ready to let the Jews out?

There may be an even more practicable proposal, in view of all the technical difficulties of moving so large a number of people: that all these Jews be kept where they are in camps under the supervision of the International Red Cross, or a neutral power, which would also assist in feeding them. For German consent to such a scheme, a monetary compensation could be offered. This would remove all the difficulties of transportation, and of getting countries to accept them during the war; moreover, it would guarantee the safety of those Jews who may have to remain where they are for the duration. The main thing is to try to save them and prevent their extermination, and there are indications from past experience that an offer of monetary compensation may be acceptable instead of the demands presented.

I am submitting these proposals for your consideration, so that you may discuss them with the British, as it would be necessary if the contact is to be maintained, to make some counter offers. I am sure that you will receive additional information from Mr. Shertok when he arrives in Istanbul and hope that you will keep me informed and give me an opportunity for further discussion with you. With many thanks for your courtesy, Sincerely yours,
Nahum Goldmann

Ankara, June 8, 1944.

No. 679.

CONTROL COPY

Subject: Transmitting a Further Report on the
Activities of Representatives of
the Jewish Community of Budapest.

The Honorable
The Secretary of State,
Washington.

Sir:

I have the honor to refer to my despatch No. 676
of June 5, 1944, and to enclose as of interest to the
Department and the War Refugee Board a further report
concerning the background and activities of Joel Brand
and Andre Gyorgy (alias Gross), prepared by Vice Consul
Leslie A. Squires of the American Consulate General in
Istanbul.

Respectfully yours,

Laurence A. Steinhardt.

Enclosure:

1. Copy of Report.

File No. 840.1 x 820.02

LAS/pe

Original only (for Ozalid machine)

DECLASSIFIED
State Dept. Letter, 1-11-72
By R. H. Parks Date SEP 27 1972

Miss Hodell

Doc. 10

99

107097

Enclosure No. 1 to Despatch No. 679, dated June 8, 1944
from the American Embassy at Ankara.

C O P Y

AMERICAN CONSULATE GENERAL
ISTANBUL, TURKEY

MEMORANDUM

Subject: Activities of André Antol Gyorgy and Joel Brand.

Date: June 4, 1944.

Introduction

On May 19, 1944, the German courier plane from Vienna arrived in Istanbul with the following persons as unlisted passengers: André Gross, alias André Antol Gyorgy, a Hungarian Jew
with a long record as a double agent; and Joel Brand, a Hungarian Jew, by vocation a small manufacturer, but by choice an active Zionist and an agent in the Jewish underground.

Gyorgy arrived on a Hungarian special passport. Brand
used a German travel document, issued a few days previously in
Vienna. Brand did not have a Turkish visa. Gyorgy's credentials in this connection are uncertain. Both, however, entered
Turkey without difficulty, and remained free until May 25, 1944.
On that date they were picked up by the Turkish secret police
for questioning, Gyorgy on a smuggling charge, Brand for entering Turkey without a visa.

Within the next few hours, Gyorgy was released from custody,
announced that the Gestapo had ordered his return to Germany,
pleaded on bended knee before Allied intelligence officers for
assistance in "escaping" to Syria, was documented for entrance
into Allied territory, and departed on a southbound Taurus express.

During the same period, Brand remained under the nominal
supervision of the Turkish secret police, but returned to the
Pera Palas Hotel each evening under guard. He was released
from custody on May 31, 1944, and departed for Syria and Palestine on June 5, 1944.

He left behind "the Brand proposals," allegedly an official
German program to free the Jews in occupied Europe in exchange
for nominal shipments of food supplies, soap and 10,000 trucks
"to be used only on the Russian front."

Background of Gyorgy

André Gross, alias André Antol Gyorgy, was born about forty
years ago in Hungary. Little is known of his background, but he
has been accepted as a double agent by both sides. (Note: A
full dossier on Gyorgy should be available through Allied intelligence channels in Istanbul).

DECLASSIFIED
State Dept. Letter, 1-11-72
By R. H. Parks Date SEP 27 1972

During . . .

100

During the past six months he has been used by Allied intelligence agencies, has certainly cooperated with the Gestapo, has operated as a contact man between Jewish agencies in Istanbul and underground Jewish channels in German-occupied Europe, and has engaged in profitable gold and diamond smuggling on his own account.

Early in 1944 Gyorgy was used by an Allied intelligence agency in Istanbul in connection with an attempt to plant a radio in Hungary. Included in this conspiracy were Colonel Hatz, then Military Attaché of the Hungarian Embassy at Ankara, and General Kadar, head of the counter-espionage section of the Hungarian General Staff.

While all details of the events transpiring after Gyorgy's departure from Istanbul with the radio set are not clear, it is at least certain that General Kadar was liquidated; his mistress, in whose apartment the radio was found by the Gestapo, was placed under arrest; and Colonel Hatz, who was recalled to Hungary, was placed in a concentration camp. Of all those involved in the conspiracy, only Gyorgy appears to have escaped with a whole skin and a new job under Gestapo supervision.

The conclusion is inevitable and unescapable. It seems clear that Gyorgy, already known as a double agent, sold out to the Gestapo, either of his own choice, or under pressure. The resulting seizure of the radio by the Gestapo led to the apprehension of all other active participants in the action. Gyorgy, on the other hand, turned up some weeks later in the German courier plane at Istanbul.

101

Background of Brand

Joel Brand was born in Transylvania about thirty-eight years ago. At an early age he moved to Germany with his family, and remained a resident of German territory until 1935. In that year he returned to Hungary where he has since resided.

Brand speaks very little Hungarian. When questioned in Hungarian, he answers in German. In explanation he states that his long residence in Germany, where he spoke German, and his relatively recent return to Hungary, have made German his mother tongue.

Following his return to Budapest in 1935, Brand established a small knit-wear factory. This plant employs a maximum of 40 employees, and appears never to have been a financial success. Brand himself states he has always been more interested in Jewish affairs than in his business.

Brand is married and has two children, a mother and three sisters in Hungary.

Shortly after his return to Hungary from Germany, Brand appears to have become interested in the Zionist movement and in other phases of Jewish affairs. Following the beginning of the

war . . .

war, he became an active member of the Jewish underground, receiving money from Jewish leaders in Istanbul, and assisting in the rescue of Jews from Poland.

Brand himself states: "I have saved many Polish Jews from the very doors of the gas chamber."

In the course of this work for the Jews, Brand came into frequent contact with the counter-espionage section of the Hungarian General Staff. He not only admits that he has been in touch with the Deuxième Bureau in connection with Jewish matters, but implies that he has been of service on more than one occasion. This is interesting in that the Hungarian Staff has been, at least since 1939, a center of pro-German activity. Brand's admission that he was in frequent touch with the G-2 of the Hungarian General Staff is the first link connecting him with the Gestapo.

Within recent months Brand has been actively engaged in Jewish rescue work in Hungary. In this connection he has been in touch with Jewish leaders in Istanbul, and has been supplied by them with funds. One such contact was made by Gyorgy on one of his trips for an Allied intelligence agency and Colonel Hatz, at that time Hungarian Military Attaché in Ankara.

While exact dates are not available, it appears probable that this was the same trip Gyorgy made to plant an Allied radio in Hungary. Since it is known that the Gestapo broke up this combination, it seems probable that the Germans were informed of the rôle played by Brand, and of the fact that he was receiving money and documents from Istanbul through Gyorgy.

This belief is confirmed by Brand's admission on one occasion that he had been arrested by the Gestapo, and that they had found gold, American currency and correspondence from Jewish leaders in Istanbul in his possession.

In any event it seems certain that Brand is linked to the Gestapo by a second bond through the discovery of his illegal pro-Jewish activities.

Explanation of Brand's Trip

Brand states that he came to Istanbul in an attempt to save the Jews of Hungary. He reports that all Jews in south and south-western Hungary have been placed in concentration camps or ghettos, and that this procedure will be extended to the other parts of the country as soon as possible. He adds that 12,000 Jews are being shipped to Poland for liquidation each day.

When asked why he was chosen for this mission rather than a prominent Hungarian Jewish leader, Brand gave this reply:

"The Jews in Hungary are divided into several camps. If any prominent leader had come, he would have represented only his camp."

If . . .

If this assumption is correct, Brand was chosen as a "dark horse," as an "unknown" who could speak, not for one group, but for all Hungarian Jews.

Whether this is an accurate explanation is perhaps open to question. Brand's obvious position in the Zionist camp, and his admission that he has been a leader, if a minor leader, in the Jewish movement in Hungary, makes his explanation a trifle illogical.

Brand's documentation indicates that he has the backing of at least some important Jewish leaders in Hungary. He brought with him two letters of introduction of a "To whom it may concern" nature from Baron Freudinger and Samuel Stern. Freudinger is believed to be the President of the Central Rat der Juden, the Jewish control organization established by the Germans. Samuel Stern, the second sponsor, has always been considered one of the leaders of the Jewish community in Hungary. He has been president of the Budapest Jewish Council and served as head of the Hungarian Jewish Committee at one time.

Brand's documentation as a Jewish emissary appears to be fairly satisfactory. It cannot be ascertained, however, whether his letters represent German manipulation or Jewish desire. It is possible that his communications are part of the German plot. It is more probable, of course, that the Jewish leaders in Hungary, aware of the peril of their situation, were willing to use the emissary provided by the Gestapo and accordingly granted him appropriate documentation.

103

Details of Brand's Trip

It is obvious from the details of Brand's trip to Turkey that his journey was actively sponsored by the Gestapo.

Brand left Budapest in the private car of Oberstandartenführer Krummei, a S.S. official. Gyorgy made the trip with him. Gyorgy held a Hungarian service passport, but Brand was without documentation of any sort. Despite this fact, the car crossed the border into Austria without delay or hesitation.

In Vienna, Brand was equipped at Gestapo headquarters with a German passport in the name of Engineer Eugene Band. Arrangements were quickly made, and there was no difficulty.

Brand and Gyorgy, who remained together in Vienna, were then taken to the airport and placed on the German courier plane for Istanbul. Their names were not included in the passenger list.

Brand was given documents and letters by the Gestapo for use in crossing the German checking stations en route to Turkey. For example, the Sofia Gestapo headquarters passed him, upon presentation of his documents, without difficulty.

Two points are of special interest here:

1. . .

1. The fact that Gyorgy was with Brand during the entire trip, including the automobile ride from Budapest to Vienna, in which they were the only non-Gestapo passengers in the car. This admission labels Brand's statement that he did not know Gyorgy, and had only met him once on the plane, as an obvious falsehood. It is certain that Brand and Gyorgy began and finished the trip together, and that their association was not accidental.

2. The fact that Gestapo agents at a number of points were obviously acting on instructions to assist Brand and Gyorgy, and facilitate their departure from German-occupied territory. Since the Gestapo in Budapest, at the Hungarian-Austrian frontier, in Vienna and en route to Turkey, all were obviously acting under orders, it is certain that Brand's mission is not the brain-storm of a minor Gestapo leader in Budapest. The orders could not have been so widespread and sure unless they came from a relatively high source.

On the basis of Brand's own account of his trip, it can be concluded that:

1. Brand and Gyorgy were fellow travelers.

2. Their mission had active Gestapo sponsorship and support.

3. The source of this support was a point relatively high in the Gestapo, rather than some local agent.

104

Nature of Brand's proposals

According to Brand, he was instructed to come to Istanbul with the following proposal:

1. The Germans are willing to consider the release of the Jewish population of Hungary as fast as the Jews can be admitted into Spain, Portugal and Turkey.

2. In exchange, the Germans expect to receive the following from the Allies:

     a. 2,000,000 bars of soap.
     b. 800 tons of coffee.
     c. 200 tons of cocoa.
     d. 800 tons of tea.
     e. 10,000 trucks.

3. Of special interest is the fact, not stressed in some reports, that Brand made clear that the Germans were willing to give a guarantee to the effect that the 10,000 trucks would be used only against the Russians, and would not, under any circumstances, be sent to the Italian or "second" fronts.

Two factors are of importance in determining the validity of this offer: (1) Does Brand take it seriously; (2) Do the German sponsors take it seriously.

As . . .

As to the first question, Brand himself seems to hesitate in making a decision. He clearly indicated, in his last interview before leaving Istanbul, that he had little hope of actually getting many Jews out of Europe. He implied that he was playing his present rôle in the hope that by "playing for time," the Jews in Hungary might be assisted. He seemed to feel that, while the proposals will have no definite result, the time consumed in connection with them may postpone the liquidation of Jews in Hungary for a sufficient period to see the turn of the tide in Europe.

When asked whether he believed the Germans would abide by their part of the proposal, Brand made an evasive answer. It seems probable that Brand himself has little faith in the success of his proposals, or in the German intention to keep their part of the bargain, even if the proposals are accepted by the Allies. He is clearly "playing for time," hoping that the time saved will be the margin that may prevent the liquidation of the Jews in Hungary.

The second question, as to the seriousness of the Germans in making the proposals, can be divided into two parts:

1. Does the proposal come from responsible German leaders?

Brand states that his proposal originated with Vessenmayer, the highest German authority in Hungary, who bears the official title of Trustee of the Greater German Reich in Hungary. While Brand did not have direct contact with Vessenmayer, he did, according to his report, secure his proposals directly from Eichman, a S.S. leader in charge of Jewish affairs in Vessenmayer's headquarters.

Brand also made it clear that the proposal came, not from the Hungarians, or from the Germans through the Hungarians, but directly from the Germans. He categorically stated, on the contrary, that the Hungarians had no knowledge of the proposals, and this his instructions came directly from the German leaders in Hungary.

If Brand is correct in stating that his proposals came from Vessenmayer through Eichman, and there is apparently no reason why this should not be considered to be factual, then it can be assumed that the Brand proposals originated with responsible German leaders.

2. Were the responsible German leaders serious in making the proposals?

From a realistic viewpoint, it is hard to see how responsible German leaders, at this stage of the war, could have the slightest belief that the Brand proposals would be accepted by the Allies, even as a basis for negotiation, much less in their entirety. Is it possible to assume that the Gestapo leaders in Hungary, who are certainly not fools, would expect the Allies to agree to the shipment of 10,000 trucks to Germany, regardless of the conditions? Is it possible to assume that the German occupiers of Hungary, whose plan of occupation was as masterful as that used in Norway, are naïve enough to believe that the Brand proposals will be successful?

On . . .

105

On the basis of logic, it is necessary to answer both of these questions in the negative. Leaving aside, for the moment, the real reason for the Brand proposals - and there was a realistic reason since the Germans do not inaugurate elaborate plans such as this without reason - it can safely be said that the fabricators of the plan must have known that it would not be taken seriously in Allied capitals.

It follows that the German originators either expected the plan to gain its ends before it reached Allied capitals, i.e.: it was intended only for the ears of the Jewish leaders in Istanbul and Palestine; or the plan was not intended to be successful, and its success had no part in the German plans.

Following this line of logic, a strictly sensible conclusion is possible. It can be assumed that the Brand proposals did originate in responsible German sources, that they were placed on the table in Istanbul through the active cooperation and assistance of the Gestapo, and that, at the same time, the originators knew that the plan had no possible chance of acceptance in Allied capitals.

If such is the case, then the Brand proposals are part of an elaborate German propaganda campaign. They will not be accepted and they were not intended to be accepted. They will not bring Germany soap, coffee, tea or trucks, and they were not intended to bring Germany these products. They will not free any Hungarian Jews, for the Germans had no intention of seeing the Jews of Hungary go free.

As to just where the Brand proposals fit into the German propaganda program, a number of theories are valid. One suggestion is that they form part of the German attempt to split the Allies from the Russians.

The handling of the guarantee that the 10,000 trucks will not be used on the Italian or "second" fronts has been tricky and careful. Brand has placed it definitely in the record, so definitely as to guarantee that it has been recorded. On the other hand, he has not pushed the theme, and has tended to leave it out of his conversation as occasion demands.

It seems possible that the German propaganda machine has planted the Brand proposals in Istanbul in the hope that they will be given sufficient attention and acceptance by the Allied representatives to enable the Germans to say to the Russians: "Look at your Allies. They are seriously considering (or even giving semi-serious attention to) a proposal that involves sending us 10,000 military trucks to be used only against you!"

At a moment when the only hope of German success lies in splitting the Allies from the Russians, it is not too far-fetched to believe that the Brand proposals form part of an elaborate propaganda campaign designed to produce the desired result.

Relationship . . .

Relationship of Brand and Gyorgy

In examining the relationship between these two men, it is important to note that Gyorgy was a regular courier between the Jewish leaders in Istanbul and the Jewish underground in Hungary. Since it appears certain that he placed himself in Gestapo hands or was caught, as proven by the radio affair, it seems probable that the Gestapo secured knowledge of the fact that he was a courier between Brand and Jewish leaders in Istanbul. There is some evidence that Brand was actually caught by the Gestapo with gold, American currency and letters brought by Gyorgy in his possession.

In any event, it is almost certain that Gyorgy led the Gestapo to Brand at the same time as he led them to Colonel Hatz and General Kadar.

If such is the case, the participation of Gyorgy and Brand in the present activity is explained. On the basis of available information and logic, it can be assumed that:

1. Gyorgy either surrendered voluntarily to the Gestapo or was caught and forced to talk.

2. The information placed in the hands of the Gestapo by Gyorgy included word of the link between Brand and the Jewish leaders in Istanbul.

3. When it became essential to the German plans that these Jewish leaders should be contacted, Gyorgy and Brand became obvious choices, since both were under obligation to the Gestapo, and in no position to claim the immunities of free agents.

4. Brand was chosen to carry the message, since he was known to have been in contact with the recipients, and since he was, by discovery of his underground actions, under the complete control of the Gestapo. He was certain to remain tractable since his wife, two children, mother and sisters would remain in Hungary under Gestapo control.

5. Gyorgy was chosen as the "escort" since he had already made contact with Allied intelligence circles in Istanbul, was known to many people here, and was persona grata with the Jewish leaders in Istanbul by virtue of his service to them as a courier.

This reconstruction satisfactorily explains the use of Gyorgy and Brand by the Gestapo and clarifies their relationship. It is collaborated by the refusal of Brand to return to Hungary without Gyorgy, and by his admission that Gyorgy was sent with him "as an escort and guardian."

Conclusions

It has been suggested that the following interpretations of this affair are possible:

1. . .

107

1. The proposals are the effort of a small group of Germans, in control of the situation in Hungary, to secure valuable supplies, and to experiment with the possibilities of gaining ransom for the release of the Jews in Hungary.

Comment: As noted above, the numerous points at which the Gestapo acted on instructions indicates that orders must have come from a relatively high source. This makes it appear improbable that the Brand proposals are the brain children of German officials in Hungary.

While it is not impossible that the element of personal profit has entered into the considerations of the German originators of the Brand proposals, it does not appear probable that this element was the dominant factor in placing in action the complicated campaign of which Brand and Gyorgy are elements.

2. The proposals are a cover for the beginning of peace proposals, and are designed to enlist the interest of persons who might be used in this connection.

Comment: Two negative factors dominate this possibility:

(A) If peace proposals are being considered, would a minor Jewish industrialist and a proven double agent be entrusted with even the preliminary negotiations?

(B) Is it likely that the Germans would consider Jewish organizations such as the Jewish Agency for Palestine a suitable intermediary with the Allies?

It seems unlikely that the Germans, even in a most repentant mood, would seek to open a channel to peace through the Jewish organizations operating in Istanbul, or, in the event such a program was in order, would use such minor characters as Brand and Gyorgy, even as preliminary negotiators.

3. The proposals are an effort to use Jewish influence to halt the Allied campaign to divert raw materials from the Axis, and to halt the flow of trade from neutral countries to Germany and her satellites.

Comment: It would certainly invalidate the Allied suggestion that the neutrals halt shipments to Germany, if the Allies suddenly made available shipments of coffee, cocoa, soap and trucks on their own account. It would certainly be bad propaganda for the Allies, and good propaganda for the Nazis, if they could even suggest that such a proposal was being considered. It would certainly call for a reconsideration of the entire Allied economic warfare program if supplies of the type indicated were made available to the Germans.

These considerations can be of value, however, only if it is assumed that the German originators of the plan actually believed that it had a chance of acceptance. Since it is clear that the Germans based their actions on the belief that the plan would not be acceptable, this suggestion does not appear to be valid, since it has value only if the Germans believed the plan would be accepted by the Allies.

4. . .

4. The proposals are a plot to place the Allies in a bad light, since they are designed to refusal, and will permit the German propagandists to say: "We offered to save the Jews, but the Allies turned us down!"

Comment: There is a possible element of truth in this supposition. It accepts the basic premise that the German originators made the Brand proposals intentionally unacceptable. It also accepts the premise that the Brand proposals are basically propagandistic in nature, a conclusion both logical and valid.

The disadvantage lies in the importance of the conclusion. Is it of sufficient value to the Germans, at this stage of the game, to be able to say: "We offered to save the Jews, but the Allies refused"?

There would be an advantage in lightening the burden on the German conscience. There would be a possible advantage in preparing for the peace table. The actual benefits, however, in war terms, would be minor. If we assume that the Germans are still placing their bets on, if not victory, at least a stalemate, then it is improbable that they would elaborate a propaganda campaign to prove a point of validity only in case of defeat.

5. The proposals are essentially an effort to prove that Germany is altering its anti-Jewish policy and is adopting a policy more favorable to the Jews.

Comment: The Brand proposals are essentially under-cover and secret in nature. They do not give the appearance of being an open propaganda attack, or of developing in that direction. Would the single Brand proposal, if revealed, counterbalance the scores of anti-Semitic actions taken in Hungary alone in recent months? Would the Brand proposal, even if blared forth with propaganda trumpets, overbalance the death cries of the Jews still being murdered in many sections of Europe? The Brand proposal is of too minor a nature to mean a complete shift in German policy. Its rightful position can be found within the framework of current German policy.

6. The proposals are an effort to lift from the Germans the burden of providing even a minimum subsistence for the Jews of Europe.

Comment: There is this possibility, that the Germans will say: "We have offered you the opportunity of saving the Jews of Europe. You have turned it down. Your action relieves us of responsibility. From here on, we are not responsible for what happens."

It is this fear that has, I am certain, led the Jewish leaders in Istanbul to consider the Brand proposals seriously. It is a valid fear, and one which fits into the basic requirements. It explains the unreasonableness of the proposals, the certainty that the Germans did not make the proposals acceptable and did not want them to be acceptable. It also explains the direction of the proposals and the means used to put them in the hands of the Jewish leaders in Istanbul.

It . . .

109

It does not, however, explain the fact that the Brand proposals are essentially under-cover in nature. Had this been the German plan, it seems probable that the proposals would have been broadcast, would have been put before the maximum audience possible, would have been placed in action as part of a propaganda campaign. This failure to capitalize the Brand proposals leads to the conclusion that the proposals are intended, not as the end, as they would be in this case, but as the means to the propaganda result for which they were designed.

7. The proposals are part of an effort to split the Allies, to divide Russia from Great Britain and the United States.

Comment: If it is accepted that Germany can win a stalemate only by dividing the Allies, then it can be assumed that every effort will be made, up to the last minute, to split Russia away from the Allied camp. Such an end can be achieved best, if it can be achieved at all, only by convincing the Russians that the Allies are not playing an open and honest game. How better could this be attained than by demonstrating that the Allies were considering a proposal that made military equipment available to the Germans for use against the Russians.

This analysis of the basis for the Brand proposals fills most if not all of the qualifications:

1. It explains the use of Brand and Gyorgy, since it is essential that men be used who can return to German-occupied territory and there give "evidence" that their proposals were listened to by Allied leaders in the Middle East.

2. It explains the obvious design of the plan, and the peculiar emphasis on "10,000 trucks" for use "only on the Eastern front."

3. It explains the elaborate campaign to put in Allied hands a plan which the Germans obviously must have considered impossible of acceptance from the first. If the Brand proposals are propagandistic in nature, it is essential that they not be accepted. It is not acceptance that interests the Germans, but a hearing.

(Signed)
LESLIE ALBION SQUIRES
American Vice Consul

110

Copied by AFH

War Refugee Board (Rfle)

Secret

no copies distributed

ORIGINAL TEXT OF TELEGRAM SENT

FROM: Secretary of State, Washington

TO: American Embassy, Ankara

DATED: June 9, 1944

NUMBER: 514

CONTROL COPY

FOR AMBADDADOR STEINHARDT'S, ATTENTION, ANKARA, TURKEY

Reference is made to your Ankara No. 63, dated May 25, for the War Refugee Board, concerning a proposal for the release of Jews from enemy territory submitted to Barlas by Joel Brandt.

This proposal was the subject of an Aide Memoire delivered to the Department by Lord Halifax on June 5. With the Aide Memoire there was transmitted the text of a telegram received by the British Foreign Office from the High Commissioner, Jerusalem, concerning the proposal in question. For your information the following is the text of the said telegram:

Telegram No. 683

From: High Commissioner, Jerusalem

To: Foreign Office

Ben Gurion and Shertok came to see me this morning and stated as follows:

Special messenger started from Turkey on May 22nd and reached Jerusalem May 24th bringing them statement from their representatives in Istanbul (Barlas etc.) to following effect.

On May 19th well known and trusted Zionist representative in Hungary Joel Brandt arrived in German aircraft in Istanbul from Vienna accompanied by a Hungarian Gestapo agent who has several aliases (e.g. Andrew George, Andrew Gross) and who so far as is known is still in Turkey. Brandt has been sent to Turkey with this man as watchdog by high German Gestapo chiefs

in Budapest

DECLASSIFIED
State Dept. Letter, 1-11-72
By R. H. Parks Date SEP 27 1972

in Budapest to place the following order before Jewish leaders in Palestine, England and America, and before the high Allied authorities.

As an alternative to complete annihilation of all Jews remaining in Hungary, Rumania, Czechoslovakia and Poland, the Nazis are ready to evacuate one million Jews from these countries to Spain and Portugal (though not, as they specifically stated, to Palestine). In return they require delivery of 10,000 motor lorries and certain quantities of coffee, tea, cocoa and soap. As an act of good faith they are prepared, once the offer has been accepted in principle to release first batch of five to ten thousand Jews before receipt of corresponding consideration. They are also prepared to exchange Jews against German prisoners of war. If the offer is rejected they will proceed with their programme of wholesale liquidation. The emissary must return to Budapest with a reply within a fortnight from May 19th.

2. Brandt has the impression that these negotiations can be prolonged if evidence is forthcoming that scheme is being earnestly considered in high Allied quarters. It is also believed that substitution of cash payments in Switzerland for deliveries in kind wholly or in part is not to be excluded and both sides barter transaction, namely evacuation and compensation can be realized by successive stages.

3. Brandt reports that 300,000 Hungarian Jews are already herded in concentration camps as a preliminary to deportation. The rounding up of other Jews is in progress. Plans have been made for daily deportation to Polish slaughter houses of 12,000 Jews of means but this is presumed to have been deferred pending negotiations. This report of the position in Hungary is said to be fully corroborated by various Hungarian Jewish eye witnesses who reached Palestine on May 24th.

4. In the light of the above and past experience agency fears that the fate of Hungarian, Czechoslovak and Rumanian Jews is sealed unless they can be saved in time and "they firmly hope that the magnitude and seemingly fantastic character of the proposition will not deter the high Allied authorities from undertaking a concerted and determined effort to save the greatest possible number. They fully realize the over-whelming difficulties but believe they might not prove insurmountable if the task is faced with boldness demanded by unprecendented catastrophe".

5. Shertok is proceeding to Istanbul as soon as he can (i.e. probably within a few days) for a more complete elucidation of the facts and will report to His Majesty's Ambassador Ankara.

6. Agency

112

6. Agency is keeping all the above information strictly secret and wishes us to do likewise but they ask that His Majesty's Government should at once communicate it on the same terms to Washington and that the sole exceptions to the official secret should be

(A) Dr. Weizman personally to be informed by His Majesty's Government.

(B) Dr. Goldman personally to be informed by the United States authorities.

I enquired whether the agency desired any other specific action than communications referred to in preceding paragraph pending Shertok's enquiries and report to His Majesty's Ambassador Ankara, and they replied in the negative.

We are informed that the British Ambassador at Ankara has been instructed to discuss this matter with you in the strictest confidence.

We have discussed this matter with Ira Hirschmann who is scheduled to leave for Turkey on June 11. He will convey our views more fully to you when he arrives.

We agree with the Biritsh that serious suggestions by the Germans to release Jews and other persecuted minorities which are compatible with the successful prosecution of the war should not be rejected outright but should be given consideration. While we have not, of course, been able to make a definitive judgment as to the character of the offer in question, we feel that it is important to keep the door open while this matter is being explored.

Although we obviously could not enter into any understanding with the Germans in a matter of this kind except after consultation with both the British and the Soviet Governments, we feel strongly that pending further developments and

discussions with

113

and discussions with these two governments every effort should be made to convince the Germans that this Government is sufficiently concerned with the problem that it is willing to consider genuine proposals for the rescue and relief of the Jews and other victims.

Accordingly, you should arrange to convey to Joel Brandt at once through Barlas or otherwise the fact that this Government is sending a Special Representative of the War Refugee Board to Ankara, who is fully acquainted with the views of this Government concerning the proposal. It should be indicated that this representative will arrive in Ankara within a fortnight.

For your information, the sole purpose of conveying this fact to Brandt is to let it be known that this Government has not closed the door. Hirschmann will, of course, act only under your instructions.

114

We are advising the British Embassy here of this action. Please advise us urgently of all developments and any further information which you may have. Foregoing was repeated to American Embassy, Moscow to be transmitted to Soviet Government.

HULL

CABLE TO AMBASSADOR STEINHART, ANKARA, TURKEY.

Reference is made to your Ankara No. 63, dated May 25, for the War Refugee Board, concerning a proposal for the release of Jews from enemy territory submitted to Barlas by Joel Brandt.

This proposal was the subject of an Aide Memoire delivered to the Department by Lord Halifax on June 5. With the Aide Memoire there was transmitted the text of a telegram received by the British Foreign Office from the High Commissioner, Jerusalem, concerning the proposal in question. For your information the following is the text of the said telegram:

[Here take in text of attached telegram]

We are informed that the British Ambassador at Ankara has been instructed to discuss this matter with you in the strictest confidence.

We have discussed this matter with Ira Hirschmann who is scheduled to leave for Turkey on June 11. He will convey our views more fully to you when he arrives.

We agree with the British that serious suggestions by the Germans to release Jews and other persecuted minorities which are compatible with the successful prosecution of the war should not be rejected outright but should be given consideration. While we have not, of course, been able to make a definitive judgment as to the character of the offer in question, we feel that it is important to keep the door open while this matter is being explored.

Although we obviously could not enter into any understanding with the Germans in a matter of this kind except after consultation with both the British and the Soviet Governments, we feel strongly that pending further developments and discussions with these two governments every effort should be made to convince the Germans that this Government is sufficiently concerned with the problem that it is willing to consider genuine proposals for the rescue and relief of the Jews and other victims.

Accordingly, you should arrange to convey to Joel Brandt at once through Barlas or otherwise the fact that this Government is sending a Special Representative of the War Refugee Board to Ankara, who is fully acquainted with the views of this Government concerning the proposal. It should be indicated that this representative will arrive in Ankara within a fortnight.

For your information, the sole purpose of conveying this fact to Brandt is to let it be known that this Government has not closed the door. Hirschmann will, of course, act only under your instructions.

We are advising the British and Soviet Embassies here of this action. Please advise us urgently of all developments and any further information which you may have.

115

6/7/44

DECLASSIFIED
State Dept. Letter, 1-11-72
By R. H. Parks Date SEP 27 1972

Handed to Mr. Stettinius
June 9, 1944 —

Mr. Pehle

ORIGINAL TEXT OF TELEGRAM SENT

FROM: Secretary of State, Washington

TO: American Embassy, Moscow

DATED: June 9, 1944

NUMBER: 1460

CONTROL COPY

There follows a repetition of the Department's 514,

of June 9, 1944 to Ambassador Steinhardt at Ankara:

(Here quotes Department's No. 514 of June 9 to Ankara).

The foregoing information should be conveyed to the

Soviet Government whose particular attention should be called

to the fact that the United States Government is interested

primarily in keeping the question open and that consultation

with the British and Soviet Governments will take place before

any understanding with the Germans is entered into.

HULL

Doc. 12

116

DECLASSIFIED
State Dept. Letter, 1-11-72
By R. H. Parks Date SEP 27 1972

DEPARTMENT
OF
STATE

INCOMING
TELEGRAM

DIVISION OF
COMMUNICATIONS
AND RECORDS

GEM-77
Distribution of ~~~ be
true reading only be
special arrangement.
~~T W)

Ankara

Dated June 12, 1944

Rec'd 11:07 p.m. 13th

CONTROL COPY

JUN 15 1944

COMMUNICATIONS

Secretary of State,

Washington.

1055, June 12, 10 p.m.
    x
FOR THE WAR REFUGEE BOARD FROM THE AMBASSADOR

Department's 514, June 9.

Ankara No. 74.
         v
I have discussed the subject matter of the Depart-

ment's telegram under reference with the British Ambas-

sador who informs me that Brand and Gyorgy proceeded

to Syria, the former on June 1 and the latter on June 5.

Although a Turkish visa for Shertok of the Jewish agency

was telegraphed to Jerusalem a week ago, he has informed

Barlas in Instanbul that he is not (repeat not) coming

to Turkey. While neither the British Embassy nor we

are informed as to Brand's present whereabouts, we assume

that he is now either in Jerusalem or in touch with the

Jewish Agency there. If Brand has not returned to

Turkey by the time Hirschmann arrives here or is not

expected immediately thereafter, it may be desirable

                        for Hirschmann

Doc. 13

117

DECLASSIFIED
State Dept. Letter, 1-11-72
By R. H. Parks Date SEP 27 1972

-2-#1055, June 12, 10 p.m., from Ankara.

for Hirschmann to go to see him.

I am entirely in accord with the view expressed by
the board that until a definitive judgment as to the
character of the offer in question has been arrived at,
it is important that the door be kept open for further
exploration of the matter and that every effort be made
to convince the Germans that our government is seriously
concerned with the problem of the rescue and relief of
the Jews and other victims and is willing to consider
any genuine proposals.

118

I have informed Barlas today of Hirschmann's impending arrival and that he will be fully acquainted with
the views of the board concerning the proposal and have
requested him to convey the foregoing to Brand.

STEINHARDT

WSB
CSB

DEPARTMENT
OF
STATE

INCOMING
TELEGRAM

DIVISION OF
COMMUNICATIONS
AND RECORDS

For security ~~~~ the
text of this ~~~~ must
be closely ~~

MJB-950
Distribution of
true reading only by
special arrangement
(~~~~~).

Lisbon
Dated June 13, 1944
Rec'd 6.30 p.m.

CONTROL COPY

DEPARTMENT OF STATE
DIVISION OF
JUN 16 1944
COMMUNICATIONS
AND RECORDS

Secretary of State,

Washington.

Doc. 14

119

1815, June 13, 4 p.m.

Proposal referred to our May 4, your May 15
came from Joel Brand from Hungary visitor Mayers.
Brand just visited Resnik Istanbul and presumably
now talking Jewish agency Palestine. Saly knows
of these travels of Brands and thinks Brand officially
represents Jewish communities Hungary and Slovakia
possibly also Roumania. This from Leavitt from Pilpel
WDC 14 WRB 68. Saly thinks Brand reliable. Payment (Comment)
after war not possible.

Union orthodox Rabbis United States Canada asked
for huge sum this purpose by Rabbi Joseph Sternbusch
in behalf Rabbi Freudiger Hungary. Brand Freudiger
members same committee but unable combine efforts.
Schwartz has all information. WRB Switzerland knows
of reference to Washington of Freudiger -Sternbusch
proposition. Sternbusch waiting for answer.

DECLASSIFIED
State Dept. Letter, 1-11-72
By R. H. Parks Date SEP 27 1972

NORWEB

BB   RR

CORRECTION ON

PARAPHRASE OF TELEGRAM RECEIVED

FROM: American Embassy, Moscow

TO: Secretary of State, Washington

DATED: June 15, 1944

NUMBER: 2152

CONTROL COPY

This message was erroneously marked 2142. Please change
the serial number from 2142 to 2152.

Doc. 15

120

DECLASSIFIED
State Dept. Letter, 1-11-72
By R. H. Parks Date SEP 27 1972

PARAPHRASE OF TELEGRAM RECEIVED

FROM: American Embassy, Moscow

TO: Secretary of State, Washington

DATED: June 15, 1944

NUMBER: ~~2142~~
2152
x

We have transmitted to the Soviet Government by a note dated June 15 the pertinent information contained in Department's cable of June 9, No. 1460, to Ankara with respect to the proposal for the release of Jews from enemy territory.

HARRIMAN

121

DECLASSIFIED
State Dept. Letter, 1-11-72

By R. H. Parks Date SEP 27 1972

Im Zusammenhang mit den Verhandlungen die Joel Brand
gefuehrt hat, uebernahmen wir die Verpflichtung an jenen Stellen,
welche die Judenfrage in Haenden haben, gewisse Warenmengen zur
Verfuegung zu stellen. Als Gegenleistung fuer die Warenliefer-
ungen, waeren "Menschenleben" d.h. die Deportierungen wuerden
abgestellt werden.

Unter den beanspruchten Waren sind hauptsaechlich solche,
welche von der Ziwilbevoelkerung benoetigt werden, wie z.B.
Cacao, Medikamente, Maennerhemden, etc.

Unseren Kontrahenten versprachen wir, diese Waren vom Ausland zu besorgen, haben aber dort sofort Erhebungen eingeleitet
und Aktionen untergenommen, diese Ware auf den Gebieten, welche
unter Kontrolle der Achse stehen, aufzubringen. Diese Aktion,
welche von Julius Link geleitet wird (er selbst habe die Sache
in dieser Form angeregt) verspricht auch Erfolg. Wohlgemerkt:
es handelt sich nicht um Waren, welche von Uebersee eingefuehrt
werden sollen (auch diese Frage war Gegenstand der Beratung von
Brand, welche Vereinbarungen er diesbezueglich draussen getroffen
hat, wissen wir noch nicht) sondern um Waren, welche auf hiesigen
Gebieten bereits vorhanden sind und nur eingesammelt und von
uns bezahlt werden muessen.

Die Bezahlung dieser Waren muss in Sfr. erfolgen zumal nur
auf diese Weise Waren gekauft werden koennen. Die erste Tranche
soll in allerkuerzester Zeit zur Abwicklung gelangen und hiezu
wird ein Rahmen von ca. 8.000.000 Frs. erforderlich zu sein. In
jenem Ausmasse, wie wir diese Ware bereitstellen werden, wird
seitens des Kontrahenten in der Judensache gewisse Erleichterungen
gestattet werden. Zunaechst geht es um die Errettung von vielen
100.000den vor der Deportation und der damit verbundenen Folgen,
es muss daher uns geholfen werden, diese Aktion zur Ausfuehrung
zu bringen.

Von JDC erwartet man die Hilfe in der Hoehe von 10.000.000
$ ein Betrag, der wohl als hoch angesehen werden kann, im

Verhaeltnis zur Groesse der Hoffnungen die daran geknuepft
sind, doch als ganz minimal angesehen werden muss.

In beiden Faellen also in den ersten erwaehnten 8.000.000
Frs. also auch in der Dollarfrage, handelt es sich, wenn anders
nicht moeglich, um ein Darlehen, welches nach Kriegsende von
dem Judenvermoegen rueckgezahlt werden koennte.

Mein Vorschlag waere:

Einige Finanzkapazitaeten moegen in beiden Faellen die
erforderlichen Summen in Form von Darlehen zur Verfuegung
stellen. Als Deckung fuer diese Darlehen wuerde die jued.
Gemeinde in Budapest, deren unbewegliches Vermoegen allein
weit ueber fuenfzig-sechzig Millionen Dollar ausmacht, mit
ihrem gesamten Vermoegen haften. Die Details moegen Eurerseits
raschest ausgearbeitet werden.

123

Noch ist die Moeglichkeit vielen Hunderttausenden von Juden
zu helfen, bezw. am Leben zu erhalten, es darf keine Zeit
verloren gehen, versuchen Sie alles im Interesse des Gelingens
dieser Aktion zu unternehmen.

Wir muessen annehmen, dass unsere Kontrahenten es mit dem
Antrag ernst meinen.

Joe

FROM: American Embassy, Moscow

TO: Secretary of State, Washington

DATED: June 19, 1944

NUMBER: 2184

CONTROL COPY

Doc. 17

124

Reference is made herewith to Department's cable of June 9, No. 1460, and Embassy's cable of June 15, No. 2152, concerning proposals of the War Refugee Board.

There has been received by the Embassy from Vyshinski a secret note dated June 18 stating that there have been brought to the attention of the Soviet Government the contents of Embassy's note dated June 15, and that Vyshinski has been instructed by the Soviet Government to state that it does not consider it permissible or expedient to carry on any conversations whatsoever with the German Government on the questions which the note from the Embassy touched upon.

HARRIMAN

DECLASSIFIED
State Dept. Letter, 1-11-72
By R. H. Parks Date_____ SEP 27 1972

My dear Mr. Secretary:

I am enclosing herewith a copy of the report of the War Refugee Board for June 5 to June 10, 1944.

I should like to point out for the record one development of the past week which does not appear in the enclosed report because of its extremely secret nature. Through Ambassador Steinhardt and the British we have been advised of a German proposal for the release of Jews from enemy territory submitted to the Jewish Agency in Palestine by Joel Brandt, a Zionist representative in Hungary who recently arrived in Istanbul accompanied by a Hungarian Gestapo agent. Brandt's message is that the Nazis are ready to evacuate one million Jews from Hungary, Rumania, Czechoslovakia and Poland to Spain and Portugal in return for the delivery of 10,000 motor trucks and certain quantities of coffee, tea, cocoa and soap. Since it is felt that serious suggestions by the Germans to release Jews which are compatible with the prosecution of the war should not be rejected outright but should be given consideration, and since we have not been able to make a definitive judgment as to the character of this offer, Ambassador Steinhardt has been advised that we feel it is important to keep the door open while the matter is being explored. The problem was discussed with Hirschmann before he departed for Turkey and Steinhardt is advising Brandt of Hirschmann's expected arrival and the fact that he is acquainted with this Government's views on the proposal. The sole purpose of conveying this fact to Brandt is to let it be known that this Government has not closed the door on the proposition. The British and Soviet Embassies have been advised of our action and it is expected that the representatives in Turkey of these countries

Doc. 18

125

will discuss the whole matter with Steinhardt. Incidentally, we have just received a cable from Steinhardt indicating that he understands our position and that he is personally handling the matter in Ankara.

Sincerely yours,

(Signed) J.W. Pehle

J. W. Pehle
Executive Director

The Honorable,

The Secretary of the Treasury.

126

Enclosure.

JH - Cleared with Du Bois
FH:lab 6/17/44

My dear Mr. Secretary;

I am pleased to send you herewith a copy of the report of the War Refugee Board for June 5 to June 10, 1944.

I should like to point out for the record one development of the past week which does not appear in the enclosed report because of its extremely secret nature. Through Ambassador Steinhardt and the British we have been advised of a German proposal for the release of Jews from enemy territory submitted to the Jewish Agency in Palestine by Joel Brandt, a Zionist representative in Hungary who recently arrived in Istanbul accompanied by a Hungarian Gestapo agent. Brandt's message is that the Nazis are ready to evacuate one million Jews from Hungary, Rumania, Czechoslovakia and Poland to Spain and Portugal in return for the delivery of 10,000 motor trucks and certain quantities of coffee, tea, cocoa and soap. Since it is felt that serious suggestions by the Germans to release Jews which are compatible with the prosecution of the war should not be rejected outright but should be given consideration, and since we have not been able to make a definitive judgment as to the character of this offer, Ambassador Steinhardt has been advised that we feel it is important to keep the door open while the matter is being explored. The problem was discussed with Hirschmann before he departed for Turkey and Steinhardt is advising Brandt of Hirschmann's expected arrival and the fact that he is acquainted with this Government's views on the proposal. The sole purpose of conveying this fact to Brandt is to let it be known that this Government has not closed the door on the proposition. The British and Soviet Embassies have been advised of our action and it is expected that the representatives in Turkey of these countries will discuss the whole matter with Steinhardt. Incidentally, we have just received a cable from Steinhardt indicating that he understands our position and that he is personally handling the matter in Ankara.

127

Sincerely yours,

(Signed) J.W. Pehle

J. W. Pehle
Executive Director

The Honorable,

The Secretary of War.

Enclosure.

FH:lab 6/17/44
Cleared with JL Dr Bris

FROM: American Consulate General, Jerusalem

TO: Secretary of State, Washington

DATED: June 19, 1944

NUMBER: 81

RECEIVED
WAR REFUGEE BOARD
WASHINGTON, D.C.

1944 JUN 22 AM 11 35

CONTROL COPY

The following repeated to Ankara.

With reference to the offer which it is reported that
the Germans recently made for release of Jews, details of
which have been given to the High Commissioner for transmission
to London also for repetition to the Department, Joel Brandt,
who acted as intermediary, has been interviewed by Shertok of
the Jewish Agency. The interview took place at Aleppo in the
presence of a British Army officer after the Foreign Office
had been consulted and subsequently Brandt was taken to
Cairo under British escort where he is now being held. It is
stated by Shertok that his release for return to Hungary is
questionable but representations have been made to the High
Commissioner by the Jewish Agency that he should be permitted
to return in order to prevent breaking off negotiations thus
gaining time to ascertain the true motives of the Germans in
making the offer. It has also been suggested by the Agency that
meeting occur between Allied and German delegations but that the
Allied delegation be selected so that no implication might be
drawn that any subject other than refugees was being discussed.
The High Commissioner agreed to send these views to London and
facilities for early traveling to London have been requested
by Shertok.

DECLASSIFIED
State Dept. Letter, 1-11-72
By R. H. Parks Date SEP 27 1972

PINKERTON

Doc. 19

128

CONTROL COPY

PARAPHRASE OF TELEGRAM SENT

RECEIVED
WAR REFUGEE BOARD
WASHINGTON, D.C.

1944 JUN 24 PM 4:25

To
FROM: Amembassy, Ankara

From
TO: Secretary of State, Washington

DATED: June 19, 1944

NUMBER: 546

FOR ATTENTION OF THE AMBASSADOR.

The Department was today informed by the British Embassy here that Joel Brand arrived Cairo June 14 and that on June 20 Shertok of the Jewish Agency is expected there. The British Embassy presumes that Brand and Shertok are proceeding to Cairo with the expectation of confering with the British Resident Minister, Lord Moyne.

Doc. 20

129

HULL

DECLASSIFIED
State Dept. Letter, 1-11-72
By R. H. Parks Date SEP 27 1972

CORRECTED COPY OF PARAPHRASE OF TELEGRAM RECEIVED

FROM: American Consulate General, Jerusalem

TO: Secretary of State, Washington

DATED: June 19, 1944

NUMBER: 82

CONTROL COPY

Doc. 21

130

It is requested by Shertok that Nahum Goldmann receive
the substance of the following message:

The British Embassy has probably informed you of
the offer by the Nazis to evacuate, primarily from
Hungary, the remnants of European Jewry. Joel Brandt,
trusted Hungarian Zionist, brought the message and was
sent to Istanbul May 19 on Wehrmacht plane with a view
to return within two or three weeks with the reply.
The offer ostensibly was to exchange Jews for goods
of specified kinds and amounts. The evacuees were to
proceed to Spain. On receipt of favorable reply concerning the whole scheme the first substantial transport
was to be sent out without consideration. The conditions
of the exchange sounded fantastic but it was decided to
explore it. We immediately informed the High Commissioner
who reported to London in full with request that
Washington and you be advised. Every possible aid was
given by the Commissioner to assist me to proceed to
Turkey for the purpose of interviewing Brandt. My

departure

DECLASSIFIED
State Dept. Letter, 1-11-72

By R. H. Parks Date SEP 27 1972

departure was delayed because of visa difficulties. At
Aleppo I eventually met Brandt. It was originally agreed
by British authorities Jerusalem Istanbul that Brandt
should return to Turkey with a view to proceeding to Hungary
from there but his transportation to Cairo, where he
is detained, was ordered by higher quarters. Istanbul
is now being informed by our friends in Budapest that
everything will be lost unless Brandt returns at once.
Following my report the conclusions of the executives
are that while the exchange proposition may be mere
eye wash and that there is a possibility of ulterior
motives, it must be assumed that it is not improbable
that even preliminary negotiations might result in a
substantial number being saved. According to information
received by us it was agreed by Eden during conversation
with Weitzmann that the policy should be to gain time to
avoid the other side obtaining the impression that the
Allies are slamming the door and refusing to even give
the matter consideration. Although the helpfulness of
this attitude is appreciated, it is felt by us that
more is warranted. It has been proposed that steps
should be taken at once with a view to exploring the
possibility of meeting with German representatives say
in Madrid or Lisbon for the purpose of discussing the
rescue of Jews urging at the same time that pending the

meeting

131

meeting deportations and slaughter be discontined at once. Intergovernmental Refugee Committee, War Refugee Board, Red Cross or any other suitable agency might be the body appearing on behalf of the Allies. It has also been urged that Brandt return at once to report that the message has been delivered and that active consideration is being given to it. I have also requested urgent priority for me to fly to London. It is requested that you act in accordance with this.

A message similar to this has been sent through the British Government to Weizmann.

PINKERTON

DCR:FDB:HL

6/28/44

132

2 - War Refugee Board
(Pehle)

CONTROL COPY

Declassified per
Kogan letter 12/8/70

PARAPHRASE OF TELEGRAM SENT

1944 JUN 24 AM 11 39

FROM: Secretary of State, Washington

TO: American Embassy, Ankara

DATED: June 20, 1944

NUMBER: 556

CONFIDENTIAL

The following is for Steinhardt's information.

Moscow has been sent Department's message Number 1460 of June 9, 9 a.m., which is a repetition of Department's Number 514 of June 9, 9 a.m. For Ankara's information, we repeat herewith Moscow's message Number 2184 of June 19, midnight.

With reference to Embassy's message Number 2142 of June 15, 3 p.m. and Department's Number 1460 of June 9, 9 a.m. in connection with proposals of War Refugee Board, a secret note from Vyshinski dated June 18 has reached the Embassy. The note declares that the details of Embassy's communication of June 15 were called to the attention of the Soviet Government and Vyshinski has been told by the Soviet Government to say that any discussions whatsoever with the German Government on the matters mentioned in the Embassy's communication are deemed neither wise nor allowable.

HULL

Doc. 22

133

DCR/GPW
6-23-44

<u>MEMORANDUM FOR THE FILE</u>

June 21, 1944

Cable No. 2184 of June 19, 1944, from Moscow, was brought to my attention about 5 P. M. on June 21, 1944.

The matter was promptly discussed and at 5:30 P. M. on June 21 I called Hayden Raynor and asked him to send the following cable immediately to Steinhardt and repeat it to Harriman in Moscow:

"There is repeated to you herewith cable No. 2184 from the American Embassy at Moscow. In this connection you will refer to our cable No. 514 of June 9.

"Please take no, repeat no, further action of any nature with respect to this matter pending further instructions."

Doc. 23

134

2-War Ref. Board
Mr. Pehle

PARAPHRASE OF TELEGRAM RECEIVED

FROM: American Legation, Cairo

TO: Secretary of State, Washington

DATED: June 22, 1944

NUMBER: 1746

CONTROL COPY

~~CONFIDENTIAL~~

Following has been repeated to Ankara.

Today Ira Hirschmann of the War Refugee Board was presented by the Legation to Lord Moyne, British Minister Resident, with whom arrangements were made to interview Joel Brandt at Steinhardt's request. Also on the same affair, Shertok of the Jewish Agency/arrived in Cairo today at noon en route to London. It was suggested by Lord Moyne that Hirschmann should also proceed there but Hirschmann is acting under instructions from Steinhardt to conside (*) nkara first although if necessary he was willing to proceed to London.

It was pointed out by Lord Moyne that as any decisions in this matter are for highest levels, London was the place where complete coordination could be secured most readily.

For the 24th we have arranged Hirschmann's return to Ankara.

TUCK

Doc. 24

135

DECLASSIFIED
State Dept. Letter, 1-11-72
By R. H. Parks Date SEP 27 1972

DEPARTMENT
OF
STATE

INCOMING
TELEGRAM

DIVISION OF
COMMUNICATIONS
AND RECORDS

CONTROL COPY

GEM-42 For security reasons the text of this message must closely guarded.

Distribution of true heading only by special arrangement. (W)

Ankara

Dated June 22, 1944

Rec'd 11:45 p.m.

Secretary of State,

Washington.

> DEPARTMENT OF STATE
> JUN 24 1944
> DIVISION OF
> COMMUNICATIONS & RECORDS

1131, June 22, 4 p.m.

FOR THE WRB FROM THE AMBASSADOR

Ankara No. 79.

Doc. 25

136

Barlas of the Jewish Agency has informed me today that he is in receipt of a telegram from the representative of the Jewish Agency in Budapest to the effect that the deportation of Jews from Hungary is continuing and that the Gestapo is "very angry" at developments as the journey of Brand and Georgy was intended "only as a preliminary to future discussions to be carried on in Lisbon by Schroder of the Gestapo". The message concludes with the statement that unless Brand and Georgy return immediately to Budapest "all efforts are useless".

STEINHARDT

WSB
RR

DECLASSIFIED
State Dept. Letter, 1-11-72
By R. H. Parks Date SEP 27 1972

DEPARTMENT
OF
STATE

INCOMING
TELEGRAM
CONTROL COPY

DIVISION OF
COMMUNICATIONS
AND RECORDS

War Rf Bl - Dahle

6 copies
Control to Hodel

GEM--112
Distribution of
true reading only by
special arrangement
(▓▓▓▓-W)

Lisbon

Dated June 23, 1944

Rec'd 9:15 a.m.

Secretary of State,

Washington.

DEPARTMENT OF STATE
JUN 24 1944
DIVISION OF
COMMUNICATIONS & RECORDS

1941, June 23, 10 p.m.

Referring JDC 19 Mayer states 100,000 Swiss

francs were intended for purchase clothing which

Barlas made through Red Cross not for Shanghai. This

JDC 22 WRB 79 referring JDC 14 from Pilpil for Leavitt.

Understand WRB attache Bern wiring Washington latest

news Joel Brandt's proposition. Schwartz consulting

Hirschman and others Palestine and Turkey. He is

hoping to clear with Saly.

Doc. 26

137

NORWEB

BB
RR

DECLASSIFIED
State Dept. Letter, 1-11-72

By R. H. Parks Date SEP 27 1972

CONTROL COPY

FROM: American Legation, Cairo

TO: Secretary of State, Washington

DATED: June 23, 1944

NUMBER: 1767

Schwartz sends the following for Leavitt of JDC for War Refugee Board.

Discussions have been held here by me with Hirschmann regarding Brandt, who according to Shertok and Hirschmann after he was interviewed by them, is believed to be entirely trustworthy and reliable. Hirschmann is now pursuing the matter vigorously with Steinhardt and highest authorities. I believe it important that Brandt should be allowed to return to Budapest. In accordance I ask that it be recommended.

TUCK

Doc. 27

138

DECLASSIFIED
State Dept. Letter, 1-11-72
By R. H. Parks Date SEP 27 1972

DEPARTMENT
OF
STATE

INCOMING
TELEGRAM

DIVISION OF
COMMUNICATIONS
AND RECORDS

CONTROL COPY

LFG-141

This telegram must be
paraphrased before being
communicated to anyone
other than a Government
Agency. (RESTRICTED)

Ankara

Dated June 27, 1944

Rec'd 8:50 p.m.

Secretary of State,

Washington.

DEPARTMENT OF STATE

JUN 29 1944

DIVISION OF
COMMUNICATIONS & RECORDS

1173, June 27, 3 p.m.

x

FOR THE WAR REFUGEE BOARD FROM THE AMBASSADOR

Ankara's 80.

Hirschmann has returned to Ankara after talking with

Brand in Cairo. His report will be forwarded by pouch

as soon as possible.

STEINHARDT

RR REP

Doc. 28

139

June 28, 1944

<u>MEMORANDUM FOR FILES</u>

On June 26, Mr. Pehle gave copies of the attached proposed cables to Moscow and Ankara to Mr. Warren.

Warren agreed to find out if the British plan to release Brandt and to find out where Gyorgy is presently located.

F. Hodel

Doc. 29

140

DRAFT OF CABLE TO STEINHARDT AND HIRSCHMANN AT ANKARA

There is repeated to you herewith cable being sent
to Moscow today, which is self-explanatory. Please
forward promptly to Harriman and Winant your despatches
Nos. 676 of June 5 and 679 of June 8.

We would appreciate a full report on recent developments in this matter and your recommendations as to how
we can proceed from here.

141

DRAFT OF CABLE TO MOSCOW FOR AMBASSADOR HARRIMAN'S PERSONAL ATTENTION.

PART ONE

Reference is made to our cables to you No. 1460 of June 9 and No.   of June 21 and to your cable No. 2184 of June 19. The following additional facts are now available with reference to this matter:

(1) Joel Brandt is presently being held in custody at Cairo after having previously proceeded to Jerusalem for discussions there. There have been discussions in Cairo between the American and British authorities, Brandt and Shertok of the Jewish agency.

(2) Gyorgy, who arrived from Vienna with Brandt on May 19, was taken into custody by Turkish officials on May 25, released in a few hours, pleaded for assistance in "escaping" to Syria, was documented for entrance into Allied territory, and departed on a southbound Taurus express. His present whereabouts are not definitely known here.

(3) Shertok of the Jewish agency is proceeding to London presumably for further discussions of this matter.

(4) Word has been received that the Gestapo are very angry about the failure of Brandt and Gyorgy to return to German territory. The Gestapo is alleged to have indicated that Brandt's journey was merely a preliminary to future discussions to be carried on in Lisbon by Schroeder, presumably a Gestapo agent.

(5) Although no such information was contained in our earlier reports with regard to this matter, it now appears that Brandt has indicated in several informal conversations that the German Government would be willing to agree that the 10,000 trucks would not (repeat not) be used on the Western front.

(6) We are requesting Ambassador Steinhardt to forward to you promptly Ankara despatches Nos. 676 of June 5 and 679 of June 8 which supply additional background information with respect to this matter.

142

2

SECTION TWO

It is requested that this matter be taken up with the Soviet Government in such manner as you deem appropriate and all of the facts brought to the attention of the Soviet Government promptly.

It should be emphasized to the Soviet Government that neither this Government nor the British Government has been deceived as to the character of this alleged offer of the German Government and that we have been convinced from the outset that the offer is part and parcel of the German psychological warfare effort. This is borne out particularly by the facts which have now come to light on the alleged German willingness to guarantee that the trucks would not be used on the Western front.

On the other hand, we do not wish definitively and preemptorily to refuse even to consider such offers as are made. It is our view that by appearing to explore such matters we not only have the possibility of saving lives while the discussions are going on, but also clearly leave the way open for further offers which we anticipate and which might possibly be ~~made in good faith.~~ *acceptance*

143

Any further developments will, of course, be promptly brought to your attention for the information of the Soviet Government and no action will be taken without prior agreement with the Soviet and British Governments.

It is suggested that you consult fully with the British Ambassador with respect to this matter and in discussions with the Soviet Government make it clear, if the British Ambassador is in agreement, that the views expressed by you are also the views of the British Government. The British authorities here are in agreement.

Repeat to Ankara, Cairo, and London. If London has not already been furnished with such cables it should be sent repeats of the following cables: (1) Cable to Moscow, No. 1460 of June 9; (2) No.   to Moscow of June 21; and (3) Cable to Moscow, No. 2184 of June 19.

CONTROL COPY

PARAPHRASE OF TELEGRAM RECEIVED

FROM: American Consulate, Jerusalem

TO: Secretary of State, Washington

DATED: June 29, 1944

NUMBER: 89

Doc. 30

144

The War Refugee Board is requested by Isaac Gruenbaum, Jewish Agency, to send the following to Rabbi Wise.

We have received information from Istanbul that confirms deportation of 400,000 Hungarian Jews to Poland and the imminent deportation of remaining 350,000 now concentrated in Budapest and neighborhood. Information that we have received expressly states that direct causes of intensified deportation is the detention of two men. Competent authorities are urged to be impressed their assistance was asked fully trusting, if they are not able to help at least it will not make things worse which they did by the detention two men. Urge therefore, first, immediate return of the two men; second, immediate agreement meeting Lisbon; and third, adoption meanwhile of extraordinary measures, including retaliatory measures, repeatedly suggested with view to interfering with deportation.

PINKERTON

DECLASSIFIED
State Dept. Letter, 1-11-72

By R. H. Parks Date SEP 27 1972

DCR:VAG   7/1/44

<u>COPY</u>

<u>Text of a telegram from Mr. Eden dated July 1st. 1944</u>

Mr. Shertok agreed in suggested method of approach to Germans but urged (a) the United Kingdom and United States Governments should make a further offer to approach the Spanish Government regarding reception and temporary maintenance of some manageable number of Jewish refugees; (b) a "carrot" should be dangled before the Germans in the shape of agreement by the United Kingdom and United States to discuss with them the question of Jewish rescue; (c) in advance of such discussion we should decide what <u>quid pro quo</u> could be offered to the Germans.

2.   In regard to (a) subject to views of His Majesty's Ambassador Madrid I see no difficulty. On (b) and (c) the reply given Shertok was that there could be no direct contact between the Allies and the Germans, to which he retorted that direct contact with the enemy was he understood in certain circumstances permissible to the War Refugee Board. On this the observation was made that, whatever the truth about the War Refugee Board's powers (on which I should be glad to be enlightened) such a conversation would ruin Soviet confidence in the Allies unless they had been asked and had agreed. The idea of compensation, trading in concert with a Gestapo agent, Jewish blood against Allied goods, looked equally dangerous. S. agreed, and said the Russians should, of course, be asked to concur, and that only compensation contemplated was that of no military or economic importance. It would be for us to discover such.

Doc. 31

145

Text of a telegram from Mr. Eden dated July 1st. 1944.

Please inform the United States Government that first discussions have been held here with Shertok. They have strengthened our conviction, supported by much independent evidence including detailed report placed at our disposal by United States Ambassador Angora, that however influential the Germans who authorised the offer, it was designed (a) to extract material concessions of war material from Allied Government, (b) to embroil United Kingdom and United States Governments with the Soviet Government by representing to the latter that the former were negotiating with the enemy (c) to elicit a rejection which would then be represented as justification for extreme measures against the Jews. Shertok appeared to agree with this analysis.

2.   The offer in fact was not serious and especially as coming through such insignificant or suspected channels, should on its merits have been contemptuously ignored. But we have kept it in play in the hope of staving off disaster and seeing whether something acceptable might not emerge.

3.   We must now consider our next steps. Choice appears to lie between (a) keeping Brandt and doing nothing in expectation that Gestapo may produce further offer, (b) sending Brandt back with message that he had found Allied circles concerned with the fate of the Jews and ready to consider any practicable scheme for alleviating the fate of the Jews and that he understood the Allies were conveying their views through the protecting power, and the German Government might shortly expect to hear something.

4.   If (b) is decided upon, as we would propose, then we suggest that British and American Ministers in Berne should be instructed to address Swiss Government as follows:-

Begins.

Reports of further extreme measures by the German authorities against the Jews are reaching the United Kingdom and United States Governments. At the same time both Governments have been informed from what appear to be authoritative German quarters that the German Government might be disposed to modify their policy if Allied cooperation in a solution could be obtained. Such cooperation would it appears take the form of transferring a stated number of Jews in conditions of particular distress to the responsibility of other countries. The United Kingdom and United States Governments would be willing with due regard to military necessities to consider practical measures in this connection and would be glad if the Swiss Government would so inform the German Government. Swiss Government should then state in particular that: (a) Swiss Government has invited the German Government to give facilities for the departure of 1500 Jewish children who would be given temporary hospitality in Switzerland. Similar offers have been made by other neutral Governments. As an earnest of good faith the German Government shall agree to give effect to all these offers (b) 5000 Jewish children from south eastern Europe with a proportion of accompanying adults would have been received in Palestine long ago in accordance with an offer made by the British Government had the necessary exit and transit permits been provided by the Governments (Bulgarian, Roumanian and Hungarian). The German Government is requested to facilitate the grant of such permits. (c) Transport of Jewish refugees to the various homes offered them has been hindered by the absence of German safe conducts for various ships proposed to be employed. The German Government is requested to withdraw its objection to safe conducts, in particular in the case of S.S. Tari which would be used solely for transport of civilian refugees. (d) For some considerable time past lists of Jews who would be given immediate entry into Palestine have been communicated to the German Government. It is suggested that as many of the persons as can be identified should now be given permits to leave and on hearing that this has been done transport arrangements will be taken in hand by the United Kingdom and United States Governments.

     Ends.

147

POINTS TO BE MADE TO THE BRITISH

1.   Upon the basis of present information, we are inclined to agree with the British analysis of the Brandt proposal. We agree with procedure suggested in point 3 (b) of the Eden telegram - i.e. that Brandt should be permitted to return. We are also prepared to make a representation to the Germans through the Swiss government along the lines suggested by the British. We feel that the particular language suggested in the British cable might be construed as limiting unduly the number of Jews which the two governments would be prepared to receive under their protection. It is the view of this Government that the Swiss should advise the Germans that the United States and the United Kingdom governments will make arrangements for the reception from German occupied territory of all Jews who can be received consistently with military necessities. As presently worded, the proposed cable to the Swiss is subject to the interpretation, and perhaps would be so interpreted by the Germans, as merely an offer to consider any proposal to release the limited number of Jews for the reception of which in Palestine and elsewhere there are present commitments. This interpretation would under the present circumstances be highly unfortunate and it is assumed that such was not intended. It is suggested that the following language be substituted for the third and fourth sentences of the proposed cable to the Swiss:

"Such cooperation would it appears take the form of transferring Jews now in German controlled territory to the responsibility of other countries. The United Kingdom and United States Governments would be willing, with due regard to military necessities, to consider measures for the reception of all Jews permitted to leave areas under the control of Germany; and would be glad if the Swiss Government would so inform the German Government."

2.   We should indicate to the British our view that the matter must be cleared in advance with the Russians and we should ask for their approval of the proposed cable to Moscow.

3.   The British should be asked to have Sir Samuel Hoare immediately approach the Spanish Government with the request that that government admit into Spain temporarily all Jewish refugees permitted to leave areas under the control of the Germans. This Government is prepared, in conjunction with the British government, to arrange for the maintenance and care of all such refugees during their stay in Spain and to arrange for their prompt removal to temporary havens of refuge elsewhere. This attitude of the United States Government has already been communicated to our Ambassador in Madrid. Sir Samuel should be requested to advise the Spanish government of these facts upon making his request.

4.   Explain to the British that Shertok's reference to the Board's authority to communicate with the enemy refers to the authorization given Board's representative under the Trading With the Enemy Act. Indicate that only use made of this authority have been discussions solely on refugee matters with Bulgarian and Rumanian Ambassadors, of which British are aware.

148

AMERICAN EMBASSY

Ankara - July 3, 1944.

Dear Mr. Pehle:

In pursuance of instructions from Ambassador Steinhardt, on June 21st I left Ankara for Cairo for the express purpose of interviewing Joel Brandt following the instructions you gave me in Washington.

Enclosed is the report which I submitted to Ambassador Steinhardt upon my return from Cairo to Ankara on June 25th.

At that time I was informed by Ambassador Steinhardt of the Department's telegram No. 557, of June 21st, to take no further action in the matter pending further instructions. We are taking no further steps whatever in this matter unless and until we receive further instructions from you. May I add that I consider it of utmost importance that Brandt be returned to Hungary without delay.

With kind personal regards,

Cordially yours,

I. A. HIRSCHMANN,
Special Attache.

Doc. 32

149

Mr. John H. Pehle,
       Executive Director,
              War Refugee Board,
                     Treasury Building,
                            Washington, D.C.

DECLASSIFIED
State Dept. Letter, 1-11-72
By R. H. Parks Date SEP 27 1972

Cairo, June 24, 1944.

Dear Mr. Ambassador,

The attached memorandum was dictated "piece-meal" as developments and conferences ensued in Cairo under the pressure of time and 118 degrees temperature. On reading the typed draft I am inclined to the opinion that it somewhat reflects the above-mentioned conditions. At the same time it fairly completely reflects the observations and views obtained from these explorations in Cairo which are believed by me to have been most useful.

Not referred to herein are telegrams which I am informed were despatched by (a) Lord Moyne to London covering the subject of our discussions. These telegrams were not shown to me but referred to in discussions. (b) Telegram from Mr. Tuck to the Department, a paraphrase of which is attached. I recommended that the latter should not be sent but I was overruled. Mr. Tuck requested of me a copy of the Interrogation of Joel Brand by me which I handed to him.

It occurs to me that en route from Cairo you may consider it desirable to confer with Lord Moyne on this matter.

Cordially yours,

I. A. Hirschmann
Special Attache

150

MEMORANDUM TO AMBASSADOR STEINHARDT

Date: June 22, 1944.

Subject: Interview with Joel Brand, Observations
and Recommendations.

Acting under your instructions I arrived in
Cairo on Wednesday, June 21, 1944, at approximately
5:00 p.m. and repaired at once to the American Legation.
When I requested an audience with Minister Tuck I was
informed by his secretary that Mr. Doolittle, First
Secretary of Legation, had been working during the
day on the matter which had brought me from Ankara.
Upon presenting the letter from you to Minister Tuck
a conference was arranged between the Minister, Mr.
Doolittle and myself.

The Minister introduced the subject by asserting that Lord Moyne, British Minister Resident in
the Middle East, had conferred that day with him on the
subject under discussion and that Lord Moyne was
acting under instructions from London on the highest
levels. He emphasized that any decisions that were
to be taken would be centralized by both the British
and American Governments in London and that I was
being requested by the British Government to proceed
at once from Cairo to London.

Here I demurred, asserting that I had instructions from the War Refugee Board, Washington and my
superior officer in Turkey, Ambassador Steinhardt to interview Joel Brand at the earliest possible moment and that I
had been despatched to Cairo with the express understanding

that

that I would be able to do so. I also stated that I
could not accede to the request of the British Government to direct me to proceed thousands of miles to
London to interview Brand when Brand was in Cairo
at this moment, and the fact that I had come to Cairo
for the express purpose of seeing him here.

I informed Mr. Tuck that the British Minister
to Turkey, Mr. St. Bennett, had requested me to commu-
icate with a Mr. Hamilton at the Office of the Minister
of State. Mr. Doolittle informed us that he had been
in communication with Mr. Hamilton that day.

At the conclusion of our conference it was agreed
that Mr. Doolittle would impress upon Mr. Hamilton
on the following day the necessity of my interview
with Joel Brand in Cairo after which I was to return
to Ankara to submit my report to Ambassador Steinhardt.
Mr. Tuck concluded the conference by stating that it
was difficult to move the British once they had
developed a program of strategy.

In the meanwhile Mr. Doolittle informed me of
the fact that Mr. Joseph Schwartz of the JDC had
arrived from Algiers to Cairo and that Schwartz
had also requested an interview with Joel Brand,
Schwartz having been unaware of my presence in Cairo
for that purpose.

At ten o'clock on Thursday, June 22nd, Mr.
Doolittle invited me to meet with Joseph Schwartz
in the former's office. After disclosing my instructions on the subject of Joel Brand, Schwartz agreed
to withdraw from active participation in the matter

at

152

at this time. In Schwartz's presence Mr. Doolittle
informed me that he had discussed the matter with
Lord Moyne by telephone that morning and ~~further~~
that it was agreed that I was to visit with Lord
Moyne at twelve noon, after which arrangements
would be made by the British for me to interview
Joel Brand.

At the meeting with Lord Moyne there were
present, in addition to Lord Moyne, Brigadier
R.J. Maunsell, Sir William Croft, First Assistant
to Lord Moyne, John Hamilton, Assistant Minister
Resident, Mr. Doolittle and myself. Lord Moyne
informed me that Shertok had requested of the British
Government that he be permitted to proceed at once
to London on the subject at hand and Lord Moyne
suggested that I prepared to accompany Shertok in
order to have the discussions, and possible decisions,
centralized in London. I emphasized that I could
not make any decision regarding my movements until
I had (a) talked with Brand, (b) reported the results
of my interview with Brand to Ambassador Steinhardt
in Ankara and (c) received instructions for my next
steps from Ambassador Steinhardt through Washington.

At the outset of this conference I referred to
the interest which was being taken in this matter
on the highest level in Washington. I referred to the
active interest of Under Secretary of State Stettinius,
the interest disclosed by President Roosevelt and the
active exploratory efforts towards which I was directed
by Ambassador Steinhardt. At the suggestion of Mr.

Doolittle

153

Doolittle I took the occasion to show the letter of
President Roosevelt addressed to me to Lord Moyne.
I indicated that the War Refugee Board and Ambassador
Steinhardt were intent in their desire to explore all
the facts with a view to (a) determining the authority
from which the offer emanated, (b) possibly "keeping
the door open," (c) the remote possibility of saving
lives in accordance with the American and British
established policy, and (d) the possibility of determining information that might be otherwise helpful.
I referred also to the need of keeping the Russians
informed.

Lord Moyne asserted that the next steps connected
with this proposal could only be taken in London
and that the moves would be out of his jurisdiction.
He referred to the implications from Brand's interviews
conducted by the British Intelligence. He and his
associates were clear in indicating that they did
not credit Brand with any unworthy motives although
there were some slight discrepancies in his stories
which they were inclined to believe had sprung from
nervousness and apprehension. When the subject of
Gross was introduced I maintained that this man was
in a different category and that we were not interested in him except for possible additional disclosures
which might relate either to our efforts in behalf of
refugees or revelations which might be of value in
other aspects of our explorations.

Brigadier Maunsell, who is in charge of Intelligence,
questioned me on this point and wanted to know what

other

other explorations we had in mind. I referred to the possibilities of other implications in the visit of Brand which might arise from his disclosures and which of course the British Intelligence would be able to ferret out.

It was agreed (1) that I was to meet first with Brigadier Maunsell to be briefed on the background of the British Intelligence investigations to date and the operations of the Gestapo, (2) that I was to meet in a private home by arrangement of Brigadier Maunsell with Mr. Brand, Major Martin Forrest and a stenographer (I suggested the desirability of a transcript), and (3) that I was to meet with Lord Moyne on Friday, June 23 at 11 a.m., (4) I was to return to Ankara to report to Ambassador Steinhardt on June 25.

In view of the emphasis which I had put on the need for returning Brand to Hungary at the first possible moment it was suggested as an alternative that a message could be sent at once through BARLAS in Istanbul to the Hungarians and the Germans referring to "the consideration which is being given the matter." It was determined that this would be decided after my meeting with Brand in the afternoon. Lord Moyne reiterated his fear of the dangers involved in the Germans exposing and exploiting the "offer" and announcing that the Allies had flatly refused by silence and delay. I replied that I thought that we would have to take this chance now until our conclusions had been reached and cleared through Ambassador Steinhardt and London.

At

155

At 4:00 p.m. I met Mr. Brand at the private apartment at which there were also present Major Martin Forrest, a British agent whose name was not disclosed as well as Brigadier Maunsell's secretary, Miss Read. Attached as Exhibit A is a fairly verbatim report of the interview. After the interview tea was served and Brand disclosed the following which was not reported in the attached notes:

Brand stated that it was of interest and ironical that the representatives of the Jewish organizations who had been dealing illegally with the Germans had now been asked to act in an official capacity by the Germans; that apparently the Germans respected those who resisted or took action against them.

156

In reply to my question to Brand: "Did you see any evidence on the part of the German leaders that they were becoming fearful or desperate?" Brand replied: "Yes, decidedly, I see it in their talk and protestations; in the fact that a high German officer tells to the Jew, Brand, 'We need things--go and get them.'" This, Brand said, appeared to him to be a great confession of weakness.

Brand asserted that Eichman represents the "top"; that Eichman has the rank of Minister representing the Government for activities against the Jews. Brand also asserted that

Hitler's

Hitler's special representatives had been present at one of the four conferences. They were Wesenmeyer and Winckelman. (The British Intelligence Officer confirmed that these men were Hitler's top representatives.) Brand further asserted that the German Minister for Foreign Affairs was not interested in this activity but that the German military and SS all the way up to the head "are in this thing." Brand stated that Wislezein is next to Himmler.

Observations and Recommendations:

Brand impressed me as honest, clear, incisive, blunt and completely frank. In my talk with him, which occupied over an hour's time, I could find no shadow of evidence to support the reservations contained in the report of Mr. Rueben B. Resnik to Ambassador Steinhardt of June 5th which asserted "I had the impression that he was not sincere and straightforward as other observers thought him to be." My impressions were distinctly the reverse. I do not wish to labor this point except that I believe it to be of utmost importance in evaluating the veracity and informative nature of Brand's disclosures.

In spite of the pressure of the British Intelligence's questioning under which he was operating during the last ten days (the questioning ensued some days for ten hours) he was open, clear, affirmative and high minded. His concern with his own family, his relatives and the possibility of reprisals for others, were he

not

157

not to be able to return, was genuine and moving,
in my opinion. In short, Brand's disclosures are to
be accepted in my view as truthful, without reservations.

On the above premises I am of the opinion that
we can offer a number of conclusions and possibilities:
(1) The proposals were made as a result of four separate
interviews by Brand with Eichman and the latter's collaborators. They cannot be considered in the realm of
fantasy. They are serious, and we must probe for the
point of view on which to explore further. (2) In at
least one of the conversations with Eichman there
appeared two representatives of the Nazi SS who are
said and believed by the British Intelligence to be
"high up". It seems that the proposals have the
sanction of Nazi officials from somewhere near the
top level. (3) Brand's statement that the proposal
connected with ten thousand lorries and other commodities
was mentioned in an off-hand way and in effect "pulled out
of the hat" by one of the German officers is a clear
indication that this is not concrete or to be taken seriously. Immunity or some reference to immunity may be
considered seriously as a bargaining point. (4) Brand's
explanation of the Nazi's recommendation to send the
refugees through Spain seems to justify the contentions
already established in other quarters that the Nazis,
for various reasons, wish to discourage additions to
the population of Palestine and do not wish to offend
the Arabs. There may be other reasons for this suggestion regarding Spain as the proposed refuge,
which may have military and political connotations
which are self evident. (5) Brand's strong conviction that something tangible could result from

a skillful

158

a skillful manoeuvre in this situation, impressed me.

Conjectures from the above:

A. A clique is making a bold and desperate attempt to secure large sums of money for itself or to save their skins; or possibly to pull a deal which would impress the top Nazi officials.

B. Under political warfare it may be a device to separate the three Allied Governments and create a misunderstanding between them.

C. It is remotely possible that the proposals have the sanction of some top authorities who were of the opinion that they might succeed in receiving the money, lorries, commodities, et cetera.

D. It is a bold effort to embarrass the Allies by publishing to the world the fact that a bona fide offer had been made through a representative and responsible Jew and had been postponed and finally denied.

159

E. On the positive side it is possible that some kind of deal might be executed, if the matter is pursued without delay. Brand indicated rather strongly such a possibility and it was my impression that he would not have left on so perilous a mission unless he could see a door which was open even though it may be a small aperture.

F. It is not outside the realm of possibility that the Nazi rulers really believe their own propaganda and have considered the Jews a soft spot in the armor of the Allies through whom they could engage the Allies in discussions that begin with the refugee subject and lead to proposals of peace. Lord Moyne does not reject this latter.

Recommendations

Recommendations

1. I respectfully suggested to Lord Moyne in my second conference today, June 23, at 11:00 a.m. that a message be transmitted at once which would reach the Hungarians and the Germans. To this he responded that a message had already been drafted and was being sent to BARLAS in Istanbul. I approved the despatch of the attached Exhibit B. I further suggested that Brand, for his peace of mind and for constructive purposes in the keeping up of his morale, be informed immediately that a message had been sent through BARLAS.

2. Lord Moyne in his conversation with me referred to Anthony Eden, the British Foreign Minister's alleged interest in "keeping the door open in this situation". It is indicated that the British will collaborate in pursuing this "open door policy". This should be exploited.

3. That Brand be retained in Cairo. There was some question in the British circles of sending Brand to London. I pressed Lord Moyne and he agreed that Brand was to remain in Cairo. Obviously the nearer he is to Hungary and his eventual destination, the better.

4. That Ambassador Steinhardt invite instructions from Washington with regard to the American representative to be despatched to London to confer with authorities along with Shertok who has been given permission and high priority to proceed to London June 25 arriving on Wednesday June 28.

5. That Brand be given careful verbal instructions to take back to Hungary at the first possible moment, indicating that consideration is being given the proposals in connection with money and possible immunity; if the

Germans

160

Germans, as Brand indicated, were prepared to make the
first steps in releasing minorities and Jews this
would be received by the Allies as an earnest ~~gesture~~
of their good will and would lead to more conclusive
negotiations.

6. That no efforts be made on our part with regard
to interrogating Giorgy (Gross). He is in a different
category, an agent with a perfidious record. He should
be kept outside this situation, as the introduction
of his testimony or activities can serve no useful
purpose.

7. Plans should be considered for a possible meeting
between the Nazi representatives and British and Americans at some neutral point as soon as desirable. Brand
should attend this meeting.

8. The suggestion made by Ben Gurion and Shertok to
the Palestine High Commissioner, which was transmitted
to London by the latter, suggesting a committee of the
Inter Governmental Committee, the International Red
Cross and other organizations to sit with German representatives contains dangerous features. I informed
Shertok and Lord Moyne that nothing expeditious could
come of such a large scale organizational group meeting
and suggested that any such conversations should be held
in the strictest confidence by highly authorized Governmental representatives in a small circle. Lord Moyne concurred.

9. In this connection it is of utmost importance to
avoid the disclosure of any of these negotiations, as
publicity would explode the entire matter and result
in a boomerang effect. I am informed by Mr. Hamilton

that

161

that an American and British newspaperman have
already asked about the matter.

    10. In our recommendations to Washington we should
urge silence in the event of a leak.

    Both Lord Moyne and I, at our first meeting, were
of the opinion that there was only the remotest possibility of something useful emanating from these explorations. On my second meeting with Lord Moyne today,
following my talk yesterday with Brand, and his careful
reading of the transcript (Exhibit A) he was (along with
me) genuinely enthusiastic regarding possibilities which
might develop provided that this matter was handled
with care and skill. He again urged me to proceed
to London and I repeated I would have to obtain any
instructions from Ambassador Steinhardt. He urged that
upon the return of Brand it would be desirable for me to
coach him about his proposed conversations with the
Germans in view of the fact that it was felt that I had
succeeded in obtaining Brand's confidence.

    Lord Moyne announced that the transcript of my
interview would be established as the basic and accepted
report on the Brand case. He asserted that new information
had been disclosed in this interview which had heretofore
been unknown to the British Intelligence. xxxxxxxxx
xxxxxxxxxxxxxxxxxxxxxxxxxxxxxxxxxx

Respectfully submitted:

I.A. Hirschmann
Special Attaché to
Ambassador Steinhardt.

Enclosures:

162

Enclosures:

1- Exhibit A: Text of Interview between Mr.
              I.A. Hirschmann and Mr. Joel
              Brandt.

2- Exhibit B: Telegram from Shertok to BARLAS.

3- Exhibit C: Memorandum concerning telegram from
              the High Commissioner of Palestine
              to London.

4- Exhibit D: Copies of telegrams left with Mr.
              I.A. Hirschmann by Shertok:

        (1) Shertok to N. Goldmann.
        (2) Shertok to Dr. Weizman.
        (3) Shertok to Russell.

ADDENDUM

Upon returning to the Legation on Saturday,
June 24 following the return of the plane en route from
Cairo to Adana due to mechanical difficulties I was
handed your telegram of June 22. Mr. Doolittle suggested that we transmit the information contained therein to the British which was done through Mr. Kirk of
the British Intelligence. It was suggested that efforts
be made to question Brand regarding Shroder, whose name
was not mentioned in Brand's interview with me but who
was mentioned by Brand frequently in testimony to the
British Intelligence.

Mr. Hamilton visited Mr. Doolittle and me at the
Legation at 5:00 p.m. He requested that in view of
my enforced incarceration in Cairo and the new possible
developments contained in your telegram from BARLAS of
June 22 that Lord Moyne desired a further conference
to which I assented.

I met with Lord Moyne at his office at 5:45 p.m.
Also in attendance were Mr. Hamilton, Colonel Kirk and
Sir William Croft. Lord Moyne informed me that he
had received a telegram from London authorizing the
telegram from Shertok to BARLAS, Exhibit B. The situation was then explored further in view of the above-
mentioned telegram from BARLAS. Shroder's real name,
it appears, is Lauffer. Lauffer is apparently the
leading Gestapo agent in Hungary. I reiterated my
view that if it was agreed to send Brand to Hungary
it should be done without unnecessary delay and that
Brand be despatched with coached information in which

he would

164

he would (a) explain that no munitions or material
can be considered as part of any discussions, (b)
promise nothing, (c) ask the Nazis to make the first
step in ceasing persecutions and deportations, (d)
following the above he could return and suggest
discussions concerning money or immunity.

To this Lord Moyne replied that he was strongly
of the opinion that the British Government would not
consent to the offer of money. I emphasized that
such money would be put in a block account and not
be used in connection with the war but for individuals.
On this point he was somewhat open-minded.

Lord Moyne requested if he might impart my views
above stated telegraphically to London. Whereupon
I requested that he would not do so as they represented
only my personal views and not the Ambassador's nor
the Government's. I agreed to recommend to Ambassador
Steinhardt that the British Ambassador in Ankara be
informed of our recommendations to be transmitted to
Lord Moyne.

165

INTERROGATION OF MR. JOEL B R A N D T BY MR. IRA HIRSCHMAN.

22 June 44

H.   I understand you speak English.

B.   Not very well.

H.   I am delighted to have the opportunity of speaking to you,
       because I hope that I can be helpful to you - as you know I
       come from America.

B.   Yes, I heard that just now.

H.   My only reason for being here is to try to be helpful in
       the refugee situation - you understand.

B.   You are not Mr. HIRSCHMAN are you.

H.   No - I wanted to talk with you to see if there was not
       some way that we could be helpful.

B.   If there was something you could do for me I should be very
       pleased -

H.   Because you have had rather a difficult time -

B.   I have had a very difficult time; everyone has been very
       polite but it is as though I have been put in a prison-
       but I can understand it is necessary to keep me away
       from other people - I can quite understand it.

H.   My impression is that you have nothing to fear - you
       have done a great deal of very valuable philanthropic
       work in Hungary for many years.

B.   I have done what it was possible to do.

H.   You have a reputation for being very helpful.

B.   I have done what I could do - it was not easy.

H.   I am sure it was not easy and it is to your credit that
       you are interested in doing such things. Are conditions
       in Hungary very bad?

B.   Very bad, yes very bad.

H.   Could you tell me something about them.

B.   Well, what has been done in Germany, Austria, Czechoslovakia
       and Poland in years has been done in Hungary in a few weeks'
       time - it all came about very quickly, all the laws and
       oppressions against the Jews came in Hungary in a very short
       time.

H.   Are the women and children being persecuted as well as the men.

B.   No difference between women and children and men- though
       children under six years do not have to wear the Ghetto star.

H.   Why did you leave Hungary?

B.   Because I had been sent to come and try to make -

H.   Who sent you.

B.   Two different sources sent me, on the one side the Germans to make a bargain, and on the other side the Jews selected me to be their emissary.

H.   It seems that the Germans made arrangements with the Jewish leaders -

B.   I was taken on first by the Jewish leaders, who had debates with the Germans that I should keep up the contact between the official German authorities and the Jewish representatives, and if it came out that somebody should be allowed to go and try to come to some arrangement about the persecution of Jews, I should be picked by the Jews as the person to go.

H.   What were the names of the Jewish representatives?

B.   STERN, Philip von FREUDIGER - President of the orthodox Jews - KOMOLY.

H.   You had been active in these organisations for a number of years - with the Zionist movement?

B.   Yes, I was active in the Zionist movement for many years and I have been active in general Jewish charities.

H.   You were a business man?

B.   Yes.

H.   The Germans also picked you-

B.   Yes, because I had been the negotiating link between -

H.   Did you know many of these German leaders?

B.   No-- I did know some of them by name, but I did not know them well.

H.   Who are the German leaders?

B.   EICHMANN, who is in Hungary now - he marched in with the German troops.

H.   Who are some of the other leaders?

B.   KLAGES, KRUMEY, Wili von WISLIZENI. WISLIZENI started to make some negotiations with our friends -

H.   What friends?

B.   Our Jewish friends - about a year ago.

H.   What kind of negotiations?

B.   The same kind as the one I have been doing now, for the Jews in Bratislava. I spoke about these negotiations - I tried this already about a year ago.

H.   Didn't you see any danger in dealing with these people?

B.   I did, but there was no other way outside the illegal way which we were already doing to try to help these people.

H.   So you decided to try.

B.   I did, yes.

167

H.   What kind of relations did you have with EICHNER and his party?

B.   EICHMANN - I spoke to him in his office, I went at his invitation - or rather at his order!

H.   Who suggested this idea that you should come here - where was it suggested?

B.   EICHMANN called me, that was the first time I was speaking to him and there he suggested that I should go and he would give an offer -

H.   Who suggested the idea of the offer?

B.   The idea of making some arrangement with the Germans - we tried to do the same type of thing - EICHNER did - about a year ago.

H.   What kind of offer was that - money?

B.   Money. We only offered money.

H.   What kind of offer did you bring from EICHMANN - a written offer?

B.   I did not have a clear offer - he only told me some kinds of goods and money which I should bring. He told me that he would be willing to set the Jews free.

H.   Was there any specific offer.

B.   Nothing specific. He did not specify that I should bring any money.

H.   How would you know what to say?

B.   He said I would find out for myself - he did not want to commit himself.

H.   Did he commit himself on things or money?

B.   Both.

H.   What did he suggest to you that he wanted?

B.   The main thing was trucks.

H.   How many?

B.   He once said ten thousand, but -

H.   What else?

B.   He only spoke about trucks. Another gentleman, I did not know his name, who was present - I believe his name was BEISMEYER (?), said once I should ask also for coffee, chocolate and tea and soap. And EICHMANN once mentioned money - dollars, Swiss francs and some South American money.

H.   You felt that you had some kind of basis for an offer to discuss in Istanbul.

B.   Yes, I had for this reason some basis, because a year ago they had already fixed this up on a basis of two million

168

dollars. When I started the negotiations I did not speak with EICHMANN, I spoke with WISLIZENI and I also suggested that this old offer should be accepted now.

H. What was the old offer -

In Slovakia, Bratislava - we had the same difficulties as we have now. The offer was two million dollars for stopping deportation and punishment for those Jews who are still living in Czechoslovakia and Poland. For my part negotiations were different. No deportation, no concentration and allowing to come to Palestine - and no shooting.

H. What happened to the original negotiations?

B. They were accepted on paper but not carried through - neither from them nor from us. For our part because we did not pay - we did not get any amount which we could pay. In Slovakia there are only sixty or eighty thousand Jews, in Hungary there are one million Jews; we wanted to make negotiations not only for the Hungarian Jews, we wanted to make negotiations for all Jews. The original negotiation was only from Slovakia. WISLIZENI -

H. He now wanted to make a plan for all the Jews?

B. Yes, not only the Hungarian Jews.

H. Where did you expect to get this money or these trucks?

B. The trucks I did not know I would be able to get, but I thought I must try and get them from the English and American governments. The money I thought I would be able to get from Jewish organisations.

H. How much money did you have in mind?

B. I thought that I could get about one million dollars, in payment, not with me but to my credit, somewhere, and that I should be able to open negotiations and it would not be necessary for me to go back with money or with goods because I had the promise from EICHMANN that it would be all right if the offer was accepted and I could make some bargain with them; he agreed before I went away that he would make the first move, that he would let out at first a certain number, ten, twenty, fifty thousand Jews, and for this reason alone it would have been a great thing -

H. That gave you confidence. Did you have confidence in his word?

B. When he is making the first move -

H. Did you have confidence that he would keep his word with you?

B. I did not have the right to question my own conscience. There is no other way besides legal means in which we can help - we cannot wait for that invasion of Budapest -

H. Then it was a matter of conscience with you, not a matter of confidence - is that correct?

B. No - there is only one chance, perhaps it is no good, but there is no other chance.

169

H.   What is your opinion of the chances of this working?

B.   My opinion is that they would keep their word.

H.   Why?

B.   First of all because they need things -

H.   How do you know?

B.   When I left Hungary, I know that they were needing all
         kinds of things.

H.   Things or money.

B.   At first I thought, I know they need things. I know from
         years of work that everyone of them can be bought. I
         know this from years of work - I am not saying that I have
         bought EICHMANN or WISLIZENI. In my work very many of
         them have been bought and I do believe that criminals of
         such a low sort as these men are always receptive to offers
         of money. It is natural that people who do such terrible
         things will not have clean hands where money is concerned
         either.

H.   You refer to some of these people having been bought before-
         in what connection?

B.   Not these people particularly, but German officials, SS
         and Nazi officials. We had our main work before the
Ger   Germans came in - bringing men from Poland and from other
         countries illegally to Hungary.

170

H.   I would like your opinion Mr. BRANDT on what you think will
         happen to this money if such money were available - I do
         not know if it in fact would be, I do not know anything
         about it - but supposing something should happen and money
         were available.

B.   Believing that it is done on a very large scale, somebody
         must go to some official places, I am certain many men will
         be there who will settle personally and make it their own
         business.

H.   Do you mean high-up sources?

B.   I have the opinion that there are very many different
         cliques within the Nazi movement and that there are certain
         circles who want to make money or more business for them-
         selves or their circle and that they will not get punished
         or anything like that. I can imagine them saying quite
         brutally, well you have had eight million Jews, we have
         killed more than six million, we will give you the rest if
         you do not punish us for killing the others.

H.   How did Mr. GIORGY come into this matter?

B.   Mr. GROSS is his real name. He brought letters from our
         friends in Istanbul and from us for a year and a half- two
         years about - that is where I met him. I knew him to be
         an official of the Hungarian General Staff at the time when
         the Hungarians' politics were considered to be fairly
favourable to the Allies. Though I think he went over to the
         Germans he had nothing to do with this except that he
         he came with me.

H. I wonder how you and he got together.

B. He was bringing letters from Turkey for us for the last year and a half.

H. Who was he working for really?

B. I do not understand you - he was working for money.

H. Are you associated with him this affair of yours?

B. He has nothing to do with this affair - he says there is some other reason why he has come here, at least I wanted to assume it this way. It is possible that the Germans have sent him for this reason too- but not to my knowledge. He was not sent by the Jews.

H. He was not working in collaboration with you in this matter?

B. No. He had nothing to do with my mission, and I had nothing to do with his.

H. It seems that GIORGY said that you had a paper to show with an actual offer. What is this paper, where is it?

B. The paper is with me.

H. No - did you leave it in Istanbul?

B. What kind of paper - to bring back or did I bring it here- it is not true. I only remember a list of goods which they are needing. I did not bring a written offer for you from them. I remember a list of things they are needing -

H. Who wrote this paper?

B. I got it from Mr. SCHROEDER.

H. Where is it?

B. When I reached Istanbul I gave it in the first instance to Mr. BARLAS - he has it. It is not an important thing- only a list of things.

H. I know - I only mentioned it offhand. What do you expect to happen now?

B. Nothing good. I am very much afraid of it.

H. Aren't you optimistic?

B. I have had to leave my wife and family - I am very much afraid - it is not easy to talk about the things they are capable of doing - the Germans. They are my kids and my wife and my mother and I am getting a little nervous -

H. What is making you nervous -

B. I cannot speak about these things.

H. You mean that if this does not work out -

B. Yes, it is already more than five weeks since I left Germany.

H. Did they say anything to you about when they expected you to return, the Germans?

171

B.   No. They said I could take my time if I saw that I had possibilities of success.

H.   Then you should not be certain-

B.   You asked me ten minutes ago if I believed everything they said. I know that I have had no contact with my wife for three or four weeks and I know what they are capable of doing.

H.   You are afraid they will do something because you are delayed?

B.   Very much afraid that they will. They always take their revenge on others. I beg your pardon for getting nervous. I know what they are like. We had problems to solve. If we did steal one man away from a camp - if one man got away they would shoot ten or twenty or fifty. We had many discussions about it, whether we should try to stop getting men away. We decided that we should go on, because we knew that they were shooting and killing them anyway.

H.   Were the Germans definite in saying that they would release these people through Spain?

B.   Yes....there are things which I know through years of work, and other things which I am only guessing, and I believe that they want to do something legal. I think perhaps they want to do some big propaganda. To say that they wanted to set the Jews free and the Allies did not want it, and so there was no other way but for them to kill them off. Understand?

H.   Yes. Now what about Spain?

B.   That is one of the reasons. It is very hard to get people over to Germany when there is an invasion going on. The mass of the Jews have to go to Spain. That is one of the reasons why I say that they are making a bargain which it would be very hard for us to fulfil, and they will have in their propaganda one more reason for killing the Jews: "Well we wanted to give you this and you did not want to take it".

H.   They might do that anyhow.

B.   There is one other reason for Spain. That is that of the Arab question - they do not want to have the Arabs against them if they sent Jews to Palestine. They did mention that to me.

H.   Did they mention any connection with Spain?

B.   Not in connection with Spain but in connection with an argument against Palestine.

H.   How often did you see EICHMANN?

B.   I saw him four times in his office. The other officers I saw very many times.

H.   I have just one or two more questions. If you were in a position now to ask and to get what you wanted to make this a successful venture, what would you ask?

B. Nothing. I only ask permission to offer, not to give, and I would ask my Jewish authorities for money for the Jews in Hungary and in Poland to to help them there. But I would not ask anything much from the Germans. I would go back and ask EICHMANN, will you release, as you said once, a hundred men for one truck, send the first transport to Spain; then you would get these things. That would be logical.

H. Do you think that you could get what you want with money and without any of these trucks or goods?

B. I do not know. Perhaps I can -

H. And that some suggestion of the possibility of this might secure immunity?

B. Immunity I have got for myself.

H. I do not want you to think that these things could be done, I have no reason to know about it - I do not want you to have any false hopes. What do you think would be the best thing to do?

B. The best thing I think would be that one, two or three officers from Hungary should come to a neutral country, say Spain, or Turkey or Switzerland, and English and American people, and myself too, and we should try to come to some sort of bargain. That is my recommendation.

H. You feel that if you went back with such a recommendation -

B. I believe I could stop persecutions - the worst persecutions - that are going on at once.

173

H. Are these persecutions still going on?

B. I am sorry to say that they were going on.

H. What number of people have been deported?

B. Until the week I went away, the week I went away they started deporting about 12,000 every day.

H. Where?

B. Kaschau, Klausenburg, Munkacs, Hust.

H. Were they in camps.

B. They were concentrated in places in such terrible conditions that they have never been known before.

H. What kind of transportation - trucks?

B. No, railway lorries, 60 and 80 men in a lorry, the lorry sealed down.

H. Did any die on the way?

B. I am certain of it.

H. Where were they taken to?

B. Auschwitz and Birkenau.

H. What other Germans were implicated.

B. Some of the highest representatives of the German military command as well as EICHMANN - the military and the SS are in this thing. WISLIZENI is a near relative of HIMMLER's.

H. Is there any evidence of desparation amongst them?

B. There is an indication of some change of attitude.

H. Does persecution of other minorities go on besides the Jews?

B. Yes - they have persecuted and have arrested all the Socialist leaders and little political leaders. The Socialist and the Liberals are feeling it as much as we are feeling it and being sent into concentration camps. They are not concentrating only on the Jews. Prisoners-of-war in Hungary who had run away from Germany - English, French prisoners-of-war have been treated pretty well. They have only to register and are allowed to live quite freely.

H. If you were detained here for a long time - though I have no reason to think that you would be - what do you think would happen?

174

B. I am afraid that in the first place my family will get persecuted in the most terrible way. Secondly my friends will get punished. Thirdly I fear that they will have executions and deportations. If for some reason or other I personally should not be allowed to be sent back, then at lease somebody else should be sent.

H. You think it would be necessary to send someone, or could a message be sent?

B. Perhaps a message on the radio or in a letter - it is terrible for me with my family there - they will take it that I have run away.

H. Your family will?

B. No, my family know - my wife knows pretty well what I am doing.

EXHIBIT B

TO :- BARLAS ISTANBUL

FROM :- SHERTOK JERUSALEM

Am summoned to London on high Government priority (.) HIRSCHMANN
may follow (.)   Meanwhile BRANDT is detained by British
authorities in MIDDLE EAST (.)

NOTE.

During his conversation with the
High Commissioner for Palestine, subsequent
to his interview with Brandt at Aleppo,
Mr. Shertok, after reporting his talk,
stressed the vital need to explore every
avenue to help these Jews in Hungary. He
thought that it was most important to
arrange a meeting with German representatives,
it being understood that political discussions
were completely barred. He suggested that
these discussions might take place on the
Allied side thro' the head of the refugee
organisation or the Red Cross authorities,
or the U.S.A. War Refugee Board.

176

19.6.1944

For Nahum Goldmann from Shertok

You have probably been informed by British Embassy of Nazi offer evacuate
remnants European Jewry primarily from Hungary. Message was brought by
Joel Brandt trusted Hungarian Zionist who was sent on Wehrmacht plane
to Istanbul May 19th, view returning with reply within two three weeks.
Ostensibly offer was exchange Jews for goods specified kinds quantities.
Evacuees to proceed Spain. First substantial transport to be sent out
without consideration on receipt favourable reply regarding whole scheme.
Exchange conditions sounded fantastic but we decided explore. Informed
immediately High Commissioner who reported fully London with request
inform Washington and you. High Commissioner did everything help me
proceed Turkey view interviewing Brandt. Visa difficulties delayed my
departure. Eventually met Brandt Aleppo. Originally it was agreed by
British authorities Istanbul Jerusalem that Brandt should return Turkey
view proceeding thence Hungary but higher quarters ordered his
transportation Cairo where he is detained. Our friends Budapest now
informing Istanbul unless Brandt returns immediately everything will
be lost. Executives conclusions after my report are that though
exchange proposition may be mere eyewash and possibility ulterior
motives must be assumed it is not improbable that even preliminary
negotiations might result in salvation substantial number. We are
informed Eden in conversation with Weizmann agreed policy should be
gain time avoid other side getting impression Allies are slamming
door refusing even consider matter. Whilst appreciating helpfulness
this attitude we consider more is warranted. Have proposed steps
should immediately be taken view exploring possibility meeting with
German representatives say in Lisbon or Madrid to discuss rescue Jews
urging same time immediate discontinuation deportations and slaughter
pending meeting. Body appearing behalf Allies might be intergovernment
l Refugee Committee or War Refugee Board or Redcross or any other suitable agency. Have also urged Brandts immediate return to report that
message has been delivered is under active consideration. Also asked
for urgent priority for me to fly London. Please act accordingly.

19.6.1944.

Following for Dr. Weizmann from Shertok

According text telegram from friends in Budapest transmitted by Istanbul unless Brandt and other person who accompanied him to Istanbul return to Hungary immediately everything will be lost. Both Brandt and other person are now in Cairo. We hold no brief for other person and must leave his fate to be decided by competent British authorities. But Brandt came as emissary remnant European Jewry who in interests its rescue accepted mission from enemies on clear understanding that he return with reply. Although realising that his return alone and with definite answer may cause his death immediately he is desparately anxious carry out bargain and return in hope that his report about delivery message and its consideration in high quarters will help gain time and prevent precipitation calamity. We consider his return most imperative if slightest chance rescue is to be preserved. We regard this as first indispensable step giving effect to line agreed by Mr. Eden of gaining time and not closing door. For same reason we consider it equally essential that some immediate indication be given to other side of readiness negotiate regarding rescue Jews urging same time immediate discontinuation deportations and slaughter pending meeting. Please do utmost regarding both matters also about my quickest return London as we all believe my first hand contact with Brandt will help clarify matters more than any telegraphic report. Cable.

178

ABWER —

J.B.R

dealing with —
German Intelligence — Corrupt — want to make money —
a no. have given up — . taken over by Himmler

Security People

Zicherhordienst (S.D.)

Gestapo
in Germ

Overseas Body —

to keep ↑ & on Germans
abroad —

overseas arm of Himmler —
have taken over ABWA —

Party Body — fanatics —
anti-Semitic — als. anti
Corrupt members —

Brandt has probably had dealings directly or incl.

R.J. Maunsell, Brig. — / Phone # 49600 - G.H. /
Col. Kirk   Ext 348 _ /
Martin Forrest —   49159

C O P Y

(l)
cover letter

TELEGRAM SENT

To: Department of State

Date: June 22, 5 p.m. 1944

No. 1746

Charge: Legation

P A R A P H R A S E

MOST IMMEDIATE - US URGENT   REPEATED TO ANKARA.

180

Ira Hirschmann of War Refugee Board was presented today by the Legation to Lord Moyne, British Minister Resident through whom at the request of Steinhardt arrangements were made to interview Joel Brandt. In regard to the same matter Shertok of the Jewish Agency arrived Cairo today also en route London. Hirschmann acting on instructions from Steinhardt feels that it is essential to return to Ankara first in spite of Lord Moyne's suggestion that Hirschmann should also proceed to London, but he was willing to go there at a future date if necessary.

It was pointed out by Lord Moyne that London was place where complete coordination could be most qickly obtained as any decisions in this matter are for highest levels.

The twenty-fourth is the date arranged for Hirschmann's return to Ankara.

TUCK

HAD:lw

C O P Y

15. 6. 1944

NLT LINTON 77 Greatrussell London

208 Waited Aleppo four days for authority see friend who arrived
Wednesday 7/6 stop Interviewed him Sunday six hours found him
onehundred percent reliable was deeply impressed by his purity
character spirit selfsacrifice factual exactness soberness stop
Came conclusion active steps now imperative view exploring
possibility achieving practical results stop After interview
friend transported Cairo myself returned Jerusalem Tuesday night
reported Executive Wednesday saw High Commissioner with Bengurion
today stop High Commissioner cabling London we asked himfor
transmission Weizmann gist our evaluation and proposals including
first immediate facilities for my flying London second arrangements for friends return home stop You will learn our main proposal
regarding line action from Colonial or Foreign stop High Commissioner
informed us regarding Charles interview stop Agreed line of keeping
door open makes friends return absolutely imperative please do utmost
your part expedite my journey stop Inform Nahum

Shertok

181

CONTROL COPY

EMBASSY OF THE

UNITED STATES OF AMERICA

Lisbon, July 4, 1944

Subject: Proposal Made by German Authorities to
Exchange Jews in Occupied Countries for
Various Supplies

The Honorable
The Secretary of State
Washington

Sir:

I have the honor to transmit herewith a copy of a report prepared by Reuben B. Resnik, an American citizen representing the American Joint Distribution Committee, which was sent to the European office of the above committee, together with a copy of covering letter from Robert Pilpel, the acting European Director of the above committee.

The Embassy assumes that the information contained in the enclosed report has already been received by the Department from Ankara with appropriate comments; however, we feel that certain observations are in order. In the first place the Embassy would like to invite attention to the objectivity with which Mr. Resnik has made his report. On the other hand, it is felt that Section V on Page 4 and 5, POSSIBLE INTERPRETA-TIONS, does not give the interpretations in their proper order or significance. The important element in the interpretation. is Section D-3 at the top of Page 5; viz., that this is a definite attempt to create an open split between the Allies. This split would be threatened by publication of the agreement, if it were made, mentioned in the second paragraph on Page 3, to the effect that the Germans would not use trucks on the western front.

In addition it seems that the Germans have created a very unpleasant situation for the United States, whatever action is taken regarding this proposal. It seems obvious that it would not be accepted under any conditions, but if it is not accepted, then as Resnik points out in D-1, the United States and the Western Allies will be accused of a lack of sincerity in their attempts to rescue Jewish refugees.

It also occurs to Americans here to query whether or not this proposal has any connection with the recent incursion into Portugal of thirty very prominent Hungarian Jews (Embassy's telegram 2054, July 1st, 1944), who came here obviously with the consent if not under the direction of the German Government.

There is one other point in Resnik's memorandum, Section H on Page 6, which this Embassy questions. Resnik states that

"everyone....

DECLASSIFIED
State Dept. Letter, 1-11-72
By R. H. Parks Date SEP 27 1972

Doc. 33

182

"everyone believes that all should be done to continue
exploration until it is definitely determined that no
further good can be served by its continuance." This is
probably the best procedure from the point of view of the
strictly limited humanitarian aim of Resnik's work but it
would seem that a continuation of these negotiations might
at any moment lead to the fact of their existence becoming known to the Russians with resultant serious difficulties.
In fact, the Germans would have every reason to see that
the Russians were advised of them.

It is felt that the War Refugee Board would be interested in this report and the accompanying letter, and if
the Department perceives no obejction, it is requested
that copies be forwarded them with the request that a
copy of the letter and the report be sent by the Board
to the Joint Distribution Committee.

Respectfully yours,

For the Ambassador:

Edward S. Crocker,
Counselor of Embassy

183

Enclosures:

Copy of letter from Robert Pilpel and
and report from Reuben E. Resnik

RCD:ew

Enclosure to despatch No. 680, dated July 4, 1944, from the Embassy at Lisbon.

EMBASSY OF THE
UNITED STATES OF AMERICA

AMERICAN JOINT DISTRIBUTION COMMITTEE

242, Rua Aurea

Lisbon, Portugal

June 27, 1944

Lisbon Letter No. 1107

184

To: AJDC NEW YORK

We send you herewith, for your confidential information, a copy of a memorandum we have just received
from Mr. Reuben Resnik regarding certain proposals
of a Mr. Joel Brand for the rescue of Jews from
German-occupied territories. This memorandum ties
up with the subject of our recent War Refugee
Board cables regarding the plan that has been
brought to the attention of Saly Mayer in
Switzerland.

(sgd.) Robert Pilpel

MSG:ms
Encs.

Via Pouch

DATE   July 5, 1944

TO   : Mr. Pehle

FROM   : F. Hodel

In your absence, I informally advised Dr. Nahum Goldman of the World Jewish Congress of the contents of the attached message from Gruenbaum of the Jewish Agency.

Dr. Goldman advised me that he had just received through commercial channels a cable from Shertok in London requesting that efforts be made to obtain the release of the two men. The cable also strongly urged that Ira Hirschmann be sent to London at once to participate in the present discussions there on the Brandt proposal. Dr. Goldman requested that the contents of this message be given to you. Before calling at your office, he advised Mr. Warren of this message.

Dr. Goldman also wished to know whether the proposals he had submitted to Mr. Stettinius with respect to a possible answer to the Brandt proposal had been sent on to Ambassador Steinhardt. I advised Dr. Goldman that I had no information on this matter but I would bring it to your attention.

F. Hodel

185

CABLE TO AMBASSADOR HARRIMAN, MOSCOW, FROM THE DEPARTMENT AND THE WAR REFUGEE
BOARD.

Please refer to our Nos. 1460 of June 9 and   of   .

The following is a recent telegram from the British Foreign Office
concerning the matter referred to in the above cables:

QUOTE Please inform the United States Government that first discussions
have been held here with Shertok. They have strengthened our conviction,
supported by much independent evidence including detailed report placed
at our disposal by United States Ambassador Angora, that however
influential the Germans who authorized the offer, it was designed (a) to
extract material concessions of war material from Allied Government, (b)
to embroil United Kingdom and United States Governments with the Soviet
Government by representing to the latter that the former were negotiating
with the enemy (c) to elicit a rejection which would then be represented
as justification for extreme measures against the Jews. Shertok
appeared to agree with this analysis.

2. The offer in fact was not serious and especially as coming through
such insignificant or suspected channels, should on its merits have been
contemptuously ignored. But we have kept it in play in the hope of staving
off disaster and seeing whether something acceptable might not emerge.

3. We must now consider our next steps. Choice appears to lie between
(a) keeping Brandt and doing nothing in expectation that Gestapo may
produce further offer, (b) sending Brandt back with message that he had
found Allied circles concerned with the fate of the Jews and ready to consider any practicable scheme for alleviating the fate of the Jews and that
he understood the Allies were conveying their views through the protecting
power, and the German Government might shortly expect to hear something.

4. If (b) is decided upon, as we would propose, then we suggest that
British and American Ministers in Berne should be instructed to address
Swiss Government as follows:-

Begins.

Reports of further extreme measures by the German authorities against
the Jews are reaching the United Kingdom and United States Governments.
At the same time both Governments have been informed from what appear to be
authoritative German quarters that the German Government might be disposed
to modify their policy if Allied cooperation in a solution could be obtained.
Such cooperation would it appears take the form of transferring a stated
number of Jews in conditions of particular distress to the responsibility
of other countries. The United Kingdom and United States Governments
would be willing with due regard to military necessities to consider
practical measures in this connection and would be glad if the Swiss

Government would so inform the German Government. Swiss Government should then state in particular that: (a) Swiss Government has invited the German Government to give facilities for the departure of 1500 Jewish children who would be given temporary hospitality in Switzerland. Similar offers have been made by other neutral Governments. As an earnest of good faith the German Government shall agree to give effect to all these offers (b) 5000 Jewish children from south eastern Europe with a proportion of accompanying adults would have been received in Palestine long ago in accordance with an offer made by the British Government had the necessary exit and transit permits been provided by the Governments (Bulgarian, Roumenian and Hungarian). The German Government is requested to facilitate the grant of such permits. (c) Transport of Jewish refugees to the various homes offered them has been hindered by the absence of German safe conducts for various ships proposed to be employed. The German Government is requested to withdraw its objection to safe conducts, in particular in the case of S.S. Tari which would be used solely for transport of civilian refugees. (d) For some considerable time past lists of Jews who would be given immediate entry into Palestine have been communicated to the German Government. It is suggested that as many of the persons as can be identified should now be given permits to leave and on hearing that this has been done transport arrangements will be taken in hand by the United Kingdom and United States Governments.

Ends.

187

Mr. Shertok agreed in suggested method of approach to Germans but urged (a) the United Kingdom and United States Governments should make a further offer to approach the Spanish Government regarding reception and temporary maintenance of some manageable number of Jewish refugees; (b) a "carrot" should be dangled before the Germans in the shape of agreement by the United Kingdom and United States to discuss with them the question of Jewish rescue; (c) in advance of such discussion we should decide what quid pro quo could be offered to the Germans.

2. In regard to (a) subject to views of His Majesty's Ambassador Madrid I see no difficulty. On (b) and (c) the reply given Shertok was that there could be no direct contact between the Allies and the Germans, to which he retorted that direct contact with the enemy was he understood in certain circumstances permissible to the War Refugee Board. On this the observation was made that, whatever the truth about the War Refugee Board's powers (on which I should be glad to be enlightened) such a conversation would ruin Soviet confidence in the Allies unless they had been asked and had agreed. The idea of compensation, trading in concert with a Gestapo agent, Jewish blood against Allied goods, looked equally dangerous. S. agreed, and said the Russians should, of course, be asked to concur, and that only compensation contemplated was that of no military or economic importance. It would be for us to discover such. UNQUOTE

This Government is inclined to agree with the British analysis of the so-called Brandt offer.

As indicated in No.   of   , in our consideration of the
procedure to be followed in this matter we have been seeking a formula which
would not (repeat not) involve any direct negotiation with the Germans, but
which at the same time would leave the door open for any subsequent offers
which might receive favorable consideration of the British, Soviet, and United
States Governments. After consideration it is felt that the suggestion that
an approach be made to the Germans through the Swiss offers the best means
available for achieving this purpose. Accordingly, this Government is prepared
to make a representation to the German government through the Swiss in conjunction with the British along the lines suggested, provided that the Soviet
government expresses no objection. Moreover, the British and United States
Governments are prepared to request the Swiss to advise the Germans that we
would be willing, with due regard to military necessities, to consider
measures for the reception in allied and neutral territory of all Jews permitted
to leave areas under the control of Germany or allies of Germany.

The foregoing information should be conveyed to the Soviet Government
and that Government should be requested to indicate whether it has any objection
to the procedure contemplated.

In order that the Soviet Government may be kept fully informed in this
and related matters, there are repeated herewith cables recently received
from our legations in Stockholm and Bern.

188

STOCKHOLM CABLE

QUOTE   Information has reached Olsen that several approaches have been
made locally by certain influential German officials connected with
Baltic affairs on the general proposition of freeing Jews in Latvia against
a cash consideration. We allowed the situation to develop and it resulted
in the following concrete proposal.

All Jews in Latvia (a guaranteed minimum of 2,000) would be free from
ghettos and allowed to come to Sweden against a cash payment of 2 million
dollars (revised later to 2 million Swedish kronor). This amount was to be
deposited in Riksbank subject to the conditions as follows.

A. Guaranteed release of these funds when and if refugees arrived safely
in Sweden.

B. Funds could be used without restriction for purchase of certain supplies
other than war materials, such as medicines, Red Cross supplies, et cetera.

C. Balance of funds available for transfer to German clearing. The group
would require assurances from Sweden, in turn, that these refugees would not
be allowed to spread anti-Nazi propaganda.

These discussions were communicated to the Swedish Foreign Office and it has advanced the following information regarding the three individuals involved. The most important individual is Kleist, said to be Himmler's man in the Baltic and reputedly one of the cleverest intelligence operators in Germany. He is also connected with the German Red Cross. The Foreign Office has had some experience with him in that, contrary to strict orders from Ribbentrop, Kleist facilitated escape to Sweden of certain Swedes in the Baltic. The name of the second individual is Boening, and he is considered somewhat of a mystery to the Foreign Office, although he is known to represent Kleist in Sweden on various matters. The third and last individual is named Klause. He is stated to have been a former member of the German Military Intelligence but recently he asked the Swedish Foreign Office to consider him a political refugee, based on the fact he is considered a Jew by the Germans. From other sources we are informed that at least on previous occasion Klause obtained funds from individuals in Sweden on the promise of rescuing certain Jews in Europe; he never fulfilled the promise. On subsequent approach, it was intimated by this group that very little, if any, of the 2 million kronor would go into the German clearing, or even to buy Swedish goods for Germany. Instead, they would use some of the funds to bribe certain minor German officials in the Baltic, and the three would pocket the balance. It was suggested by Olsen, simply to explore the mysterious background of these negotiators, that the German group be informed that it was impossible to raise the money in Sweden and then to ask whether there was any objection to exploring the possibilities of securing American funds. This could be done only by raising the problem with Olsen at the American Legation who probably would want to get all the details directly. It was then stated by the group to this proposal, that money was not necessarily a consideration, that perhaps no money at all would be needed. The important consideration was stated to be that the Swedish Foreign Office must express a strongly sympathetic attitude towards this rescue operation, a willingness to receive these refugees gladly, and to promise that the refugees would not agitate against the German authorities. While baffling and not a little fantastic in scope, the foregoing situation presents the following interesting intelligence aspects. If the government of Germany is behind these feelers, it becomes a simple ransom proposition from which they would hope to trap us into a series of other extortions on a much larger scale. We know that the Germans are extremely pressed for foreign exchange and are experimenting with all possible devices to ease the situation. Too, if German authorities are behind these negotiations, they may be setting a trap for anti-Jewish propaganda in the United States — playing these refugees against prisoners of war, et cetera. On the other hand, the individuals involved may simply be making a last minute effort to purchase good will in the United States and Sweden. (The Swedish Foreign Office believes this latter to be the true basis of the feelers made locally.) At least Kleist is a marked man and the situation in the Baltic may have prompted him to look towards the immediate future. Treasury should be informed and also War Refugee Board as our No. 41. Johnson   UNQUOTE

189

BERN CABLE

QUOTE   McClelland Sends the following for WRB.   Reference is made herein to the Legation's cable of June 24, no. 4041.

The Jews of Budapest have no illusion as to the fact that deportation is probably in store for the majority of 300,000 Jews concentrated in houses and restricted blocks all over that city, according to information dated June 18 and received from responsible Jewish circles in Budapest.   It is openly admitted by the Germans that selection of those to be deported will be made on a basis as follows: (A) men who are able-bodied, (B) children, women and girls who are able-bodied, (C) all persons unsuited for work and children.   No doubt the last mentioned category will be sent to Auschwitz for extermination while the first two groups will be used as forced labor in occupied territories and Germany.

There seems to be some possibility, as result of recent discussions in Budapest between responsible Jews and Germans, of the following: (1) rescue of a small number of children and prominent persons who will be allowed to leave Hungary in an initial convoy of 1000 persons; and (2) rather than being immediately exterminated, the lean concession that 30,000 Hungarian Jews unsuited for work will be maintained in three camps in Germany.   The success of these two proposals depends in turn on two conditions: (1) That there can be secured for the initial group of 1,000 and for others to follow emigration possibilities via Spain; and (2) that the three camps of 10,000 persons each in Germany can be supported by the supply of funds from Jewish organizations.   To do this it is estimated that at least 500,000 Swiss francs monthly would be necessary.   It was intimated by the Germans that further contingents would be allowed to leave Germany from these camps as Spanish transit and overseas (Palestine, North Africa or elsewhere)emigration visas became available.

These propositions have been discussed with Salymayer of Joint to whom appeal has been addressed, to find funds required for the support of such camps in Germany.   We both feel that a serious attempt should be made to secure initial block of 1,000 or more Spanish transit visas at least for the children, even though we both consider them highly improbable and incomprehensible from many angles.   To care for such transit groups arrangements should be made in Spain and for further destinations also.   A great many have Palestine certificates, according to information we have received from Budapest. We recommend that approach be made to the Spanish Government.

In at least trying to comply with requests of persons sur(*) place in Hungary there is nothing to lose and possibly something to gain, even though these propositions may seem to be far fetched.   Even though remote, every channel of aid must be explored in view of the desperateness of the situation of Jews there.   Over 400,000 have already been deported, according to reports.
(*) Apparent omission - Harrison. UNQUOTE

190

You will note that these cables appear to indicate that the Germans are putting out additional feelers somewhat comparable to the Brandt proposal. You may indicate to the Soviet Government that we will not negotiate with the Germans on these proposals or any others which may be received without the previous agreement of the Soviet Government.

The British government has been informed of the contents of this cable and the British Ambassador in Moscow is being advised thereof by his government.

JBF:AA:LSL:ro 7/6/44

Sent to Mr. Warren of State
after telephone Conversation.
5/7/44 - 3:30 PM - JBF

MEMORANDUM

Mr. Eden's telegram of July 1, 1944, with regard to the so-called Brandt proposal and discussions with Shertok, has been carefully considered. The following are the views of the United States Government with respect to this matter:

1. Upon the basis of present information, the United States Government is inclined to agree with the analysis of the Brandt proposal contained in Mr. Eden's telegram.

2. The United States Government is in accord with the suggestion contained in paragraph 3 (b) of the Eden telegram that Brandt be permitted to return to enemy territory with the message that the allies are conveying their views to the German government through the protecting power. This Government is also prepared to join with the British in making a representation to the German government through the Swiss government along the lines suggested in paragraph 4 of the Eden telegram. This Government, however, suggests that the following be substituted for the third and fourth sentences of the proposed instructions to be sent to the British and American ministers in Bern:

> "Such cooperation would it appears take the form of
> transferring Jews now in German controlled territory
> to the responsibility of other countries. The United
> Kingdom and United States Governments would be willing,
> with due regard to military necessities, to consider
> measures for the reception in allied and neutral territory
> of all Jews permitted to leave areas under the control of
> Germany or allies of Germany and would be glad if the
> Swiss Government would so inform the German Government."

3. The United States Government is of the opinion that neither of the steps mentioned in point 2 should be taken until the Soviet Government has been fully informed of the procedure contemplated and its approval obtained. Attached hereto is a proposed cable to Ambassador Harriman in Moscow which outlines the situation and requests that the views of the Soviet Government with respect thereto be obtained. It will be appreciated if the British Government will indicate its concurrence in the proposed cable.

4. The United States Government has noted that Mr. Eden sees no difficulty in Shertok's suggestion that a further approach be made to the Spanish Government regarding the reception and temporary maintenance of some manageable number of Jewish refugees. This Government is of the opinion that this suggestion should be followed vigorously and it will be appreciated if the views of the British ambassador in Spain are obtained as soon as possible.

JBF:ro 8/8/44

Sent to Mr. Warren of State
after telephone conversation
5/7/44 — 3:30 P.M. JB7

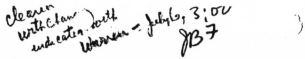

DRAFT OF CABLE TO MOSCOW FOR AMBASSADOR HARRIMAN's PERSONAL ATTENTION

SECTION ONE

Reference is made to Dept.'s 1460 of June 9 and 1529 of June 21 and to your cable 2184 of June 19. The following additional facts are now available.

(1)   Joel Brandt is presently being held in custody at Cairo after having previously proceeded to Jerusalem for discussions there. There have been discussions in Cairo between the American and British authorities, Brandt and Shertok of the Jewish Agency for Palestine.

(2)   Gyorgy, who arrived from Vienna with Brandt on May 19, was taken into custody by Turkish officials on May 25, released in a few hours and departed for Cairo where he is held in custody with Brandt.

(3)   Shertok of the Jewish Agency is in London pursuing conversations with officials of the British Government.

(4)   Word has been received through the Jewish Agency, that the Gestapo are very angry about the failure of Brandt and Gyorgy to return to German territory. The Gestapo is alleged to have indicated that Brandt's journey was merely a preliminary to future discussions to be carried on in Lisbon by Schroeder, presumably a Gestapo agent. The British Government has proposed that Brandt and Gyorgy be permitted to return to Budapest with message that Allied circles are concerned with the fate of Jews and ready to consider any practicable scheme for relieving their fate and that Brandt understands that the Allies will convey their views through the protecting power and that the German Government might shortly expect to hear something through this source.

(5)   Although no such information was contained in our earlier reports with regard to this matter, it now appears that Brandt has indicated in several informal conversations that the German Government would be willing to agree that the 10,000 trucks would not (repeat not) be used on the western front.

(6)   We are requesting Ambassador Steinhardt to forward to you promptly Ankara despatches to the Department Nos. 676 of June 5 and 679 of June 8 which supply additional background information with respect to this matter.

(7)   British Ambassador in Moscow has cabled the British Foreign Office suggesting that the information on the trucks will increase the possibility of a completely negative response from the Soviet Government. Nevertheless it is the feeling here that information with respect to the trucks ~~will eventually become known to the Soviet Government through other sources and might therefore better~~ be presented directly at this time. He also believes that Brandt and Gyorgy should not be permitted to return to Budapest until the attitude of the Soviet Government on this point has been determined. /should

(8)   Two additional proposals for the release of ~~2000~~ Jews from enemy territory in order that the Soviet Gov't will be fully informed.

193

as promptly as possible

~~Latvia to Sweden~~ has been received ~~and Sweden has been received~~ through Stockholm, the details of which will be sent to you for transmission to the Soviet Government later.

SECTION TWO *and Bern,*

It is requested that this matter be taken up with the Soviet Government in such manner as you deem appropriate and all of the facts brought to the attention of the Soviet Government promptly within your discretion and after concurrence with your British colleague.

It should be emphasized to the Soviet Government that neither this Government nor the British Government has been deceived as to the character of this alleged offer of the German Government and that the two governments have been convinced from the outset that the offer is part and parcel of the German psychological warfare effort. This is borne out particularly by the facts which have now come to light on the alleged German willingness to guarantee that the trucks would not be used on the Western front.

You will understand the reluctance of the British and American Governments to shut the door completely on any offer. Other offers of this nature are expected and eventually one may be received which can be given serious consideration. It is our view that by appearing to explore such matters we not only have the possibility of saving lives while the discussions are going on, but also clearly leave the way open for further offers which we anticipate and which might possibly be made in good faith.

You should inform the Soviet Government that we are fully aware of the undesirability of such direct contacts with representatives of the German Government and we are searching for a method of rescue through the intermediary of the Swiss. Details of any practical proposal will be communicated to the Soviet Government and the Soviet Government will of course be currently informed of developments and no action will be taken without prior agreement with the Soviet and British Governments.

It is suggested that you consult fully with the British Ambassador with respect to this matter and in discussions with the Soviet Government make it clear, if the British Ambassador is in agreement, that the views expressed by you are also the views of the British Government. The British authorities here are in agreement.

Sent to Moscow. Repeated to Ankara, Cairo and London.

CODE ROOM: Repeat to London for Winant, to Ankara for Steinhardt and Hirschmann and to Cairo for Tuck.

194

*I-War Refugee Bd.
m. Pehle*

FROM: Secretary of State, Washington

TO: AMEMBASSY, MOSCOW

DATED: July 7, 1944

NUMBER: 1641

CONTROL COPY

SECTION ONE

Reference is made to Dept.'s 1460 of June 9 and 1529 of June 21 and to your cable 2184 of June 19. The following additional facts are now available.

(1) Joel Brandt is presently being held in custody at Cairo after having previously proceeded to Jerusalem for discussions there. There have been discussions in Cairo between the American and British authorities, Brandt and Shertok of the Jewish Agency for Palestine.

(2) Gyorgy, who arrived from Vienna with Brandt on May 19, was taken into custody by Turkish officials on May 25, released in a few hours and departed for Cairo where he is held in custody with Brandt.

(3) Shertok of the Jewish Agency is in London pursuing conversations with officials of the British Government.

(4) Word has been received through the Jewish Agency, that the Gestapo are very angry about the failure of Brandt and Gyorgy to return to German territory. The Gestapo is alleged to have indicated that Brandt's journey was merely a preliminary to future discussions to be carried on in

Lisbon

Doc. 35

195

DECLASSIFIED
State Dept. Letter, 1-11-72
By R. H. Parks Date   SEP 27 1972

Lisbon by Schroeder, presumably a Gestapo agent. The British Government has proposed that Brandt and Gyorgy be permitted to return to Budapest with message that Allied circles are concerned with the fate of Jews and ready to consider any practicable scheme for relieving their fate and that Brandt understands that the Allies will convey their views through the protecting power and that the German Government might shortly expect to hear something through this source.

(5) Although no such information was contained in our earlier reports with regard to this matter, it now appears that Brandt has indicated in several informal conversations that the German Government would be willing to agree that the 10,000 trucks would not (repeatnot) be used on the western front.

(6) We are requesting Ambassador Steinhardt to forward to you promptly Ankara despatches to the Department Nos. 676 of June 5 and 679 of June 8 which supply additional background information with respect to this matter.

(7) British Ambassador in Moscow has cabled the British Foreign Office suggesting that the information on the trucks will increase the possibility of a completely negative response from the Soviet Government. Nevertheless

it is

it is the feeling here that information with respect to the
trucks should be presented directly at this time in order
that the Soviet Government be fully informed. He also
believes that Brandt and Gyorgy should not be permitted to
return to Budapest until the attitude of the Soviet Government on this point has been determined.

(8) Two additional proposals for the release of Jews
from enemy territory have been received through Stockholm
and Bern, the details of which will be sent to you for
transmission to the Soviet Government promptly.

SECTION TWO

It is requested that this matter be taken up with the
Soviet Government in such manner as you deem appropriate
and all of the facts brought to the attention of the Soviet
Government promptly within your discretion and after concurrence with your British colleague.

It should be emphasized to the Soviet Government that
neither this Government nor the British Government has been
deceived as to the character of this alleged offer of the
German Government and that the two governments have been
convinced from the outset that the offer is part and parcel
of the German psychological warfare effort. This is borne
out particularly by the facts which have now come to light

on the alleged

197

on the alleged German willingness to guarantee that the
trucks would not be used on the Western Front.

You will understand the reluctance of the British and
American Governments to shut the door completely to any
offer. Other offers of this nature are expected and eventually one may be received which can be given serious consideration. It is our view that by appearing to explore such
matters we not only have the possibility of saving lives
while the discussions are going on, but also clearly leave
the way open for further offers which we anticipate and
which might possibly be made in good faith.

You should inform the Soviet Government that we are
fully aware of the undesirability of such direct contacts
with representatives of the German Government and we are
searching for a method of rescue through the intermediary
of the Swiss. Details of any practical proposal will be
communicated to the Soviet Government and the Soviet Government will of course be currently informed of developments and
no action will be taken without prior agreement with the
Soviet and British Governments.

It is suggested that you consult fully with the
British Ambassador with respect to this matter and in
discussions with the Soviet Government make it clear, if
the British Ambassador is in agreement, that the views
expressed by you are also the views of the British Government.
The British authorities here are in agreement.

Repeated to Ankara

RECEIVED
WAR REFUGEE BOARD
WASHINGTON, D.C.

-5-

Repeated to Ankara as no. 614 for Steinhardt; Cairo
as no. 1727 for Tuck; and London as no. 5353 for Winant.

HULL
(GLW)

CODE ROOM: Repeat to London for Winant, to Ankara for
Steinhardt and Hirschmann and to Cairo for Tuck.

199

C O P Y

███████████

Paraphrase of Telegram from American Embassy,

London, as No. 39, July 7, 6 p.m.

The following is for Barlas from Shertok and is
with reference to your June 30 telegram:

"Message sent by you has been received. Without
British Government's authority Bader will not be able
to proceed. The Foreign Office has been urged to grant
permission and promises an early reply. No definite
decision has been made with respect to Brandt since
Washington's reactions are being awaited by British
Government. Copies of my reports to Jerusalem by telegraph regarding negotiations made here are being transmitted by the Foreign Office through the British
Embassy at Ankara to Kaplan at my request. It would be
appreciated if you would inform Hirschmann that we
urged inter alia that authorization should be given
WRB representatives to meet at Istanbul representatives
of Brandt's backers. This is suggested with a view to
clarifying the whole matter but it is likely that more
determined and admittedly unorthodox steps even of
explanatory nature will not here be accepted."

Doc. 36

200

WVM MB

DECLASSIFIED
State Dept. Letter, 1-11-72
By R. H. Parks Date_____ SEP 27 1972

<u>Memo for Discussion with Admiral Leahy</u>

1. Joe Brandt with agent arrived in Ankara in May by German plane.

2. Discussions held at Ankara, Palestine and Cairo.

3. Brandt and agent now held in Cairo.

4. Significant points of offer:

    a. 10,000 trucks--possible guarantee
    b. 2 million cakes of soap
    c. 200 tons cocoa
    d. 800 tons coffee
    e. 200 tons tea

5. Germans would agree to stop deportation and extermination of Jews and agree to exit of Jews principally through Spain

6. Background of Brandt dubious.

7. Jewish Agent now in London for conversation.

8. Russians promptly advised--Russian reply: neither permissible nor expedient to discuss such matters with Germans.

9. Russians now being advised more fully: also to be advised that we appreciate undesirability of dealing through these channels and may wish to deal directly through Swiss. Asking Germans to show good faith by accepting previous proposals principally relating to children.

10. Germans having indicated they are very angry with Allied detention of their agents and that it was proposed that further discussions be conducted in Lisbon.

11. Similar proposals now coming from Sweden and Switzerland.

12. British and American views are that Germans were merely attempting to split the Allies, but we cannot afford to slam the door on any conceivable negotiations.

13. 35 prominent Hungarian now in Lisbon

Doc. 37

201

7/8/44

Memorandum for the Files

At Secretary Morgenthau's suggestion, I discussed with Admiral Leahy today the various offers that have been received from German sources on the rescue of the Jews, particularly the offer received from Joe Brandt. I told Admiral Leahy how these matters are being handled and he agreed fully and said that we could rely on the State Department keeping him advised on phases of such matters which are of military significance.

He said that he would mention the matter to the President when convenient.

202

Attached hereto is a memorandum of points which I discussed with Admiral Leahy.

I-rael Refugee Bd.
M. Riehl

FROM: The American Consul General, Jerusalem

TO: The Secretary of State, Washington

DATE: July 11, 1944

NUMBER: 97

CONTROL COPY

7/18/44
Per Riehl as
well as (Clun
Do. etc
on etc. JH

~~SECRET~~

I have been asked by Bengurion, Chairman of the Jewish
Agency Executive, to transmit through the War Refugee Board the
following message to Nahum Goldman:

On behalf of the Jewish Agency Executive, please transmit to
President Roosevelt the following:

A proposal emanating from apparently influential enemy sources
at Budapest has been received by this agency. The readiness of the
Nazis to release one million Hungarian Rumanian Jews, after two
years of continuous slaughter of European Jews, on the condition
known to the Department of State and proposing negotiations to
that end is indicated in this proposal. Jewish Agency immediately transmitted this proposal to the Governments of America and
Britain. A well known Budapest Zionist was the Jewish Emissary
whom the Nazis sent with this proposal. At the present time he
is detained in Cairo by British security authorities. The Jewish
Agency earnestly appeals to you not to allow this unique and
possibly last chance of saving the remains of European Jewry to
be lost although it is fully realized that the exigencies of war
are primary consideration. Even if there may be some doubts concerning the proposal in its present form we would urgently and

                                        respectfully

Doc. 38

203

DECLASSIFIED
State Dept. Letter, 1-11-72

By R. H. Parks Date SEP 27 1972

RECEIVED

respectfully submit that suitable arrangements be made to discuss
the proposal with representatives of the enemy group from which
it emanated, and that the door should not be closed. Therefore
we plead that you may see fit to give your support to the following proposals which the Jewish Agency has also submitted to
the Government of Britain: (1) Through appropriate channels to
intimate to other side immediately, readiness to nominate representative to discuss rescue and transfer the largest number of
Jews possible, and (2) to intimate to the other side that the
preliminary condition to any discussion is the discontinuance of
deportations immediately.

204

                                        PINKERTON

DCR:MPL
7/13/44

2 War Refugee Bd.
Mr. Pehle

FROM: American Consulate General, Jerusalem

TO: Secretary of State, Washington

DATED: July 12, 1944

NUMBER: 98

CONTROL COPY

It is requested by the Jewish agency that the following
information, which has also been sent to the British Government, be sent to the War Refugee Board with particular reference message for Goldman contained in my cable of July 11,
no. 97.

One. With a view to meeting the contingency that the
Budapest proposal may emanate from some Nazi organization independent of the German Foreign Office, the proposal should
also be sent concerning meeting of representatives of the
War Refugee Board with members of the Budapest group at Istanbul. Two. The emissary should be allowed to return to Budapest at once. Three. Although it is obviously preferable
that the emissary should carry with him a decision of readiness to negotiate, if this will further delay his return he
should be sent back at once with instructions to report to the
other side that his message had been delivered, it was being
considered by the highest quarters, and that prompt action
would follow. Four. So as not to give any excuse to the enemy
which is not necessary, the second emissary should also be returned if possible.

Doc. 39

205

We have
requested
this from
State

PINKERTON

DECLASSIFIED
State Dept. Letter, 1-11-72
By R. H. Parks Date SEP 27 1972

C
O
P
Y

BRITISH EMBASSY

WASHINGTON 8, D.C.

18th July, 1944.

Dear Mr. Warren,

    I enclose herein a copy of a personal message which His Majesty's Ambassador at Moscow has been instructed to hand to M. Molotov. His Majesty's Ambassador was to show this message, before delivering it, to his United States colleague, and to explain that the reason for this action was that the suggestion was pressed on His Majesty's Government with particular earnestness by high and responsible Jewish circles here.

    I also enclose, for your information, a paraphrase of a telegram from His Majesty's Ambassador at Stockholm about the approach made through the Swedish channel.

Yours sincerely,

K. I. POATE

Mr. G. Warren,
    Department of State
      of the United States,
        WASHINGTON, D.C.

Doc. 40

206

DECLASSIFIED
By Authority of *British*
Gov't. telegram, 1-12-72
By *RHP* Date SEP 27 1972

COPY

TEXT OF TELEGRAM RECEIVED
FROM THE FOREIGN OFFICE
DATED 18th JULY, 1944
- - - - - - - - - - - -

Please inform United States Government that since
receiving their views we have had fresh evidence which in
our view compels us to take a different attitude. Details
of this evidence will be passed by British Security in the
Middle East to their American opposite numbers. From the
beginning we have shared the view of the United States
Government that proposals brought by Brandt constituted a
political warfare trap set up by the Gestapo, but that we
should investigate them and retain Brandt in the hope that
a serious proposal might emerge or that in the interval the
murder of the Jews would cease. Neither has occurred. On
the other hand in the last few days we have had our suspicions
confirmed and the conviction forced upon us that it would be
highly dangerous to give even the appearance of a response to
the Gestapo's suggestions. For we now have evidence that
the Brandt mission was intended as cover for an approach to
us or to the Americans on the question of a separate peace
not seriously intended no doubt except in an attempt to
prejudice our relations with the Soviet Government. (Another
of our original suspicions confirmed). In view of this we
feel that it would be extremely dangerous to send Brandt
back with any message or send any message through Protecting
Power which would inevitably be interpreted as a response to
the Gestapo. We feel furthermore that it would be both
unfair and unwise to place on the Soviet Government any
responsibility for a rejection which we are sure they would
strongly advocate.

2.   His Majesty's Government therefore propose that the Gestapo
agent should be retained in any case and that Brandt if he still
wishes to return and the security authorities have no objection
should be told before departure that the British and United
States authorities cannot be expected to take any cognizance
of suggestions he brought or channels through which they were
conveyed.

3.   If this results in German propaganda to the effect that
a scheme of saving the Jews had been suggested but contemptuously
rejected by the United States and British Governments, then we
should be ready with an exposure of the Gestapo's plot and a
reiteration of all our respective Governments have done and are

207

willing to do to relieve Jewish suffering. Meanwhile such
schemes of assistance as we have drawn up independently or
through inter-Governmental Committee would proceed and when
possible publicity would be given to these, but never in such
a way as to appear to be connected with the Gestapo initiative.

4.   Please obtain United States Government's views urgently.
If they agree we propose to inform Dr. Weizmann and instruct
His Majesty's Ambassador to concert with his United States
colleague, similarly instructed, to inform the Soviet
Government that as nothing worth taking seriously had emerged
from the Brandt proposals and as slaughter of the Jews was
apparently continuing we had decided to have nothing further
to do with Brandt's suggestions but for security reasons
would keep the Gestapo agent in custody.

208

July 19, 1944.

To Washington, Moscow.

Repeated to Ankara, Cairo and Jerusalem.

Please inform Government to which you are
accredited that two American press correspondents
in London (Chicago Sun and New York Herald Tribune)
have secured and are sending their papers fairly
accurate accounts of Brandt's proposals about
Jews and that in answer to inquiries we are giving
the press immediate guidance contained in my
immediately following telegram. Considered formal
statement for publication will be suggested as soon
as possible for concurrence of United States
Government.

209

Following is guidance, not a hand-out.

For some time past, concurrently with well-substantiated stories of horrible maltreatment of Jews, vague suggestions have been put about in certain neutral capitals that Germany, or this or that satellite Government, was preparing to modify its Jewish policy. Recently, in particular, two (? Bulgarians) arrived from Hungary in Turkey bringing proposals for the release on certain conditions of large numbers of Jews and a cessation of extermination. These proposals were found to have no serious backing or practical meaning. They amount in fact to blackmail and threats designed to confuse the Allies and to prejudice efficient conduct of the war.

CONF~~IDENTIA~~L

July 19, 1944

From Mr. Hirschmann to Mr. Pehle

War Refugee Board

For your information Bader of the Jewish Agencies who is
liaison officer with the Jewish communities and groups in
occupied territories received the following free translation
of a coded telegram dated July 15 from Kastner who is an
important member of the Jewish Relief Committee in Budapest
and is reported to be well known to other communities as a
reliable figure.

"Consult Schroeder's friend Istanbul about your flight
to Budapest Saturday stop Your proposal about a purely
financial arrangement uninteresting repeat uninteresting
stop Cable whether Schroeder meeting next week with Schwartz
at Lisbon would lead to quick results. Schroeder's proposed
meeting with Schwartz who should have full power is urgently
important stop In matters of emigration am also in contact
with Dobkin stop Regret Bader's trip here impossible."

Concerning the above we are informed that Bader had been
urgently invited by a member of the German Consulate in
Istanbul to proceed to Berlin or possibly to Budapest to
discuss matters relating to the Hungarian Jews stop Bader
acting under the direction of his superiors in the Jewish
Agency referred the matter to Shertock in London who I am
informed discussed it with "highest authorities" and cabled
back that Bader was not to proceed under any condition.

211

DECLASSIFIED
State Dept. Letter, 1-11-72
By R. H. Parks Date SEP 27 1972

"During Bader's exchange of telegrams on the subject with Budapest he inquired whether it would be possible to negotiate on the basis of a financial arrangement instead of commodities. The telegram quoted above gives the reply that this suggestion is not acceptable but indicates that Schroeder himself would like to discuss the matter in Spain or Portugal preferably with a representative of the Joint Distribution Committee.

In this connection Joseph Schwartz of the Joint Distribution Committee received today the following free translation of a coded telegram from Pilgel in Lisbon transmitting a message from Kastner dated July 15:

"Seventeen hundred people are waiting for a solution by the Germans stop Cable whether Schwartz and Dobkin are ready to proceed to Spain in order to meet with a German representative to settle the matter Advise whether Madrid or Barcelona shall be the meeting place in ten days time."

The reference to the above seventeen hundred seems to have connection with information from several sources, namely Schwalb in Switzerland, Dobkin in Lisbon and Kastner in Hungary and also from passengers recently arrived on the S. S. Kazbek. Joseph Schwartz is proceeding to Lisbon from Turkey July 22 and is requesting my advice and your authorization to meet with Schroeder or his representative in connection with the above matter.

I have informed Schwartz that my instructions preclude any action at this time connected with the above situation andthat I am reporting the complete information to Washington and requesting for Schwartz advice from you regarding the possibility of his meeting in Portugal or Spain with Schroeder. Schwartz will report

212

to the American Embassy in Lisbon upon his arrival there
which he expects will be approximately July 29. We are
assisting Schwartz in arrangements for his early arrival
in Lisbon.

From the above telegrams there appears to be a concrete
possibility which could result in the rescue of some designated
refugees and which suggests the possible usefulness of such a
meeting. Schwartz requests that Baerwald be informed of these
developments if it meets with your approval.

213

COPY

TEXT OF TELEGRAM ADDRESSED BY
FOREIGN OFFICE TO MOSCOW, DATED
JULY 13th, 1944.
- - - - - - - - - - - - - - - - -

You will remember that on December 17, 1942 a declaration was
issued in the names of the Governments of the Soviet Union, United
States and United Kingdom and of the other Allies calling attention
to the bestial measures of extermination which the German authorities
were applying to the Jewish population in areas occupied by them and
solemnly affirming that those responsible for these crimes should not
escape retribution.

2.   In spite of an unbroken series of military reverses during the
past two years and the certainty of final defeat the Germans are in
no way desisting from their barbarous treatment of the Jews. Indeed
the contrary would appear to be the case. All our information goes
to show that since the Germans occupied Hungary measures of gassing
and burning have been applied with increasing ferocity by the Germans
and that the present Hungarian Government are collaborating as willing
accomplices in these outrages. As a result appeals are frequently
made to His Majesty's Government to issue some further declaration
condemning these crimes. It has occurred to me that given victorious
advance of Soviet armies a declaration by your government couched in
terms of unambiguous frankness and proclaiming that Soviet armies
and retribution for these crimes would enter Hungary together might
have effect at least of reducing the scale of these horrible outrages
against the Jewish population.

214

PARAPHRASE OF TELEGRAM RECEIVED

CONTROL COPY

SECRET

FROM: American Embassy, London

TO: Secretary of State, Washington

DATED: July 19, 1944

NUMBER: 5691

Transmission of following paraphrased message to Nahum
Goldberg, Jewish Agency Office, 1720 16th Street, N. W., Washington,
is requested by Shertok of the Jewish Agency for Palestine:

No decision has yet been made with regard to
Brandt but even if he is permitted to return, he will not be given
authority to give any information. The offer made to Bader Istanbul
to proceed to Budapest clearly indicates that other side ready discuss
release. It may be your desire to talk over with WRB the possibility
of contact with Bader Istanbul being made by them. Suggestion that
Kullman go to Budapest refused. Fear it is now too late Hirschmann
come here view his first-hand impression Brandt, as originally proposed.

WINANT

Doc. 41

215

DCR/GFW

7-20-44

DECLASSIFIED
State Dept. Letter, 1-11-72
By R. H. Parks Date SEP 27 1972

Istanbul, July 19, 1944

Dear Bob:-

I would appreciate it if you would arrange
for the prompt transmission of the enclosed
telegrams to Washington.

Cordially yours,

Doc. 42

216

I. A. Hirschmann

Robert F. Kelley, Esquire
    Charge d'Affaires
        American Embassy
            Ankara

████████████████

July 19, 1944

I. A. Hirschmann to S. Pinckney Tuck,
    Cairo

    Joseph Schwartz of American Joint Distribution Committee
is arriving in Cairo approximately July 25 on urgent matter.
He requires transportation and high priority to proceed without
delay to Lisbon. I should appreciate it if you would accord him
all possible assistance.

217

DECLASSIFIED
State Dept. Letter, 1-11-72
By R. H. Parks Date SEP 27 1972

References:

5353 - repeat message - in
secret file under 1641 to
Moscow.

4283 - instructions - transmits
cable to London 676, June 5,
cable from Ankara 679, June 8

218

2-War Refugee Bd.
Mr. Fehle

PARAPHRASE OF TELEGRAM RECEIVED

FROM: American Embassy, London.

TO: Secretary of State, Washington.

DATED: July 20, 1944.

NUMBER: 5721.

CONTROL COPY
(Secret)

Please refer to secret instruction of July 8,
Number 4283, and telegram from the Department, July 7,
Number 5353, when reading telegram from the Embassy
dated July 20, regarding recent German proposal to
exchange Jews for war materials, as reported in the
British press.

219

                    WINANT

DCR:LCW   7/24/44

DECLASSIFIED
State Dept. Letter, 1-11-72
By R. H. Parks Date SEP 27 1972

My dear Mr. McCloy:

I am sending to you herewith, for the attention of Military Intelligence, a copy of a report from our representative in Ankara, Mr. Ira A. Hirschmann. The report deals with various phases of recent discussions on the so-called Brandt proposal for the release of the Jews of Hungary.

Sincerely yours,

(Signed) J. W. Pehle

J. W. Pehle
Executive Director

Honorable John J. McCloy,

Assistant Secretary of War.

Enclosure.

*Original signed
by Mr. Pehle.*

FHodel/sg 7/19/44

DEPARTMENT
OF
STATE

INCOMING
TELEGRAM

CONTROL COPY

DIVISION OF
COMMUNICATIONS
AND RECORDS

War Rg J Bank-Hie

1 Copy only

FE-119

PLAIN

London

Dated July 20, 1944

Rec'd 12:30 p.m.

Secretary of State,

Washington.

DEPARTMENT OF STATE
JUL 21 1944
DIVISION OF
COMMUNICATIONS & RECORDS

5724, Twentieth

Doc. 44

221

Several newspapers today carry articles regarding recent German proposal to spare lives of remaining Jews in Hungary in exchange for war materials including 10,000 trucks "not to be used on the western front". All articles strongly condemn the proposal under such terms as "monstrous", "blackmail" etc. All point out that the British Government has kept American and Russian Governments fully informed. None gives the names of the emmisaries who reached Turkey with the proposal.

Diplomatic correspondent of the TIMES calls the offer to "barter Jews for munitions" one of the "most loathsome" stories of the war. He states that the British Government knows that only defeat of Germany will provide security for Jews and other oppressed peoples in Europe and concludes that the proposal "seems to be simply a fantastic attempt to sow suspicion among the Allies".

Diplomatic

Diplomatic correspondent of DAILY TELEGRAPH is more objective, giving a concise outline of the story and stating that "it is characterized in authoritative British quarters as a barefaced attempt to blackmail the Allies".

Article in MANCHESTER GUARDIAN covers fully the facts of the proposal as known, which it describes as "a recent German attempt to barter human lives in order to secure a negotiated peace or to secure, at any rate, a split in the United Nations". In short editorial in same paper, entitled "Blackmail", it is stated that the proposal shows that German persecution of Jews in Hungary was not due to mere hatred of Jews but that it was part of a wider scheme to split the Allies by attempting to range the tender-heartedness of the Anglo-Saxons against the realism of the Russians. "The plot failed".

DAILY HERALD reporter characterizes proposal as "cold-blooded", "fantastic" and "incredible" and, after discussing possible German motives, concludes "whatever the evil purpose it is bound to fail".

DAILY MIRROR's article is equally condemnatory. Its conclusion is that proposal represents effort by Nazis to discover how far Allies may be "blackmailed" in an attempt to save lives.

Ar request

-3- #5724, July 20, from London.

    At request of ASLOR, please furnish copies to
Secretary of the Treasury and Pehle, War Refugee Board.

                                WINANT

MRM

DEPARTMENT
OF
STATE

INCOMING
TELEGRAM

DIVISION OF
COMMUNICATIONS
AND RECORDS

LC - 303
Distribution of
true reading by
special arrangement
(████ W)

For security reasons the
text of this message must
be closely guarded

Ankara
Dated July 20, 1944
Rec'd 11:38 p.m.

DEPARTMENT OF STATE
DIVISION OF
JUL 22 1944
COMMUNICATIONS
AND RECORDS

Secretary of State,

Washington.

Doc. 45

224

1320, July 20, 2 p.m.

FOR PEHLE WRB FROM HIRSCHMANN.

Ankara No. 98.

For your information, Bader of the Jewish Agency

who is liaison officer with the Jewish communities

and groups in occupied territories, received a telegram

dated July 15 from Kastner who is an important member

of the Jewish Relief Committee in Budapest and is

reported to be well known to other communities as

a reliable person. The following is a translation

of the telegram.

"Consult Schroeder's friend Istanbul about your

flight to Budapest Saturday. Your proposal about

a purely financial arrangement uninteresting (repeat

uninteresting). Cable whether Schroeder meeting next

week with Schwartz at Lisbon would lead to quick

results. Schroeder's proposed meeting with Schwartz,

who should

DECLASSIFIED
State Dept. Letter, 1-11-72
By R. H. Parks Date   SEP 27 1972

who should have full power, is urgently important.
In matters of emigration I am also in contact with
Dobkin. Regret Bader's trip here impossible".

Concerning the above we are informed that Bader
had been urgently invited by a member of the German
Consulate in Istanbul to proceed to Berlin or
possibly to Budapest to discuss matters relating
to the Hungarian Jews. Bader, acting under instructions
from his superiors in the Jewish Agency, referred
the matter to Shertock in London who, I am informed,
discussed it with "highest authorities" and cabled back
that Bader was not to proceed under any condition.

In his exchange of telegrams on the subject
with Budapest, Bader inquired whether it would be
possible to negotiate on the basis of a financial
arrangement instead of the supply of commodities.
The telegram quoted above gives the reply that this
suggestion is not acceptable but indicated that Schroeder
himself would like to discuss the matter in Spain or
Portugal, preferably with a representative of the JDC.

In this connection, Joseph Scwartz of the WRB
received today the following telegram from Pilpel
in Lisbon transmitting a message from Kastner dated

July 15.

225

July 15.

"1700 people are waiting for a solution by the
Germans. Cable whether Schwartz and Dobkin are
ready to proceed to Spain in order to meet with a
German representative to settle the matter. Advise
whether Madrid or Barcelona will be the meeting place
in ten days time".

The 1700 mentioned above have been referred to
in information received from several sources namely
Schwalb in Switzerland, Dobkin in Lisbon and Kastner
in Hungary and also from passengers recently arrived
on the SS KASBEK. Joseph Schwartz is proceeding to
Lisbon from Turkey July 22 and is requesting my advice
and your authorization to meet with Schroeder or
his representative in connection with the above matter.

I have informed Schwartz that my instructions
preclude any action at this time connected with the
above situation and that I am merely reporting the matter
fully to Washington and requesting for Schwartz advice
from you regarding the possibility of his meeting in
Portugal or Spain with Schroeder. Schwartz will report
to the American Embassy in Lisbon upon his arrival
there which he expects will be approximately July 29.

We are assisting

226

-4-   #1320, July 20, 2 p.m., from Ankara

We are assisting Schwartz in arrangements for his
transportation to Lisbon.

From the above telegrams, there would appear
to be a potentiality which might result in the rescue
of some refugees and which suggests the possible
usefulness of such a meeting. Schwartz requests that
Baerwald be informed of these developments if it meets
with your approval.

KELLEY

JJM WMB

227

STANDARD TIME INDICATED

RECEIVED AT

TELEPHONE YOUR TELEGRAMS
TO POSTAL TELEGRAPH

THIS IS A FULL RATE TELEGRAM, CABLE-
GRAM OR RADIOGRAM UNLESS OTHERWISE
INDICATED BY SYMBOL IN THE PREAMBLE
OR IN THE ADDRESS OF THE MESSAGE.
SYMBOLS DESIGNATING SERVICE SELECTED
ARE OUTLINED IN THE COMPANY'S TARIFFS
ON HAND AT EACH OFFICE AND ON FILE WITH
REGULATORY AUTHORITIES.

Postal Telegraph

Mackay Radio   All America Cables
Commercial Cables   Canadian Pacific Telegraphs

F· W·BA159 B·PDC444NL=WY JACKSON NHAMP 20

1944 JUL 20 PM 8 44

DR JOHN W PEHLE=

WAR REFUGEE BOARD TREASURY (WASHDC)=

:HAVE CABLED MR STETTINIUS TODAY AS FOLLOWS AM INFORMED BY DR

WEIZMANN THAT HE SUGGESTED TO BRITISH GOVERNMENT THAT

CHARLES KI ULLMAN ASSISTANT HIGH COMMISSIONER FOR REFUGEES IN

LONDON BE AUTHORIZED PROCEED MEET KRAUS FROM BUDAPEST TO

EXPLORE POSSIBILITY SAVING HUNGARIAN JEWS IN LIGHT OFFER

MADE BY KRAUS STOP URGE YOU RESPECTFULLY IN SYMPATHETIC

CONSIDERATION THIS PROPOSAL WHICH NOW BEING CONSIDERED BY

BRITISH GOVERNMENT REGARDS UNQUOTE REGARDS==

DR NACHUM GOLDMANN·==

COPY

TEXT OF TELEGRAM RECEIVED FROM

MADRID, DATED JULY 20th, 1944.
- - - - - - - - - - - - - -

Mr. Dobkin has received a telegram from Keesztner in Budapest saying that a representative of German authorities is anxious to meet him and Doctor Schwartz of American J.D.C. in Spain on July 25 to discuss emigration of Jews from Hungary.

2.   He has asked whether there would be objection to this meeting from the point of view of His Majesty's Government. If not he is anxious to be fully briefed on recent German proposal to release these people against deliveries of goods (reported by Joel Brandt) and on His Majesty's Government's attitude to it or to any other proposal involving for example money payments. For this purpose he suggests he should visit London first or else that someone should be sent out from Jewish Agency in London with necessary detailed information.

3.   Please inform Shertok of Jewish Agency.

)

TEXT OF TELEGRAM FROM FOREIGN OFFICE

TO MADRID, DATED 20th JULY, 1944

- - - - - - - - - - - - - - - - - -

These proposals have just been made public both here and in
the United States and have been exposed as blackmail. Further,
we have secret evidence which we are conveying to the United States
Government that the Nazi authorities are using Jews in order to
make contact with British and American authorities as a cover for
peace proposals with the obvious motive of dividing His Majesty's
Government and United States Government from the Soviet Government
whose suspicions the Nazi authorities desire to arouse. In these
circumstances His Majesty's Government, who at once informed the
Soviet Government of German and Hungarian approach are proposing
to the United States Government to refuse to have anything to do
with these "proposals" and there would in our opinion be every
objection to Dr. Schwartz or to anybody else making contact with
the German Authorities. But Dr. Schwartz is an American citizen
and you should discuss the matter at once with your United States
colleague informing him of all the foregoing and asking him whether
he agrees or will submit the point to his Government. If the
Germans or Hungarians, who are credited with having made offers
to the International Red Cross in regard to exit permits for
refugees, who possess visas for other countries, are serious, they
can easily pursue their schemes without involving Allied citizens.
We are in consultation with the United States Government and Jewish
Agency about the reported Hungarian intentions. In the meantime,
it is essential especially in the interests of our relations with
Moscow that no suspicions should be aroused that Allied persons
are negotiating with the enemy.

230

July 21, 1944.

MEMORANDUM FOR THE FILES

Dr. A. Leon Kubowitzki, World Jewish Congress, called me from New York yesterday afternoon and told me that Dr. Nahum Goldmann called him from New Hampshire to say that he had received a message from Shertok to the effect that the British were not permitting Bader to go to Budapest and the suggestion had been made that Kullmann be allowed to go in his stead. Dr. Kubowitzki explained that this was in connection with the Brandt matter and when I asked who Bader was, he indicated that he was connected with the Histadruth. Dr. Kubowitzki asked me whether the War Refugee Board was prepared to support the suggestion that Kullmann be permitted to go to Budapest. I told Dr. Kubowitzki that I was not familiar with this proposal and asked whether the message that Dr. Goldmann had received was available in Washington or New York. Dr. Kubowitzki replied in the negative, stating that Dr. Goldmann had received the message personally in New Hampshire. I told Dr. Kubowitzki that I would check and see what I could find out. He said he would call me this afternoon.

Neither Mr. Pehle, Mr. Friedman, nor Miss Hodel had any knowledge as to any proposal to permit a man named Bader to go to Budapest, nor of any suggestion that Kullmann be permitted to go. I have asked Mr. McCormick to make a search in Censorship and the State Department for the message that Dr. Goldmann was supposed to have received in this connection.

Since dictating the above, Mr. McCormick was able to procure from Censorship the following telegram from Shertok in London to Dr. Goldmann in New York City:

"BADER PROPOSAL NEGATIVED STOP HAVE PROPOSED KULLMANN SHOULD PROCEED MEET KRAUS EXPLORE POSSIBILITIES THIS BEING CONSIDERED PLEASE ASSIST YOUR END ALSO WITH RUSSIANS".

It is assumed that this is the message that Dr. Kubowitzki had reference to. A copy thereof is attached.

L. S. Lesser.

Attachment

Doc. 48

231

DEPARTMENT
OF
STATE

INCOMING
TELEGRAM
CONTROL COPY

DIVISION OF
COMMUNICATIONS
AND RECORDS

HM-911
Distribution of true
reading only by special
arrangement. (7)

1 Copy only

Ankara

Dated July 21, 1944

Rec'd. 6:35 p.m. 22d.

Secretary of State

Washington, ...

DEPARTMENT OF STATE
DIVISION OF
JUL 24 1944
COMMUNICATIONS
AND RECORDS

1335, July 21, 3 p.m.

FOR PEHLE WRB FROM HIRSCHMANN. Ankara no. 102

If you deem it advisable I would like to be

informed regarding the proposal received through

Stockholm and Bern referred to in paragraph numbered

eight of your 614 July 7.

KELLEY

BB

Doc. 49

232

DECLASSIFIED
State Dept. Letter, 1-11-72
By R. H. Parks Date SEP 27 1972

July 26, 1944

<u>MEMORANDUM FOR THE FILES</u>:

I spoke to George Warren about the attached cable No. 1320 of July 20. Warren said the matter had just come to his attention and that in the meantime the British had furnished him with a cable from the British Embassy, Madrid, to the British Foreign Office, and the Foreign Office's reply which also related to a proposed meeting of Schwartz with the Germans. Warren said that the British were very clear in their view that no civilian should have any contact of this nature with the Germans but that Schwartz, being an American, should of course receive appropriate instructions from the United States Government.

I have urged Warren to immediately dispatch a cable to Lisbon repeating cable No. 1320 of July 20 from Ankara, and indicating that Schwartz should not take any steps toward a meeting pending definitive instructions from Washington.

Warren indicated he would take this action promptly.

(Signed) J.W. Pehle

Doc. 50

233

JWPehle:lhh   7/26/44

July 27, 1944

TO: Mr. Stettinius

FROM: J. W. Pehle

Late in the afternoon of July 26, George Warren called to my attention a telegram from the British Mission in Madrid to the British Foreign Office dated July 20, and the reply of the Foreign Office thereto of the same date, both with respect to a proposed meeting between Dr. Schwartz of the JDC and a representative of the German authorities to take place in Spain or Portugal in the near future.

This same matter is also referred to in a cable from Ankara No. 1320 of July 20.

I promptly requested Warren to despatch a cable to Lisbon requesting the Embassy to instruct Schwartz not to have any meeting whatsoever with the German authorities pending instructions from Washington.

After carefully considering this matter it is our firm view that Schwartz should be given definitive instructions not to have any meeting with the German authorities. There is at least a reasonable chance that the Germans are attempting to maneuver us into a situation which would enable them to create suspicions in the mind of the Soviet Government that the British and American Governments are trying to establish an independent contact with the German Government, not limited to refugee matters. Particularly at this stage of the war it seems to me imperative that any possibility of this happening should be avoided. Secondly, even assuming that the Germans are in good

faith willing to negotiate on refugee matters, cable No.
1320 of July 20 from Ankara indicates that the Germans are
not interested in a purely financial arrangement but are
going to insist on some supply of commodities. There is
no disposition here or elsewhere in this Government to
my knowledge to even negotiate on supplying the Germans
with commodities. Thirdly, it is my view that no such
meeting should be held without the prior approval of the
Russian and British Governments. In view of the attitude
which both of these governments have expressed and the
time factor involved it seems clear that no such approval
could be obtained.

Accordingly, I strongly urge that definitive instructions be sent which will effectively prevent any
meeting between Schwartz and the German representative.
I would also urge that the American Missions in Lisbon,
Madrid and Ankara be advised of this action and the British
be informed of our decision.

I am sending a copy of this memorandum to Assistant
Secretary McCloy of the War Department for his information.

235

(Signed) J.W. Pehle

noted
JBF

July 27, 1944

Dear John:

Thank you for your memorandum of July 27 regarding the proposed meeting between Dr. Schwartz and a representative of the German authorities in Spain and Portugal.

I think you have made the right decision and we have already sent appropriate instructions to the missions at Lisbon, Madrid, and Ankara. We have also advised the British.

With best wishes,

Sincerely yours,

E

Mr. John Pehle,
 Executive Director,
  War Refugee Board,
   Executive Office of the President,
    Washington, D. C.

236

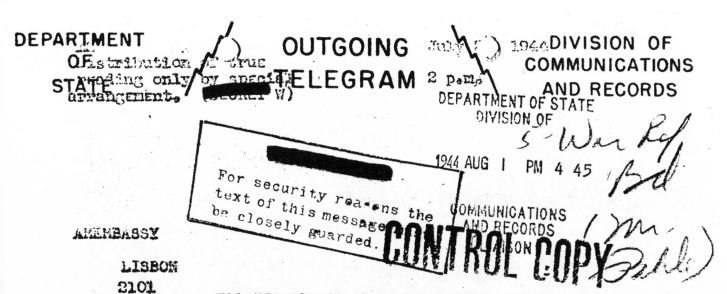

DEPARTMENT OF STATE

OUTGOING TELEGRAM

DIVISION OF COMMUNICATIONS AND RECORDS
DEPARTMENT OF STATE
DIVISION OF

1944 AUG 1 PM 4 45

COMMUNICATIONS AND RECORDS

Distribution of true reading only by special arrangement. (SECRET W)

For security reasons the text of this message be closely guarded.

CONTROL COPY

AMEMBASSY

LISBON
2101

FOR NORWEB AND McCLELLAND FROM PEHLE

Ankara's 1320 to the Department on July 20 for Pehle from Hirschmann follows for your information:

QUOTE For your information, Bader of the Jewish Agency who is liaison officer with the Jewish communities and groups in occupied territories, received a telegram dated July 15 from Kastner who is an important member of the Jewish Relief Committee in Budapest and is reported to be well known to other communities as a reliable person. The following is a translation of the telegram. INNERQUOTE Consult Schroeder's friend Istanbul about your flight to Budapest Saturday. Your proposal about a purely financial arrangement uninteresting (repeat uninteresting). Cable whether Schroeder meeting next week with Schwartz at Lisbon would lead to quick results. Schroeder's proposed meeting with Schwartz, who should have full power, is urgently important. In matters of emigration I am also in contact with Dobkin. Regret Bader's trip here impossible. END INNERQUOTE

Concerning

Doc. 52

237

DECLASSIFIED
State Dept. Letter, 1-11-72
By R. H. Parks Date SEP 27 1972

Concerning the above we are informed that Bader had been urgently invited by a member of the German Consulate in Istanbul to proceed to Berlin or possibly to Budapest to discuss matters relating to the Hungarian Jews. Bader, acting under instructions from his superiors in the Jewish Agency, referred the matter to Shertok in London who, I am informed, discussed it with 'highest authorities' and cabled back that Bader was not to proceed under any condition.

In his exchange of telegrams on the subject with Budapest, Bader inquired whether it would be possible to negotiate on the basis of a financial arrangement instead of the supply of commodities. The telegram quoted above gives the reply that this suggestion is not acceptable but indicated that Schroder himself would like to discuss the matter in Spain or Portugal, preferably with a representative of the JDC.

In this connection, Joseph Schwartz of the JDC received today the following telegram from Pilpel in Lisbon transmitting a message from Kastner dated July 15.

INTERQUOTE 1700 people are waiting for a solution by the Germans. Cable whether Schwartz and Dobkin are ready to proceed to Spain in order to meet with a German

representative

representative to settle the matter. Advise whether
Madrid or Barcelona will be the meeting place in ten
days time. END INNER QUOTE

The 1700 mentioned above have been referred to in
information received from several sources namely Schwalb
in Switzerland, Dobkin in Lisbon and Kastner in Hungary
and also from passengers recently arrived on the SS KASBEK.
Joseph Schwartz is proceeding to Lisbon from Turkey
July 22 and is requesting my advice and your authorization to meet with Schroeder or his representative in
connection with the above matter.

I have informed Schwartz that my instructions preclude any action at this time connected with the above
situation and that I am merely reporting the matter fully
to Washington and requesting for Schwartz advice from you
regarding the possibility of his meeting in Portugal or
Spain with Schroeder. Schwartz will report to the
American Embassy in Lisbon upon his arrival there which
he expects will be approximately July 29. We are assisting Schwartz in arrangements for his transportation to
Lisbon.

From the above telegrams, there would appear to be

a potentiality

239

a potentiality which might result in the rescue of some refugees and which suggests the possible usefulness of such a meeting. Schwartz requests that Baerwald be informed of these developments if it meets with your approval. UNQUOTE

You are requested to advise Schwartz that he is not (repeat not) authorized to make any contact with Schroeder or any other German agent in Lisbon or any other place. If and when any such action by Schwartz is decided upon by the War Refugee Board specific directions will be sent to Lisbon for him.

240

HULL
(GLW)

PARAPHRASE OF TELEGRAM SENT

FROM: Secretary of State, Washington

TO: American Embassy, London

DATED: July 28, 1944

NUMBER: 5949

CONTROL COPY

RECEIVED
WAR REFUGEE BOARD
WASHINGTON D.C.

You are advised, with further reference to Department's
cable of July 7, 1944, No. 5353, and specifically to the second
sentence of numbered paragraph four, that as a result of communications from/Budapest the Jewish Agency for Palestine has recently
proposed that Josepth Schwartz, American Jewish Joint Distribution
Committee representative, meet in Lisbon with Schroeder for the
purpose of further discussion regarding the Brandt proposal. We
also wish to inform you that we have requested the American Embassy in Lisbon to advise Schwartz that he does not have authority
to have any aommunication or contact with Schroeder or any other
German agent at Lisbon or anywhere else. The Foreign Office and
the British Embassy Madrid have recently exchanged communications
regarding this matter and information regarding the message to
Lisbon has been given to the British Embassy here.

The foregoing message was repeated to Moscow as No. 1812
referring to Department's cable dated July 7, 1944, No. 1641.

STETTINIUS
Acting

Doc. 53

241

DECLASSIFIED
State Dept. Letter, 1-11-72

By R. H. Parks Date SEP 27 1972

DEPARTMENT
OF
STATE

OUTGOING
TELEGRAM

DIVISION OF
COMMUNICATIONS
AND RECORDS

5 - War Ref
Bd (mm
Pehle)

MAE
Distribution of true
reading only by special
arrangement.
AMEMBASSY,

July 28, 1944

5 p.m.

CONTROL COPY

AUG 1 1944

LISBON

2112

FOR NORWEB AND DEXTER

With further reference to Department's 2101 of July 27

you are requested to advise Schwartz representative of

Joint Distribution Committee that after thorough considera-

tion of all available facts decision has been reached that

Schwartz should not (repeat not) have any contact xxxx or

communication with Schroeder or any other German agent at

Lisbon or at any other place.

Doc. 54

242

STETTINIUS
ACTING
(GLW)

S/CR

WRR:GLW:OMH
/44

WE   SE   NE

DECLASSIFIED
State Dept. Letter, 1-11-72
By R. H. Parks Date SEP 27 1972

DEPARTMENT
OF
STATE   KEH

OUTGOING
TELEGRAM

DIVISION OF
COMMUNICATIONS
AND RECORDS

War Refugee Board

Distribution of true
reading only by special
arrangement. (~~~~~ W)

TO BE SENT IN ~~~~~ "W"

July 28, 1944

5 p.m.

AMEMBASSY,

ANKARA

x 664

FOR KELLEY AND HIRSCHMANN

After full consideration of all information available
concerning contents your 1320 July 20 you are advised that
American Embassy Lisbon has been requested to advise Schwartz
that he is not (repeat not) under any circumstances or at
any time or place to make contact with or communicate with
Schroeder or any other German agent.

Doc. 55

243

STETTINIUS
ACTING
(GLW)

DEPARTMENT OF STATE

AUG 1 1911

DIVISION OF
COMMUNICATIONS & RECORDS

WRB:GLW:CMH
7/28/44

NE   SE   WE   S-CR

DECLASSIFIED
State Dept. Letter, 1-11-72
By R. H. Parks Date SEP 27 1972

DEPARTMENT
OF Distribution or true
STATE
sending only by
special arrangement.
W)

OUTGOING
TELEGRAM

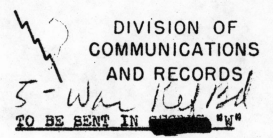

DIVISION OF
COMMUNICATIONS
AND RECORDS

5 - War Ref Bd

TO BE SENT IN ~~CODE~~ "W"

War Refugee Board

AMEMBASSY,

MADRID

2121 x

July 28, 1944

DEPARTMENT OF STATE

AUG 1 1944

AND RECORDS

CONTROL COPY

The Department has been advised by the British Embassy
here that your British colleague has been in communication
with the British Foreign Office with respect to a proposal
of the Jewish Agency for Palestine that Joseph Schwartz
representative of the American Jewish Joint Distribution
Committee meet with a German agent named Schroeder with
respect to the emigration of refugees from Hungary. For
your information and that of your British colleague, the
American Embassy Lisbon has been requested to advise Schwartz
that he is not (repeat not) to have any contact or communication with Schroeder or any other German agent at Lisbon
or at any other place.

Doc. 56

244

Noted
JB/

STETTINIUS
ACTING
(GLW)

DECLASSIFIED
State Dept. Letter, 1-11-72
By R. H. Parks Date SEP 2(1972

WRB:GLW:OMH
7/28/44

WE

NE   S/CR

DEPARTMENT
OF
STATE

INCOMING
TELEGRAM

DIVISION OF
COMMUNICATIONS
AND RECORDS

MAE-694
Distribution of true
reading only by special
arrangement. (▓▓▓▓W)

Lisbon

Dated August 1, 1944

Rec'd 3:56 p.m.

1944 AUG 2 PM 12 45
COMMUNICATIONS AND RECORDS
(LIAISON)

DEPARTMENT OF STATE
DIVISION OF

Secretary of State,

Washington.

2374, August 1, 1 p.m.

Have given Schwartz orally conclusion Department's

2112, July 28, 5 p.m. This is WRB 131. He apparently

reluctantly accepts Department's decision.

NORWEB

Doc. 57

245

EH

EMB

For security reasons the
text of this message must
be closely guarded.

DECLASSIFIED
State Dept. Letter, 1-11-72
By R. H. Parks Date SEP 27 1972

DEPARTMENT
OF
STATE

OUTGOING
TELEGRAM

DIVISION OF
COMMUNICATIONS
AND RECORDS

August 5, 1944

BAS
Distribution of true
reading only by special
arrangement. (W)

7 P.m. TO BE SENT IN "W"

CONTROL COPY

AMEMBASSY,

ANKARA.

682

For security reasons, the
text of this message must
be closely guarded.

The following for Hirschmann is WRB 99.

Reference is made to your 1335 of July 21 requesting
information about the proposals received through Bern and
Stockholm which were mentioned in our 1641 of July 7.

The Bern proposal is similar to the one set forth
in your 1356 of July 24 and to the Joel Brandt proposal
with which you are familiar. After due deliberation,
Bern was advised that it was not (repeat not) feasible
to undertake the transaction in question.

Through Stockholm a vague proposal was made by some
dubious individuals to exchange Latvian Jewish refugees
for money or non-military supplies or both. Existing
conditions in Latvia render it unnecessary to go further
into this proposal.

STETTINIUS
ACTING
(GHW)

WRB:MMV:KG
8/5/44

S/CR

NE

WE

NOE

DECLASSIFIED
State Dept. Letter, 1-11-72
By R. H. Parks Date SEP 27 1972

MEMORANDUM OF CONVERSATION with Mr. Joel Brandt in Jerusalem
on October 7, 1944.

While in Jerusalem I had been informed that Mr. Joel Brandt
had been released by the British from Cairo and was a free agent
in Jerusalem. He requested permission of the Jewish Agency to
talk with me and I saw him first at the home of Mr. Eleazer Kaplan,
an official of the Jewish Agency. In order to talk with him
quietly and ~~talk with him~~ in confidence, I invited him to my
suite at the Hotel King David. Brandt disclosed the following:

1. He had been held in a prison in solitary confinement by the
British since June 5. In the last two weeks he was released to
a prison camp, from which place he wrote a letter to the Jewish
Agency officials (intended for the hands of the British Intelligence), which he read to me. In effect it stated that were he
not released by October 5 he would regard himself as an enemy of
the British and act accordingly. Brandt had been on two hunger
strikes and informed me that he had made arrangements to make a
break for freedom or to commit suicide.

Mr. Kaplan of the Jewish Agency had informed me that they
were given the choice of sending Brandt back to Hungary or permitting him to go to Palestine. They chose the latter. Apparently Brandt was not aware of this when I talked with him.

2. I asked Brandt why he had chosen to go to Syria while in
Turkey, since he should have known that he would be captured by
the British. He stated that after the Turks had arrested him,
prior to my arrival in Ankara, he was given the choice of returning to Hungary, but had he done so it would have been interpreted
as a definite refusal by the Allies of his proposals, and he saw
only dangers of additional reprisals from this eventuality. Now
Brandt contends that even in spite of the great trials occasioned
by his incarceration that he made the right decision; that at least
he accomplished something connected with the cessation of the deportations, and the 1,700 refugees who did come through Hungary.
Brandt believes that the British continued to infer that he was
insincere and playing a "double game" in order to keep him in
Cairo so that he could not further his project.

3. Brandt, in spite of his arduous experience, is still intent
on breaking the ring around Hungary for refugee release. He
asked me to propose that someone should directly contact Tito.
He would like to see Tito and states that he knows the situation
and people in Hungary who could arrange easy access from Hungary
through Yugoslavia; that there are peasants who could arrange
quick access for messengers through to Budapest. Brandt said he
also has friends who can reach Tito.

Doc. 59

4. Brandt states his reliable information is such that it is much easier to travel within Germany and outside of Germany to Switzerland than is imagined. He asserts that, with armies and German evacuees on the move constantly, it is constantly possible for groups to slip out of Germany.

5. Brandt is emphatic in his insistence that a deal could have, and can yet be worked out with the Germans. He wishes to return to Hungary and to talk with the German leaders with whom he was conferring--to say that if they will release fifty to a hundred thousand Jews, that as an evidence of their determination to play the game, a meeting could be arranged, probably in Switzerland within three days, and that then they could come to terms. He believes he could have made such a deal, and that it still can be made. He has apparently been informed of the activities of Saly Meyer, who, he claims, is not the man for this type of negotiation; that Meyer is an old man; and that unorthodox methods are needed in dealing with these bandits.

6. I questioned Brandt further regarding the background of his previous activities and negotiations with the German leaders. He states categorically that Eichman had been reaching the "top man", namely, Himmler, who eventually had to contact Hitler; that it was impossible for these men to make any such moves as the kind that were in contemplation without orders from the top. Brandt also insisted that he knew that the Hungarians alone could not make any deal without the Germans, which he interprets as the reason for the failure of release of refugees from Hungary. Brandt wants assistance in being released from Palestine to go to Hungary to continue his proposals. He believes that he can bring out at least fifty thousand Jewish refugees. He would like then to go to Switzerland and asked that he could meet with me or some representative of our Government in Switzerland. He insists that he has connections in Switzerland which will help him to bring out refugees through this area. He asserted that he believes it is necessary now to forget Rumania through Istanbul as an exodus route.

7. The nature of the proposal that Brandt now wishes to make was as follows: That for every week that they will let out X number of Jews that they will be paid X dollars thereafter. He believes such a deal can be made without delay.

It was after some hesitation That I determined to confer with Brandt since he was released and apparently not under British surveillance, in order to secure any additional information that might be of value to the War Refugee Board in its program; also for purposes of the record and confirmation, I deemed it desirable to answer any question that may have resulted from the testimony taken with Brandt in my interview, and to determine if any efforts could be made through him or his associates to break the bottleneck in Hungary. While in Istanbul in the last months, there had been

248

several unconfirmed rumors that Brandt had confessed to being
a double agent.   This was categorically denied by the British
Intelligence Officer, Colonel Gibson, and the release of Brandt
by the British demonstrated that he was no longer suspect.

In my conversation with Brandt I was again convinced without reservation of his frankness and integrity; that he was an
impassioned young man, ready to risk his life for the sake of
his people. His testimony taken in Cairo by me has now been
confirmed as having been truthful.

I am not convinced that Brandt can be especially useful
at this time, since he is a marked man. What impresses me is
his zeal and resourcefulness. I am confident now that he
represents the leaders of the Hungarian Jewish community; that
he has connections in Hungary which could render any possible
illicit movement of refugees out of Hungary a feasible
operation.

American Legation, Cairo, October 10, 1944.

249

I. A. Hirschmann